SOCIAL WORK IN EXTREMIS

Lessons for social work internationally

Edited by Michael Lavalette and Vasilios Ioakimidis

First published in Great Britain in 2011 by

The Policy Press
University of Bristol
Fourth Floor
Beacon House
Queen's Road
Bristol BS8 1QU
UK

Tel +44 (0)117 331 4054
Fax +44 (0)117 331 4093
e-mail tpp-info@bristol.ac.uk
www.policypress.co.uk

North American office:
The Policy Press
c/o International Specialized Books Services (ISBS)
920 NE 58th Avenue, Suite 300
Portland, OR 97213-3786, USA
Tel +1 503 287 3093
Fax +1 503 280 8832
e-mail info@isbs.com

British Library Cataloguing in Publication Data
A catalogue record for this book is available from the British Library.

Library of Congress Cataloging-in-Publication Data
A catalog record for this book has been requested.

ISBN 978 1 84742 718 2 hardcover

Cover design by The Policy Press
Front cover: image kindly supplied by www.reportdigital.co.uk
Printed and bound in Great Britain by TJ International, Padstow
The Policy Press uses environmentally responsible print partners.

Contents

List of contributors   iv

Acknowledgements   v

Introduction: Social work in extremis – disaster capitalism, 'social shocks'   1
and 'popular social work'
Michael Lavalette

one   'Popular social work' in the Palestinian West Bank: dispatches   15
           from the front line
           Chris Jones and Michael Lavalette

two   Samidoun: grassroots welfare and popular resistance in Beirut   31
           during the 33-Day War of 2006
           Michael Lavalette and Barrie Levine

three   Grassroots community organising in a post-disaster context: 51
           lessons for social work education from Ilias, Greece
           Maria Pentaraki

four   Grassroots community social work with the 'unwanted': the case of   65
           Kinisi and the rights of refugees and migrants in Patras, Greece
           Dora Teloni

five   In search of emancipatory social work practice in contemporary   81
           Colombia: working with the *despalzados* in Bogota
           Carmen Hinestroza and Vasilios Ioakimidis

six   Addressing social conflicts in Sri Lanka: social development   93
           interventions by a people's organisation
           Ashok Gladston Xavier

seven   International organisations, social work and war: a 'frog's perspective'   105
           reflection on the bird's eye view
           Reima Ana Maglajlic

eight   Welfare under warfare: the Greek struggle for emancipatory social   115
           welfare (1940–44)
           Vasilios Ioakimidis

nine   Social welfare services to protect elderly victims of war in Cyprus   133
           Gregory Neocleous

ten   Worker's eye view of neoliberalism and Hurricane Katrina   143
           Marla S. McCulloch

eleven   Social work, social development and practice legitimacy in Central Asia   153
           Terry Murphy

Conclusion: Social work in extremis – some general conclusions   167
Vasilios Ioakimidis

References   173

Index   187

List of contributors

Carmen Hinestroza is a social work practitioner, activist and academic in Bogata, Colombia.

Vasilios Ioakimidis is a Lecturer in Social Work and Social Pedagogy at Liverpool Hope University. He is also a member of the Social Work Action Network (SWAN) steering committee.

Chris Jones is Emeritus Professor of Social Work at Liverpool University and Adjunct Professor of Social Work at Liverpool Hope University.

Michael Lavalette is an Associate Professor of Social Work at Liverpool Hope University. He is also the national coordinator of the Social Work Action Network (SWAN).

Barrie Levine is a Lecturer in Social Work at Glasgow Caledonian University.

Reima Ana Maglajlic is a Senior Lecturer in Social Work in the School of Human and Health Sciences, Swansea University.

Marla S. McCulloch is a Clinical Adjunct faculty member at Widener University. She is also a volunteer disaster mental health worker in Louisiana.

Terry Murphy is Senior Lecturer in Health and Social Care at Teesside University.

Gregory Neocleous is a Lecturer in Social Work at the University of Nicosia, Cyprus.

Maria Pentaraki is a Senior Lecturer in Social Work at Liverpool Hope University. She was previously Head of the Social Work Department at the ATEI in Patras, Greece.

Dora Teloni is a social work academic at the ATEI in Patras, Greece.

Ashok Gladston Xavier is a social work academic at Loyola College of Chennai, India.

Acknowledgements

We would like to take this opportunity to thank a number of people for helping us put this collection together. We would like to record our thanks to each of the chapter authors for meeting the various deadlines that we set them. At The Policy Press, Karen Bowler has been very supportive of the project and Leila Ebrahimi very patient in dealing with our various requests. We would like to thank our colleagues at Liverpool Hope University Social Work Department. Academic life is increasingly pressured; their support has made it easier for us to get this book out in time. We would also like to record our thanks to Laura and Natalia, who have had to put up with us while we completed this project.

Michael Lavalette
Vasilios Ioakimidis

Social work in extremis – disaster capitalism, 'social shocks' and 'popular social work'

Michael Lavalette

> In the wake of an earthquake, a bombing, or a major storm, most people are altruistic, urgently engaged in caring for themselves and those around them, strangers and neighbours as well as friends and loved ones. The image of the selfish, panicky, or regressively savage human beings in times of disaster has little truth to it. (Solnit, 2009, p 2)

Introduction

This book sets out to look at what we have termed 'social work in extremis'. It is an attempt to bring together a number of case studies that look at social work responses in 'extreme' or crisis situations. There is no single common perspective in the chapters that follow. In total we look at what social work institutions, social workers and community activists do during episodes of war, military occupation, environmental disaster, forced migrations and political and economic restructuring. Some of the authors look at the response of state social work and welfare institutions in these circumstances (Murphy and Neocleous), others provide reflective accounts of their work as social work academics and practitioners in crisis situations (Teloni, McCulloch, Xavier, Maglajlic, Hinestroza and Ioakimidis), two look at the extent to which social work students and educators can engage with campaigning movements in post-crisis situations (Teloni, Pentaraki), while three of the chapters, perhaps more controversially, look at alternative forms of 'popular social work' that can develop in the face of extreme circumstances (Lavalette and Levine, Ioakimidis, and Jones and Lavalette).

This last themed element, especially as it includes the volume editors, may need some further elaboration. In these chapters it is suggested that, faced with crisis situations, there is an immediate requirement to establish a social work that can engage with communities and meet people's needs. Faced with these immediate needs, communities and social movements act to create an engaged popular social work, and the chapters by Lavalette and Levine, Ioakimidis, and Jones and Lavalette provide a glimpse (and sometimes it is no more than that) of a 'popular social work', one that is flexible, open, reliable, non-stigmatising and non-conditional and hence stands in sharp contrast to the worst practices and manifestations of 'official' social work.

This poses an important question: What is social work? In many of the chapters that follow (though not all) those who provide the social work we discuss are not professional, qualified workers. Is this a problem?

'What is social work?' is a question that is regularly asked, but which has not produced any definitive answer; as Cree and Myers note: 'An examination of social work's history demonstrates that social work has always been "up for grabs"; its task and direction by no means self-evident' (2008, p 1).

The majority of social work text-books attempt to define social work by reference to the training undertaken by students (and their relationship to international definitions and national occupancy standards), the main areas of employment and the qualifications and professional recognition obtained by practitioners. Such definitions refer to the (important) world of state social work. This is certainly the case for Britain, where from the early 1980s state social work agencies have, as the major employers of social work, largely determined the content and purpose of the social work curriculum.

Within the academy, debates rage over the differences between the methods, approaches and perspectives of professional practitioners – and whether social work is an essentially conservative, critical, transformative, therapeutic or radical profession (compare Fook, 2002; Payne, 2006; Cree and Myers, 2008). Debates also focus on the impact on social work of neoliberal social policy regimes (Jordan, 2000; Ferguson, 2008), and the consequences (for both workers and service users) of imposed changes to the working environment of front-line workers (Harris and White, 2009). These debates are important – and, indeed, they are ones that I have engaged in at different levels and in a range of contexts (Lavalette and Ferguson, 2007a; Ferguson and Lavalette, 2009; Lavalette, 2011).

However, despite their strengths, these approaches focus on debates within, and changes to, state-directed social work and this raises a further important question: Should the definition of social work be restricted only to those activities carried out by 'qualified professionals' in this narrow range of employment outlets? Indeed, there is a bigger problem. Given the changes that have taken place in social work qualifications in Britain over the last 25 years (from CQSW to DipSW to BA Social Work), any such narrow definition would, in effect, mean that many of the training practices, placement opportunities and jobs carried out by CQSW-trained staff would now not be deemed 'proper' social work, given the present narrow definition of appropriate and regulated social work education and employment tasks.

If this is a problem within Britain, the difficulties of providing an acceptable definition of social work internationally grow exponentially. The International Federation of Social Workers' definition of social work, which has been widely quoted and has garnered support from national associations and affiliates, doesn't define the profession simply as a narrow, state-directed activity. Rather, it argues that social work:

> promotes social change, problem solving in human relationships and the empowerment and liberation of people … [It] addresses barriers, inequalities and injustices that exist in society. It responds to crises and emergencies as well as everyday personal and social problems … Social work interventions range from primarily person-focused psychosocial processes to involvement in social policy, planning and development. …[Including] counselling, clinical social work, group work, social pedagogical work and family treatment and therapy … Interventions also include agency administration, community organisation and engaging in social and political action. (IFSW, 2000)

Does this definition apply only to those who carry a 'recognised qualification' from a national regulatory body? If this definition is what is expected of a social worker, then many state social workers in Britain today could not be said to be undertaking social work. Or could there be organisations, networks and individuals who engage in social work activities – even though they do not hold official accreditation?

In an earlier contribution to this debate (writing with Iain Ferguson) I suggested that there were a number of well-known social movement activists from the early twentieth century in Britain who were involved in social work practice: people such as Clem Attlee, Sylvia Pankhurst, Mary Hughes and Emmeline Pethick (Ferguson and Lavalette, 2007). These people were involved in more popular forms of social work engagement but have been written out of the social work canon that reflects a history of 'professional' social work that excludes radical practitioners who combined social work with political activity.

In Britain, the drive to 'professionalise' social work was part of an attempt to inoculate the professionals against those they worked with and to stop the possibility of 'contamination.' The concern was to stop middle-class professionals identifying with their clients and locating the source of their difficulties in the structural inequities of society (Jones, 1983; Ferguson, 2008). Thus the drive to 'professionalise' and to get access to state resources has been combined with an attempt to distance social work from its more 'popular' forms and to insist that such activities not be called *social work*.

And so this raises a bigger question: Is it possible that there are 'popular forms of social work' that exist outside (or even partially outside) the formal, regulated fields of practice?

To ask this question is to raise the possibility that 'social work' is actually a range of activities and actions that different groups in the community can engage in. Some of these will be trained professionals carrying out statutory tasks ('official social work'), but what about those who work to provide, for example, a community café as a provider of cheap, high-quality, nutritious food in a setting that brings isolated people together to share experiences and discuss what they (individually and collectively) need to do to improve their lives and their environment? Is this social work, even if the volunteers and workers are not professional social workers? In Preston, in the north of England, there are two such community café projects. Both are located in the poorest parts of the city and both are run by small, voluntary sector organisations. One has a qualified social worker as part of its team, but the other doesn't. Both have a large number of community volunteers who staff and help to run the project. Both cafés have substantial 'service user involvement' on their organising committees. Are either of these social work projects? Is one a social work project because a 'professional' is involved, and the other not?

During the great miners' strike in Britain in 1984/85 the mining communities organised soup and food kitchens, pantomimes at Christmas and parties and entertainment on occasional weekends. The intention was, above all, to survive, both physically and mentally; to keep up spirits and morale; to stop people feeling isolated; to help counter individual trauma, frustration and depression, and to meet basic needs (ensuring people had food, and fuel for heating). Was this social work? My suggestion is that these activities are a form of 'popular social work' that is creative, vibrant, energetic and built upon a firm basis of community solidarity.

If these types of activities are a form of popular social work – albeit one that has been ignored and written out of the history of the 'profession' – is it not worth re-assessing and re-evaluating their worth for any insights they provide as to what good social work might look like? Furthermore, as state social work becomes ever more degraded and, in the case of Britain, moves ever further away from the understanding of social work provided by the IFSW, then it is even more compelling to look at and learn from popular social work.

It is these issues and questions that this book sets out to address – though it does so from a variety of perspectives. It is a collection where we are united in our assessment that 'social work in extremis' offers valuable lessons, and are all committed to opening up debate in this area, even though we do not share or present a single take on the events' significance or their lessons for 'official' social work.

We suggest that disasters and catastrophes shine a light onto the nature, structure and order of societies. They pose immediate questions: Who has been killed and who has been saved? How can we meet survivors' immediate needs? Is the existing social structure a help or a hindrance to the relief programme? What are the immediate priorities for society (meeting human need? economic revival? maintenance of law and social order?). The problem is that in the midst of such crises 'solutions' can be posed from a variety of different organisations and interest groups.

Naomi Klein has recently suggested that such crises ('social shocks') are exploited by the powerful for political motives, to aid economic restructuring: 'shocked societies often give up things they would otherwise fiercely protect'. (2007a, p 17). On her website she summarises this in the following way:

> At the most chaotic juncture in Iraq's civil war, a new law is unveiled that would allow Shell and BP to claim the country's vast oil reserves.... Immediately following September 11, the Bush Administration quietly out-sources the running of the 'War on Terror' to Halliburton and Blackwater.... After a tsunami wipes out the coasts of Southeast Asia, the pristine beaches are auctioned off to tourist resorts.... New Orleans's residents, scattered from Hurricane Katrina, discover that their public housing, hospitals and schools will never be reopened.... These events are examples of 'the shock doctrine': using the public's disorientation following massive collective shocks – wars, terrorist attacks, or natural disasters – to achieve control by imposing economic shock therapy. (Klein, 2007b)

Many of the chapters that follow trace elements that reflect aspects of Klein's case (see, for example, Pentaraki).

By way of a contrast, Rebecca Solnit suggests that in the midst of disasters we get a glimpse of a 'paradise built in hell'. She argues that while

> disasters are ... terrible, tragic, grievous ... [and] not to be desired ... [they] drag us into emergencies that require we act, and act altruistically, bravely, and with initiative in order to survive or save the neighbours.... The positive emotions that arise in those unpromising circumstances demonstrate that social ties and meaningful work are deeply desired, readily improvised, and intensely rewarding. (2009, pp 6–7)

Again some of these themes are reflected in the chapters that follow (Ioakimidis, Lavalette and Levine).

What determines whether a society suffers post-disaster 'social shock' or a 'paradise built in hell'? There is no simple answer. But the case studies that follow do suggest that in this vortex politics matters. Where there are traditions of social movement activity, where there is a collective memory of 'alternative ways of living', where there is what political sociologists call a complex and known 'repertoire of contention', then there is a greater possibility that these traditions of resistance can be used to resist social shock and to address the immediate needs of the community and, in the process, advocate for alternative solutions. But these are often unpredictable events where participants will have to address a wide range of difficult and challenging issues by thinking on their feet – they will continually have to ask and try to answer the question: What is to be done? The answers they find and suggest will have a bearing on the events that follow.

But whether disasters open up societies to 'social shock' or offer a vision of 'paradise built in hell' they also open up a debate over the nature of social work and the suitability of social work practices. As Michelle Herbert-Boyd notes (in a study of social work responses to the Halifax explosion in 1917, in Canada):

> Crises force individuals and [social work] professionals to examine their role in the social order, and they can be a catalyst for effective community development, progressive social policy, and social change. Conversely, they can lead to conservatism, fear and the maintenance of the *status quo*. (Herbert-Boyd, 2007, p 5)

So the chapters that follow look at a number of case studies which look at the responses of 'official social work', models of 'popular social work' and the response of local state agencies to 'extreme' circumstances. The aim is to look at social work and grassroots welfare projects under extreme social, economic and political circumstances. It is our contention that in these 'extreme' (and therefore, unusual) circumstances we can catch a glimpse of an alternative form of social work – but one, it is suggested, that can provide insightful lessons for those involved in social work, welfare work and community development across much of the globe. Our examples indicate that in these periods it is possible to establish projects that are organic, creative, politically informed and trusted by 'service users'; projects that are community oriented and informed by collective values and a local knowledge base. We therefore contend that the various popular social work responses 'in extremis' offer valuable experiences and lessons which can enrich mainstream 'official' social work theory and practice.

A Haitian case study

As I started to write the introduction to this book the television news was filled with horrific images of the aftermath of the Haitian earthquake that struck on 12 January 2010. As the crisis unfolded it was clear that the situation raised many of the themes and issues that we were exploring in the book.

The disaster in Haiti was a natural one, the scale of the devastation almost beyond comprehension: over 230,000 people killed, two million homeless, somewhere in the region of 300,000 people injured, hundreds of thousands living in makeshift camps, and the destruction of an already devastatingly poor, highly indebted country (*New Statesman*, 2010; Carroll et al, 2010). David Peppiatt (2010) from the Red Cross described Haiti as:

> The worst disaster zone I have ever seen…. Port-au-Prince [the Haitian capital] looks like it has been bombed to a pulp; the city is the epitome of Ground Zero.

Yet, although the earthquake was a 'natural' event it was one where the immediate effects, initial responses to and longer-term consequences of what happened were all affected by the social structure and the social relations of the society within which the disaster took place: the scale of the suffering was a reflection of the way in which Haitian society is organised and its relationship to the rest of the world. As Younge argues:

The recent earthquake was an act of nature. But the magnitude of the devastation, the consequent human toll and the inability of the country to recover unaided are the product of its political and economic marginalisation. (2010)

In other words, the catastrophe was as much a socio-economic and political episode as a natural disaster. This is something that is explored in each of the chapters in this collection – the events that each author describes cannot be understood outside of the history, the social structure and the political and economic relations of the society within which the 'extreme circumstances' occurred.

In Haiti, the earthquake did not hit all people 'equally'. The victims were overwhelmingly drawn from among the poorest sections of this very poor country (a theme addressed below, in particular, in the chapters by McCulloch, Lavalette and Levine, Jones and Lavalette, Pentaraki, Xavier, Teloni, Hinestroza and Ioakimidis). Of course, some wealthy people died and a number of UN workers were killed when the building they were working in collapsed; but generally, less-crammed, better-built homes protect the wealthiest from the effects of earthquakes.

Geographer Kenneth Hewitt has argued that the victims of earthquakes are overwhelmingly drawn from among the poor, and he has termed them not earthquakes but 'classquakes'. He gives the 1978 earthquake in Guatemala as an example:

[Here] 1.2 million people lost their homes. In Guatemala City, nearly all of … [the] 59,000 destroyed homes were in urban slums built in ravines, above and below steep, unstable bluffs, or on poorly consolidated young fluvio-volcanic sediments. Losses to the rest of the city, and among more expensive homes, were negligible. (1997, pp 217–18)

The Haitian capital, Port-au-Prince, was grossly overcrowded. Sixty per cent of the housing was sub-standard. It had the infrastructure for a city of somewhere between 300,000 and 400,000 people – but 3 million lived there. This 'excess population' was living in badly built shanty towns, like Cité Soleil, which housed approximately 300,000 people. These were migrants from the rural areas who had been forced to leave their land and come to the city to try and find work. They came in increasing numbers from the mid-1980s onwards because the Structural Adjustment Programme that Haiti was forced to go through opened the country up for cheap US agricultural products to flood the local market and undercut Haitian farmers and peasants. In turn, the migrants looked for work in the Export Processing Zones (EPZs) that the government set up, with US backing, to provide tax-free havens for US multi-nationals. In the EPZs US garment firms sweat cheap Haitian labour (Gonzalez, 2010a).

The result is that, prior to the earthquake, over half the population lived on less than $1 a day and the price of staples such as rice, beans, water, cooking oil and gas had risen sharply, to the point that many Haitians were struggling to eat

(Gonzalez, 2010b). This is a country 'that spent more in 2008 servicing its debt than it did on health, education and the environment combined' (Younge, 2010).

In order to understand Haitian levels of poverty – and hence the social impact of the quake – we need to recognise the history of slavery, dictatorship and US intervention in Haiti.

Haitian history is steeped in the heroic struggle of the slave rebellion under the leadership of Toussaint L'Ouverture that freed the country and its slaves from Spanish, French and British rule (James, 1938/1980). Haiti became the world's first black republic. But it was isolated and was allowed to resume trade with the European powers only on condition that it agreed to pay compensation to French slave owners of 150 million francs (the equivalent of about $35 billion today) for their lost property (that is, slaves). Haiti continued to pay this price until 1947 (Robinson, 2010).

Haiti was run by a series of dictatorships throughout the nineteenth and twentieth centuries. In 1957 the Haitian army supported 'Papa Doc' Duvalier and his brutal regime. In 1971 Papa Doc passed power over to his son, Baby Doc, who stayed in power until a massive uprising threw him out of office in 1986. The Duvaliers borrowed vast sums from international banks and the IMF. They diverted this into their own bank accounts and personal projects – yet the debt they ran up is still being paid by the Haitian people. In 1988 a US district court in Miami found that Baby Doc had 'misappropriated more than $504,000,000 from public monies' (Klein, 2010).

> Haitians, of course are still waiting for their payback … For more than two decades, the country's creditors insisted that Haitians honour the huge debts incurred by the Duvaliers, estimated at $84 million … In debt service alone, Haitians have paid out tens of millions every year. (Klein, 2010)

In the late 1980s a popular movement shaped by ideas drawn from anti-imperialist traditions and liberation theology fought for greater social justice and liberation under the leadership of Jean-Bertrand Aristide. But the army staged a coup and regained control; it stayed in power from 1991 to 1994 and killed thousands of activists during that time. Aristide was forced into exile in the US and had to accept a number of neoliberal measures to 'restore and restructure Haiti' before the US sent troops back in 1994 on a 'humanitarian mission' to restore democracy; they stayed for six years.

In 2000 Aristide was returned to government in what are generally viewed as the most constitutionally legitimate elections in Haiti's history. In response, Haitian and US banks ran a disinvestment campaign, which saw the budget plummet and GDP halve. On 28 February 2004 the US kidnapped Aristide and replaced him with Gerard Latortue, who proceeded to push through neoliberal economic reforms.

US military intervention is not a recent phenomenon. In order to meet its 'slave debts' to France, Haiti borrowed heavily from US banks. The US invaded Haiti in 1915 in order to police the repayment. It stayed until 1934. US troops returned again in 1959 to prop up Papa Doc's regime. They have left and returned with monotonous regularity ever since, propping up dictatorships and 'restructuring' Haitian society in the interests of US capital (Gonzalez, 2010b).

These historic themes continued in the immediate aftermath of the earthquake. After the disaster struck, what the people of Haiti needed was food, water and shelter. What they got was lots of US troops – few with any expertise in disaster relief. As John Pilger noted in the days after the quake:

> The airport in the capital, Port-au-Prince, is now a US military base and relief flights have been re-routed to the Dominican Republic. All flights stopped for three hours for the arrival of Hilary Clinton. Critically injured Haitians waited unaided as 800 US residents in Haiti were fed, watered and evacuated. Six days passed before the US air force dropped bottled water to people ravaged by thirst and dehydration. (2010)

The relief effort was also directed at the wealthier areas of Haiti (Kimber, 2010). On the same island, in the Dominican Republic, as Haitians fought for their lives wealthy tourists – drawn from the American and Caribbean elites – bathed on the beaches, swam in the sea and lived their lives untouched in luxury hotels. In the aftermath of the quake, there were several reports that drew a sharp contrast between the starving, thirsty and homeless masses and the conditions at the US-controlled airport and in the UN compounds where there was beer, food, water, blankets, internet access, generators and other aid relief from around the world (Kimber, 2010). This issue, of the misuse of aid and the failings of state forces and NGOs features in the chapters by McCulloch, Maglajlic, and Lavalette and Levine below

The main concern of the government, UN and US troops was the 'restoration of order' and the prevention of 'looting'. But, as Rebecca Solnit (2010) argued:

> After years of interviewing survivors of disasters, and reading first hand accounts and sociological studies from such disasters as the London Blitz and the Mexico City earthquake of 1985, I don't believe in looting. The great majority of what happens you could call emergency requisitioning. Someone, who could be you, someone in desperate circumstances, takes necessary supplies to sustain human life in the absence of any alternative. Not only would I not call that looting, I wouldn't even call that theft.

Similar issues – of human need requiring breaches of 'normal' rules, laws and codes of conduct – are covered in many of the chapters below (see in particular the chapters by Teloni, Xavier and Murphy).

Haiti is an hour's flight away from Florida, yet the recovery operation was painfully slow. Aid was flown in from Cuba and Venezuela, only to be turned away by US forces due to geo-political considerations (Gonzalez, 2010b). Two months after the disaster only 40% of the 1.3 million in need had received tents, tarpaulins or shelter tool-kits, yet the economic zones were back up and running – their expansion likely under the rubric of 'reconstruction' (Carroll, 2010).

In 2010 the tragedy of Haiti was palpable, but it was a tragedy shaped by Haiti's history and social structure. These factors also make Haiti potentially vulnerable to those who wish to exploit the catastrophe to further 'reconstruction' along neoliberal lines – again a theme that will be addressed in many of the chapters below.

'Shocked' societies

In her powerful critique of the modern world, Naomi Klein (2007a) traces the violence committed against humanity by a combination of wars and neoliberal globalisation. In particular she looks at the ways in which a series of 'social shocks' – 'natural' disasters and political, military and economic crises – have been exploited by powerful global and corporate elites to restructure economies and produce:

> huge transfers of public wealth to private hands, often accompanied by exploding debt, an ever-widening chasm between the dazzling rich and the disposable poor and an aggressive nationalism that justifies bottomless spending on security. (2007a, pp 14–15)

The use of the term 'social shock' is deliberate. Klein is attempting to draw an analogy with 'electric shock treatment' that has been used to control prisoners and make them receptive to prison regimes. So she argues:

> Like the terrorised prisoner who gives up the names of his comrades and renounces his faith, shocked societies often give up things they would otherwise fiercely protect. (2007a, p 17)

Klein gives numerous examples to show that 'social shock' has been exploited by the powerful to further increase their wealth, power and influence. In essence, Klein is arguing that during episodes of 'social shock', corporate elites use the chaos and confusion to reorganise and restructure society to make it more susceptible to the demands of neoliberalism. Countries that are desperate for any kind of aid find themselves without any leverage to negotiate the terms of the aid they get. This process Klein terms 'disaster capitalism'.

With regard to Haiti, for example, in a document entitled 'Amidst the suffering, crisis in Haiti offers opportunities to the US', the conservative think-tank the Heritage Foundation suggested that:

> In addition to providing immediate humanitarian assistance, the US response to the tragic earthquake in Haiti offers opportunities to reshape Haiti's long-dysfunctional government and economy as well as to improve the public image of the United States in the region. (Eaton, 2010)

Pentaraki's chapter on corruption and the misdirection of public funds in the aftermath of the Greek fires in 2007 raises similar issues.

Gary Younge notes a recent UN study that considers the impact of 21 natural disasters on heavily indebted countries, which concludes that rebuilding costs leave long-term financial burdens. The report suggests that:

> Shocks on such a scale can lead to a vicious cycle of economic distress, more external borrowing, burdensome debt servicing and insufficient investment to mitigate future shocks. (Cited by Younge, 2010)

Klein's thesis is that neoliberalism is a manifestation of the 'inner logic' of corporate capitalism, which exploits social shocks to bring about the conditions for its realisation. Her descriptions of the Chilean coup (1973) or the invasion of Iraq (2003) emphasise the ways in which brutal 'social shocks' are used to usher in neoliberal corporate capitalism.

The strength of Klein's argument is that she shows, in example after example, that the opening up of societies to 'free-markets', 'civil society' and neoliberal forms of regulation has been accompanied by brutality and coercion 'inflicted on the collective body politic as well as countless individual bodies' (2007, p 15) and the formation of new, interdependent relationships between the state and capital (see also Ferguson and Lavalette, 2007).

Yet, despite its many strengths, her argument can seem overly conspiratorial – a criticism made by, among others, Joseph Stiglitz when he suggested that 'there are no accidents in the world as seen by Naomi Klein' (2007).

In this respect, the 'shock doctrine' metaphor is too unidirectional. So despite the centrality of the events in Chile and Iraq to her argument, it is not simply the case that both events were prefigured on their potential to open both countries up to the world market and neoliberal economics (the Chilean coup was primarily a reaction to the strength of the organised working-class movement in Chile [Barker, 1987]; while the Iraqi war was as much to do with American military and political strategy as it was to do with economic restructuring [Callinicos, 2009]). It's also not the case that a 'social shock' is necessary to bring in neoliberal regimes of regulation. Neither Britain nor the US (or countries like India or Egypt) suffered 'social shock' in the sense outlined by Klein prior to their attachment to neoliberalism (Klein's attempt to equate the Falklands War fought by the UK or the 9/11 events in the US as the necessary 'shock' stimuli simply doesn't stand up to much analysis).

Neither is it true that 'social shocks' always produce, or necessarily produce, neoliberal outcomes. Solnit (2009), for example, suggests that 'social shocks', disasters and crises pose innumerable questions about the nature of society and its priorities; questions which can be answered in countless ways by local communities in the midst of such catastrophes. Thus she argues that during such 'moments of social upheaval ... the shackles of conventional belief ... [can] fall away and ... [vast] possibilities open up' (2009, p 9). She suggests that people suffering unimaginable misfortune in the midst of 'social shocks' often resort not to savagery and brutal competition (an assumption which reflects a Hobbesian notion that people in such circumstances find themselves in an archaic 'state of nature') but to 'an almost beatific selflessness, comforting themselves in extremis by aiding others' (2009, p 14).

In the case of Haiti, for example, Peppiatt (2010) argues that 'through the death and destruction shines the sheer strength and resilience of the courageous Haitian people ... even in the middle of a disaster, communities still have the ability to start rebuilding their lives'. In the weeks that followed the disaster there were numerous appeals for aid that were organised via the major relief agencies. However, within Haiti there was growing anger that aid was being directed to large NGOs who had also been involved in the prior privatisation of welfare and the local state in the country (see also Maglajlic, this volume). Some seven months after the disaster – despite billions of dollars being pledged in aid to the 23 biggest charities operating in Haiti – an ABS News report claimed that only 2% of the monies had been released and just 1% had been spent on operations (Adams 2010). In response, the Haitian trade union organisation, in conjunction with its Latin American sister organisations, started to argue among its global affiliates that all aid should be diverted through trade union organisations. On the ground both trade union and community organisations started to organise the relief process in opposition to that provided by the US and UN troops and the global NGOs (ITUC, 2010; TUC 2010a, 2010b).

Interestingly, however, one international project seemed to gain better results than others: the J/P Haiti Relief Organisation camp for the displaced. This project received considerable publicity because it was initiated by Hollywood celebrity Sean Penn – who left his home in the US to go to Haiti and work in the organisation's tent city.

> With a fraction of the money of mainstream relief organisations and almost no experience of the aid game ... [Penn] created what is widely regarded as the most vibrant and by some distance the best-run humanitarian project in Haiti. (Adams, 2010)

Adams reports that in Camp Penn there are more schools, hospitals, latrines and water stations than in any of the other 1,300 tent cities. It is, he suggests: 'tidier … safer … and better designed than any other … [with] a real sense of community' (2010). And at its heart are two key principles. The first is that volunteers should live in the camps where they work:

> NGOs pay thousands of dollars a month to billet staff in air-conditioned houses (the cost of leasing a home with a pool in Port-au-Prince has doubled since the quake), the Hollywood A-lister and his volunteers sleep in identical tents [within the camp]. (Adams, 2010)

The second is that money raised should go directly to the relief effort. J/P Haiti Relief employed only four people (paid by the organisation, and not directly out of relief funds). The vast majority of the work was done by volunteers – the majority of whom came for a two-week 'tour of duty'.

Standing behind these principles is a relatively simple set of values:

> [It] isn't just about spending money wisely. It also reflects a desire, surprisingly rare in the aid industry, to be seen as something approaching an equal by [those in the camps] … Traditional agencies might parachute into disaster zones with aid deliveries, and then vanish for days. Penn strongly believes that he can only help a community if he lives in it and understands what makes it tick. (Adams, 2010)

Adams's article focuses on Penn 'the Hollywood A-lister', but the approach of the J/P Haiti Relief Organisation chimes with some of the themes covered in chapters below (Lavalette and Levine, Jones and Lavalette, Teloni, Maglajlic, McCulloch and Xavier).

But such approaches do not necessarily require the input of Western organisations. Naomi Klein notes how communities potentially have the resources to organise themselves to meet their needs and to stop social shocks being exploited by powerful interest groups. She looks at the aftermath of the Asian tsunami of 2004, where she suggests:

> Despite all the successful attempts to exploit the 2004 tsunami, memory … proved to be an effective tool of resistance in some areas where it struck, particularly in Thailand. Dozens of coastal villages were flattened by the wave, but unlike in Sri Lanka, many Thai settlements were successfully rebuilt within months. The difference did not come from the government. Thailand's politicians were just as eager as those elsewhere to use the storm as an excuse to evict fishing people and hand over land tenure to large resorts. Yet what set Thailand apart was that villagers approached all government promises with intense skepticism and refused to wait patiently in camps for an official reconstruction

plan. Instead, within weeks, hundreds of villagers engaged in what they called land 'reinvasions.' (2007a, pp 463-4)

And this is a central theme in each of the chapters that follow – faced with war, crisis and 'social shocks', local communities can, and do, create alternative solidarities and means of meeting community need. Central to these activities are people engaged in social and welfare work. They may have a 'professional qualification', but many don't, though what they are doing and what they are engaged in is clearly popular social work.

The argument in this book is that social shock may create the conditions which the powerful try to exploit to restructure societies and economies, but the same events can also produce resistance and alternative ways of thinking about the world which challenge the interests of the powerful.

Enriched by catastrophe?

This dichotomy poses questions for social work and welfare activists operating in crisis situations. Professional social workers have to decide what their priorities should be (and who should decide them) and how their professional skills can help the aid process. But it is also likely to bring 'professionals' into contact with popular forms of social work activity and, rather than appear from the outside with special knowledge and exclusivist practices, social work in extremis will be enriched if it engages fully with those popular welfare forms and therefore confronts the questions: Who should they listen to? And, ultimately, whose side are they on?

Herbert-Boyd (2007) has argued that working in such extreme circumstances tests social workers and their guiding theory and practice to their limits. But, she suggests in the title of her book, social work can be 'enriched by catastrophe' if it is adaptable, dynamic, geared to meet human need and shaped by a commitment to social justice.

It's a conclusion we share. The chapters in this book open up questions about the nature of social work, about social work in extremis and about the relationship between official professional social work and forms of popular social work that have, for too long, been ignored by the professional canon.

ONE

'Popular social work' in the Palestinian West Bank: dispatches from the front line

Chris Jones and Michael Lavalette

"The Israelis want the occupation to infiltrate every area of our life: our homes, our work, our businesses, our free time, our schools, our universities ... they want to turn the camps into prisons and then into graveyards. But we have turned them into universities, to learn our history, to maintain our struggles, to survive, to live and to smile." (Firas, Am'ari Refugee Camp, interview with authors, 16 September 2006)

Introduction

Over the last four years (2006–10) we have travelled back and forth to the Palestinian West Bank. Our purpose has been to interview Palestinian young people about their experiences of life under occupation. But in the process we have come across some magnificent welfare projects and have spent considerable time observing and talking to a range of workers in various projects, asking them how they understand their role and the importance of the work they do. The majority of those we spoke to had no formal qualifications in social work, yet the quality of the work they undertook, we believe, holds lessons for social workers everywhere.

This chapter is based on interview material with six workers at the Yaffa Centre, Balata, with three workers at the Jenin Disability Centre and with three workers at the Am'ari Children's Centre. We spoke with each group three times, each interview lasting for at least two hours. In what follows, whenever possible we quote directly from the workers at the project. We have changed all the names of our interviewees to protect the workers from the threat of arrest – or worse.

Setting the context

For the Palestinians of the West Bank life is extreme. Poverty, oppression and occupation provide the backdrop against which daily life becomes a battle to survive, to live, to hope and to dream. Yet amid this maelstrom the Palestinians have managed to organise a range of grassroots welfare projects that meet some of the complex needs of the communities they serve.

The three projects we focus on are all in refugee camps: the Yaffa Centre based in the Balata Refugee Camp in Nablus, the Children's Centre in the Am'ari Refugee Camp next to Ramallah and the Disability Project in the Jenin Refugee Camp. The impact of the Israeli occupation is felt by all Palestinians – army incursions; killings and injuries; arrests and imprisonment; acute poverty and restricted mobility, due to checkpoints and barriers (Lavalette, 2006). But the refugee camps are without doubt the most targeted and stressed of all Palestinian communities both in the West Bank and in Gaza (although we focus only on the West Bank.)

The living conditions in all three camps are extremely difficult. While the physical area of the camps (1 sq km) has remained the same since they were established under United Nations' auspices in the early 1950s, the populations have multiplied. Originally homes to 5,000–6,000 refugees, the camps now house up to 22,000 people (UNRWA, 2006). The tents and shacks have been replaced by more robust block buildings that, in the most haphazard manner, crowd on top of one another and reach skywards. Going up is the only option. Hence the camps are like mazes, with narrow pathways dividing the homes. Many homes see no daylight, as additional stories are built to accommodate the growing numbers. Ibrahim, one of the youth workers in Balata told us:

> "All the people are crammed into 1 km square. In the camp we have to have mosques, schools, some shops, we have the centres – these are all important, but they eat into the space. So each house is reduced to 60–70 metres – and you often find a family of 10 living in it. Some of the houses in the middle of the camp are built so close together, and they are all built up two or three levels, that there is no natural light, no sun and little ventilation. All these conditions cause physical and mental ill health." (Balata, September 2006)

The overcrowding is exacerbated by poverty and unemployment (PCBS 2008). The World Bank estimates Palestinian unemployment rates at 40%, but because of a strangled economy, due to roadblocks and checkpoints and Israel's decision from the start of the Second Intifada in 2000 to eschew cheap Palestinian labour, unemployment in the camps is around 70% (ifamericansknew, 2006). For those in work, their incomes are low and the work is often short term and insecure. Consequently, most people stay in the camps, day in and day out. Moreover, as we saw in June 2008, the camps are full of children all day and this will continue throughout the 3-month summer school break. Most, we were told, don't leave the camps. Families won't even go to the municipal park because they have no money for snacks and ice creams.

The climate does not make it any easier: intense heat through the summer and cold and damp in the winter. But the biggest misery multiplier is the Israeli occupation. The Israeli army and state regard the camps as 'evil' and, since the beginning of the Second Intifada in 2000, have systematically targeted them. All the camps we visited are raided on a daily basis and in 2002 were subjected to major attacks – the case of Jenin being especially notorious, when around a hundred people[1] were killed and injured and over 400 buildings were destroyed (Baroud, 2003). Since 2000, over 150 people have been killed, 650 imprisoned and over 1,200 injured in the Balata Camp (Balata, nd). The consequences are unimaginable. Tariq, a youth worker at the Yaffa Centre, told us:

> "You know all the children are brought up in such strange and difficult circumstances. They have all seen dead bodies and body parts. They have all witnessed shootings, bombings and attacks from Israeli forces. They all have brothers, cousins, uncles or fathers who are martyrs or prisoners. Many of them have been hurt – if not physically, then mentally and emotionally." (Balata, February 2008)

Trauma is widespread and manifested in a wide range of difficulties, especially bed-wetting, nightmares and sleep disturbance. Play is often violent and tense. Firas, a worker at the youth project in Am'ari, told us:

> "We have a lot of angry children. We have a lot of aggressive children. We have a lot of depressed children. We have a lot who behave in a crazy way because they have no way of releasing their anger and anxieties. Sometimes it is difficult to talk to them, they are often nervous." (Am'ari, September 2006)

While Ahmed, a qualified social worker in Nablus, told us the story of Maha:

> "Maha was 11 when her older brother was killed by the Israelis. She had always looked up to her brother and thought he would always be there to protect her. One day the Israeli soldiers raided the family home and killed her brother. She was deeply traumatised and started having problems sleeping and she started to wet the bed. We were able to work with her using music and drama therapy, which allowed her to express herself in different ways. She gained in confidence and was able to start talking about what had happened. By the end we had cured her problem." (Nablus, September 2006)

How can you play and relax when there is no space and when you never know when the army is going to sweep in? This has implications for the play that the children engage in. Hamed told us:

> "If we run a workshop, for example, for 5/6-year-olds to 15/16-year-olds – we might start by drawing. But the kids don't draw a tree or a Luna Park. Instead they draw jeeps, APCs [armoured personnel

carriers], guns, war games. How do we break this psychological barrier? His life leads him to think this way – and we cannot change this in a few hours of a course. But we have to find a way to give the young people a glimpse of a better life. To run classes and groups which take them, even for a short while, away from the horrors of our lives in the camps." (Balata, February 2008)

At the Yaffa Youth Centre Tariq told us that such stresses take their toll on the very fabric of the centre:

"This is a children's centre. We can't tell them all the time 'don't do this, don't do that'. Our children are often frustrated and sometimes they get angry, sometimes excited and then things break. But they are children – and they are children who live in the most trying situations. What can we do?" (Balata, June 2008)

What makes matters worse is that so many of the shootings and arrests are completely random (Chomsky, 1999). The Israeli demonisation of all Palestinians, and especially the residents of the refugee camps, means that the Israeli soldiers tend to shoot and attack as their first response (Veracini, 2006). So many of the people we have interviewed who have been injured or arrested have simply been in the wrong place at the wrong time.

The sheer randomness of the Israeli army's actions and the subsequent shootings means that the young have keen ears and know the sound of a jeep or Humvee (an armed military vehicle), or an Apache helicopter. They also know how to recognise the weapons used against them, such as which rifles fire tear gas, rubber bullets or live ammunition. They know what to do in the case of tear gas, including the use of onions to counter its worst effects. They have had soldiers in their homes in the early hours of the morning. They have seen their parents humiliated, pushed out of their homes in their underwear and made to stand outside as their homes are ransacked.

In addition, schooling is continually disrupted by the occupation (King, 2005). Closures and curfews mean that schools are unable to open for periods of time. Curfews are always difficult, entailing being confined to the home, but when the home is extremely overcrowded the pain of curfew is deepened. All three camps have experienced periods of extended curfew. Moreover, within the camps, the schools which are run under the auspices of the UN are underfunded and the buildings are often in poor condition. Class sizes of around 45 students also add to creating a difficult learning environment.

The consequences for the children and young people are varied and many. Young boys become obsessed with computer war games; large numbers have been wounded; many more have been beaten by soldiers; some have been arrested and imprisoned (there are currently 337 children in Israeli prisons [dci-pal, 2008]); many have brothers and fathers in prison (Cook et al, 2004). One result is that young people spend a great deal of time in their homes when they are not in school or college. This is especially true for young children, and girls and young women.

Organic projects

The three projects we visited all operate within this context. All of them can be described as *organic* initiatives in that they have been created within the camps and are run by groups of volunteers who all live in the camp. Each of the centres developed during the First Intifada (1987–93). This first uprising took place throughout Israel and the occupied territories (that is, it included the Arab towns within Israel, such as Nazareth, for example). The uprising, described by Marshall as an 'unprecedented level of general collective activity' (1989, p 153), involved large numbers of people and included their involvement in demonstrations, strikes, calls for boycotts of Israeli goods and the creation of 'autonomous' schools, welfare and cultural centres (Marshall, 1989, p 151). Each of the centres reflects its roots in this collective, popular movement. Thus, Khalil told us:

> "[The Yaffa Centre] was established in the early 1990s. It originated in the camp organisation to highlight the issue of refugee rights and the right of return. By the 1990s we realised that we had to do something for the people in the camp, and the children in particular … There are two main themes in the centre's work. The first is to do with Palestinian identity: to teach the children who we are, where we come from and what we are doing here. We are Palestinians, we are refugees, we live in refugee camps for particular reasons – and so we run courses and classes that explore all of this…. The second theme in our work is to develop and train young people. We have courses on leadership, on IT, on homework skills [i.e. support for school homework], on writing for the media. These are very much about education and its importance to us…. But even here, the education we teach them is deeper than they get in school. For example in geography the curriculum defines Palestine as the West Bank and Gaza only … it doesn't include the rest of Palestine, the place where the majority of families in the camps come from. So we have to teach the full geography of our land and country. And this means knowing about our history and the fact that Palestine exists from the river [Jordan] to the sea [Mediterranean] and that is what we must strive to get back: all of ancient Palestine." (Balata, February 2008)

Similar themes were taken up by Yousif, who runs a disability project in the Jenin Refugee Camp.

> "Prior to the First Intifada people with disabilities were stigmatised within Palestine. But we were able to challenge this during the First

Intifada. Because of the attacks on the camps more people were being disabled and injured and we were able to show that all were victims of the Israeli occupation and incursions. There was nothing for disabled people in the whole of the north of the West Bank. So in 1992 we formed a committee to build a centre. By 1992 we had lots of international contacts, so when we built our centre we looked at examples from Britain and elsewhere to see what we might learn. We started work with injured people inside the camp. We made some simple aids, made home visits and helped with rehabilitation. But gradually we moved out to tackle other forms of disability, like providing services for people with cerebral palsy." (Jenin, February 2008)

Baraa, from the Am'ari Youth Centre, had a similar tale:

"The centre was started in the early 1990s during the First Intifada. It was important to find a space where the children could be children, where they could have a bit of childhood. The centre concentrated on trying to help the children understand what was happening to them and their community – it provides a space where young people can engage in sport, IT, drama and educational activities." (Am'ari, February 2008)

Each of the projects is still shaped by its original commitments. The centres rely on local volunteers who live in the camps, work in the centres and, increasingly, have formerly been 'service users'. In all three projects, many of the current workers were at one time or other users of the centre. One simple example is the speech therapist in the disability project in the Jenin camp, who was a user after she lost her arm during an army incursion. After her 'recovery' she was helped by the centre to train to work with it as a speech therapist. Tariq told us:

"The youth workers all live and were brought up in the camp. We know what it is like and we know what difficulties the children face." (Balata, February 2008)

This means that the workers, while they have developed specialist skills, often self-taught, see themselves as one with all the refugees and there is absolutely no 'professional' distance between the workers and those that come to their centres.

All the projects take a determinedly non-sectarian position. This has proved to be essential in the current climate, where relations between Fatah and Hamas are bitter and divisive. Their stance has meant that their centres are able to reach all the refugees in the camp. As one worker told us, "people have to leave their politics at the door". He went on:

"We are not political in the sense of being for any political grouping. The centre is for the camp – everyone in the camp whether they are PFLP [Popular Front for the Liberation of Palestine], Hamas, Fatah or none. Here we work for Balata camp and the right of return. If people are politically engaged, that is their right, but they must keep it out of the centre." (Tariq, Balata, February 2008)

This does not imply they have an apolitical stance. Indeed, another key characteristic of all these social work initiatives is that they are all determinedly *partisan*. They abhor the occupation and the damage it causes to their lives and their aspirations. They all recognise that it is the occupation which is at the root of their difficulties and, as with all other Palestinians, they have a duty to resist and fight back in whatever ways they can. Their principal concern is to work for all Palestinians and, with respect to the children and young people, to give them some kind of 'normal' childhood in a most abnormal context. Thus Ahmed, the qualified worker in Nablus, told us that with most of the children on the music and drama therapy course he runs:

"In most cases the trauma is [a] direct consequence of the occupation – it is the occupation in all its consequences that produces this extreme trauma in the children." (Nablus, February 2008)

This orientation ensured that the social work activity we witnessed was free of the individual pathologisation which is so evident in Anglo-American social work. The enveloping nature of the occupation in the lives of the refugees means that this is always the starting point for analysing and approaching any difficulty. This is their operating assumption, rather than to assume that problems result from some deficit in the individual and/or household. Such a baseline informs all their practice and activity.

Funding

These principles extend to their approach to funding. All the projects are starved of resources. The growing impact of poverty means that many of their volunteer workers are unable to commit time to the projects, as they need to hunt for any kind of paid work so as to assist their own families. For the disability project, artificial limbs, other aids and adaptations are very expensive, and the workers are outraged that such crucial items are priced to give the suppliers very high profits. For this reason, they have created their own workshop where they can make quality equipment for half the cost. Khalil told us:

There is a great need for artificial limbs in our community. But the price of such limbs is very expensive and the people who need them [are] very poor. When we researched into this matter we found that

> the main suppliers of the limbs were nothing more than traders; they weren't interested in the people who needed the artificial limbs. They were only interested in money. We also found that when people did get their limbs from these traders they provided no instructions or after-care, so the devices would often fail to work properly and cause even more frustration. So we got people to look at the limbs and we thought that for what we were being charged 70,000 NIS [shekels] we could make for about 30,000 NIS. We have now created a unit which includes physiotherapists, occupational therapists, a rehabilitation worker and specialists in artificial limbs." (Jenin, June 2008)

They have also successfully ensured that every public centre within the camp is now accessible to those with a disability.

Despite their acute funding concerns, none of the projects will accept external funding that in any way compromises their work or principles. One of the projects told us that USAID promised them a virtually blank cheque, but with the proviso that they had to sign a clause concerning 'terrorism' which was offensive and biased. They refused.

> "USAID have tried – on more than one occasion – to place certain restrictions or limits on our activities. They offered us a lot of money if we signed a decree against 'terrorism'. They had an open cheque and told us to write our own figures in – but the condition was to sign the decree. Now we are happy to sign against terrorism, but the problem was their definition. They defined the national resistance movement against the occupation as terrorism. The incursions weren't described as terrorism, but our resistance movement was! So we rejected their offer. We can survive without them." (Tariq, Balata, February 2008)

In Jenin we found similar outrage at the way money was offered, but tied to political agendas. But as well as suspicion at the activities of international aid agencies, here there was also a conscious distancing from the Palestinian Authority. Hamed told us:

> "We take no money from the PA [Palestinian Authority]. We don't trust them. They have no link with us. They are not interested. I think they would like us to go away because we are a constant reminder of their failings…. We have a saying: 'During the day we are under the controls of the PNA, they restrict us and tell us what to do. During the night we are under the control of the Israelis and they tell us what to do.' This is called the division of labour." (Jenin, June 2008)

Similarly, each project encounters NGOs that come to them with offers of funding but also with their own agendas which, if they were to accept, would divert them from what they have identified as their principal objectives. We ourselves were at one of the camps when an NGO worker came to discuss a proposal on governance and women's participation. Not only did we find her proposal incomprehensible, but she came with a fully worked-out project based on the assumptions of her NGO. Tariq told us:

> "Many NGOs want to come and run projects that will 'save our women'. They have an idea that we treat our women so badly; that they are just breeding factories; that they are weak and have no voice; that they have no place to meet and to raise their own issues. Of course there are issues here – like there is in your country or America, do you have complete equality? – but the NGOs exaggerate in our case. You wouldn't guess, for example, that in the An Najah University 60% of the students are female. It's not as simple as they make out." (Balata, June 2008)

All of the projects work from the *bottom up* and reject the top-down approaches of many of the larger NGOs. Each of the centres is run by a committee made up of camp delegates, workers and volunteers and it is this committee that decides on the priorities of each centre. Here are Rami, Hamed and Tariq in an excerpt from one of the interviews in Balata:

> **Rami**: "We have regular meetings when we discuss what we need to do, what courses we should run, what issues we should address. For example I was involved in a workshop – healing through music – and at the end entire families were coming up to us and asking us to run the workshop again. They told us they could see the difference it was making to their children."

> **Tariq**: "We don't have a restrictive agenda about what we should do. We will try anything. We will consider all sorts of ideas that people come up with, to try and help the kids. When we get a new idea – we try it and see what happens. We need and want to be dynamic in our approach to working with the children."

> **CJ**: *"So all of you, as workers, you have meetings and brainstorming sessions where you come up with new ideas or projects?"*

> **Tariq**: "Yes, we are always talking and thinking about these things and thinking about what we have done and what we could do better.!

> **Hamed**: "The activities are the most important thing, and then after we all sit around the table and think about what we have done and

what is next. Most of us are here every day, so if we need to meet or if there is an issue we can arrange this easily." (Balata, February 2008)

The fact that the projects are based in the refugee camps is a further hindrance to funding. Many NGOs which had been active in the camps in earlier years have been pressured by the Israeli state not to fund work in the camps. The Israelis claim that to do so aids terrorism. Hence, it is common within the camps to see rusting and old play equipment that was once funded by an NGO, but then abandoned. We also learnt that the projects in the north of the West Bank (in Jenin and Nablus, for example) feel neglected by many funders, who prefer to invest their resources in Ramallah (the 'capital' of the West Bank) or Bethlehem. These places are considered to be 'where the action is' and are of course much closer to the centre of power – it also means that NGO workers can easily travel to the projects while living in the relative comforts of Jerusalem. Here is Tariq again:

> "The other issue is where the international NGOs send their funding. They fund projects in Ramallah and the surrounding area, or Bethlehem. But then you come to the northern sector and there is very little. The Hawarra checkpoint keeps us in Nablus, but it also acts as a barrier – not many NGOs come across that barrier. I would guess the proportion is 10 to 1. For every 10 projects funded in the Ramallah area we get 1." (Balata, June 2008)

The funding problems are serious and limit what can be done. As Khalil put it: 'Our centre has no resources. It is not only non-profit, it is no profit' (Jenin, September 2006). But the renowned steadfastness of the Palestinians means that they will endure. Their resilience is helped by the knowledge that what they do can make a difference to those they work with.

Their rootedness in the camp means they get much positive feedback, such as in the case of the music classes one project started, which resulted in many parents coming to the centre to tell the workers that their children had changed. In particular, they told how their children were more relaxed and less aggressive. Much of their work has a ripple effect within the camp and this is especially evident in their work with children and young people in respect of their history and culture.

The importance of memory

Although young people learn much from their parents as to why they are living in the camps and in these conditions, all the projects believe that a deep knowledge of their history and culture is critical to sustain any semblance of well-being. Their *undefeated* dismay (to borrow a term from John Berger, 2007) is essential. So, in addition to the learning that comes from their families and daily experiences, all the projects engage in history and cultural work. Children and young people gather testimonies from the older people who left their homes during the Nakba (the 'Catastrophe', as the ethnic cleansing of 1948 is referred to [Pappe, 2006]). They produce poems, pictures and booklets which detail the history of those in the camp. In turn, such activities draw parents and grandparents into the centres, as they come to tell their stories or record them on tape or film (see for example, www.yafacult.org). As Basim put it:

> "We start the process here and then the kids go home and talk about their own family case. In turn we then often see other brothers and sisters coming and sometimes the mothers and fathers come and look at what is going on and add their stories to what we are discussing. You know, we have worksheets which we give to the children and they have to go home and talk to their parents and grandparents: 'tell me about where we come from', 'tell me about our village' etc. We turned this into a documentary, we had cameras and we had a group who made a short filming about all this – with the support of international volunteers. One of the films won first prize in the Chicago Film Festival. They were competing against films that cost $60,000 – ours cost $500 – and our children won! We do humble work – but it works. If we had more money we could do more but …" (Balata, June 2008)

The artwork produced in the centres abounds with the symbols of the refugees' plight. Pictures of old, ornate keys are especially prevalent. These are the keys to the homes from which their parents and grandparents fled during the Nakba. Many homes in the camp display their keys and many still have the documents issued by the Ottomans, and then by the British Mandate, which document the ownership of land and buildings which were taken from them by Israel. Through compiling their own families' history and experience, the young come to learn of their own rootedness in the country; to know of their exile; to learn how Balfour's letter in November 1917 to Lord Rothschild promised that Britain would create a homeland for Jews on their lands. As the workers in all the projects told us, they deeply believe that to have a clear understanding of your history, of how you ended up living in a refugee camp, is vital to one's sanity. Moreover, in the camps where the UN-managed schools are not allowed (under Israeli pressure) to celebrate Palestinian history or touch such 'sensitive' issues as the Nakba or the 1967 war, the centres' work takes on additional importance. It is perhaps not such a surprise, then, that we met so many young people who had a deep sense of their history and of contemporary politics concerning Palestine.

The children and young people also learn about their rich cultural traditions, whether this be dance, song, music, literature or art. They form dance and theatre groups in the camps. On one of our visits we watched a performance by 12- to 16-year-old boys and girls of a play written by them that portrayed what happens when they are arrested and interrogated. They also paint, play music, film and photograph. And they play in a safe place.

The concern of the centres is to give the children a chance to have some sort of 'normal' childhood. They believe that the theft of Palestinian childhood is one of the major wounds of occupation and that the Israeli targeting of children and young people has been one of the weapons to undermine Palestinian resistance and encourage them to migrate.

It is important to recognise that such activities also defy the ongoing onslaught of Israeli propaganda which portrays the Palestinians as a people without a culture or history. Cultural activities have also allowed some of the participants to travel out of the camps, to art and dance festivals and to young peoples' summer camps, especially within Western Europe. It is impossible to overestimate the meaning of any travel in a country where movement is so highly restricted and perilous. Many have no knowledge of their country outside of their camp and its immediate area. Organising trips, picnics and summer camps is given a high priority. Some succeed, but many fail. We heard painful stories of coaches of young people full of anticipation about getting out of the camp and their town, even if just for the day, being turned back at checkpoints. But we also witnessed some of the successes. We were at one of the centres when a group of 25 boys and girls aged between 12 and 15 had just returned from a three-day trip into Israel to visit the lands their grandparents had fled in 1948/49. The trip had been funded and organised by a US-based NGO which had managed to extract all the necessary permits. The youngsters were buzzing when they returned. They had been moved to see their land, villages and towns within Israel. And they were ecstatic about seeing the sea and swimming. The yearning for the sea is widespread and, though it is so close, none had ever seen it before: two of the young girls told us of their surprise to find that the water was salty!

Trust

One notable characteristic of all three projects is that they are *trusted*. This has crucial implications for their work, and none more so than in the area of psychological trauma. In all three camps we were told that problems such as enuresis, sleep disturbance, speech difficulties, anxiety and aggression were kept within families and seen in some respects as shameful.

This is now breaking down, as the workers in the centres have been able to persuade families that these are as much injuries of the occupation as is a bullet wound. The result is that families are now increasingly prepared to come to the centres and to seek help with these issues. But even with this new awareness, it is evident that without trust, parents would not make contact. We were told by the social work coordinator in the city of Nablus that such lack of trust prevents many families from seeking social work assistance provided by the Palestinian Authority for a wide range of psychological trauma conditions. Here is Rami discussing how the centre has been able to address the problem of bed-wetting and sleep problems:

> "The centre has a reputation as being trustworthy. We are from the camp and people in the camp know us. So what generally happens is that they come to the centre – usually when there is an event – and you know they want to speak to you … and they often speak quietly and tell you the problem.… The parents confide in us. They tell us that they have a problem with their children who are peeing the bed, or who seem fine but then start screaming when the lights go out at night, or who wake up with terrible nightmares. Some of the parents, at least, will now come and talk to us about these types of issues.… The other thing is that I think these kinds of problems are now recognised as being a problem associated with the occupation. That the occupation has given all sorts of problems and now we have to deal with these problems. In the past people thought if you were in prison, or had a bullet wound – that was it – and these were injuries of the occupation. But now we know that there is more to it than this." (Balata, June 2008)

Trust is also evident in the ways in which families allow the centres to work and travel with their children. This is particularly so for young girls and women, who are often kept close to the home and face greater restrictions than boys with respect to their time outside the home. All the centres attracted boys and girls and were self-evidently safe places for all.

But trust is something which is not given unconditionally. The centres and the workers are trusted not only because they are of and for the camps but also because of the tangible impacts of their activities. They have been able to improve significantly the lives of the disabled in Jenin; they have helped children realise their talents in Balata and Am'ari; they have enjoyed success with helping children manage their traumas; to relax more; to sleep better; and given them historical and cultural resources which build their steadfastness.

The facts that all these social work initiatives come from within the camps, are managed by those who live in the camps, and are seen as responding to real needs all contribute to this building of trust. But there is more. There is considerable expertise among the workers and those closely associated with the centres (such as board members). Much of this expertise has developed from the work, but in most cases is added to by self-study or university education. There is no assumption that they know all the answers, and the projects have benefited from attachments of people with skills in therapies, art and cultural work and education. Some of this assistance has come via NGOs but much has also come from 'internationals' who, in solidarity with the Palestinian cause, have worked in the camps as volunteers. What is so refreshing about these initiatives is the absence of 'ego'. There is no preciousness about what they know and have experienced; there is no distancing between the 'experts' and the rest and there is, of course, no careerism. There is a sense of humility that comes from knowing that the challenges facing them are enormous and their contribution to their amelioration is small. These factors, it seemed to us, were crucial contributors to the success of their work. They ensured an accessibility and a form of accountability that did not rely on formal events (meetings and the like) but was part of the daily life and processes of their work. Whether things worked out or not was realised immediately, and did not await some evaluation report.

They also contributed to highly respectful practice. On many occasions we witnessed workers in deep conversation with children and young people. The young were being listened to; their ideas were respected and considered. There were no mediating barriers of deficit and pathology, or closed professionalism and authoritarianism.

Undefeated dismay

Difficulties and setbacks stalk many of their initiatives. This is a social work 'in extremis'. Take, for example, the sword-fencing team at the Am'ari centre in Ramallah. This centre had been given some fencing equipment by a French NGO, which was seized upon by some of the young people who managed to find a coach and in time developed some fine fencers, who went on to represent Palestine. Now only one of the fencers is left in the camp. All the others are in Israeli prisons. It seems that success in sports is not tolerated by the Israelis and leads to able sportspeople being targeted for arrest. This also applies to those working in the centres. The Yaffa centre's office has photographs of its board members and workers who are currently imprisoned, their offences, in each case, being no more than that they were trying to make life better for refugees.

In this respect, the centres are no different from the rest of Palestinian society. The overwhelming experience of occupation is setback and failure. Despite all the talk of a peace process, the Palestinians have received virtually nothing. They have an emasculated Palestinian Authority, they have ever-expanding Israeli settlements on their land and hill-tops; the barriers and checkpoints have multiplied and the Wall continues to steal more of their land. And of course there is more. But the point is that social work initiatives, as with the rest of Palestinian society, have to face the choice of either giving up or enduring such ongoing setbacks. As with the majority of the population, they choose endurance, or what the Palestinians call *sumoud* (steadfastness). The fact that they don't give up in the face of an enveloping occupation is celebrated and seen as one of the core aspects of their resistance. It is steadfastness which recognises the significance of even minor victories; it is a steadfastness that celebrates any attempt at the normal in a context of abnormality – whether it is going to work, to university or to school – or rebuilding once more the community centre after it has been ransacked by Israeli troops, or going on with the work despite the imprisonment of key workers.

Thankfully, most welfare and community workers don't have to practise in such extreme circumstances. But it seemed to us that some of the qualities we identified in these projects do provide important insights into what makes for successful practice more generally. They demonstrate that effective social and community work is built on partisanship and being absolutely clear as to 'whose side we are on'. It resonates with Wright Mills' work on private ills and social problems and the therapeutic value of understanding traumas of all forms in their appropriate socio-political context. It highlights the importance of trust and practice free of stigma. It provides insights into how practice can be thorough and skilled while avoiding the dead hand of professional superiority and power. It is a practice which is historically informed so as to allow people to understand their predicament without resorting to self-blame. And, despite all the setbacks, it is a practice that does make a difference.

Note

[1] It remains unclear how many people were killed in the Jenin Massacre. As Baroud notes: 'Israel still holds hundreds of Palestinian men from the Jenin refugee camp in prisons in the West Bank and in Israel. Most of these prisoners are confirmed alive, yet the fate of others remains unknown.... There are still names to be accounted for and missing to be found. Some fighters reportedly rushed to Jenin to help defend the camp prior to the Israeli invasion in early April 2002. These fighters might be reported missing in Tulkarm and Ramallah, but they actually went missing in Jenin. Because Israeli soldiers destroyed Palestinian records in hospitals, schools and government buildings, this question [how many died] may never be answered' (2003, p 21).

TWO

Samidoun: grassroots welfare and popular resistance in Beirut during the 33-Day War of 2006

Michael Lavalette and Barrie Levine

Being neutral in a time of war becomes an inhuman act. (Chit, 2008)

Introduction

This chapter tells the story of a remarkable social welfare movement that emerged in Beirut during the 33-Day War waged on Lebanon by Israel from 12 July to 14 August 2006. This was the third time that Israel had invaded Lebanon (with previous invasions in 1978 and 1982), and the effect on the Lebanese people was catastrophic. During the war: 'At least 1,140 civilians – 30% of them children under 12 – [were] killed' (*The Daily Star*, 2006). According to Human Rights Watch (2007), Israel showed 'reckless indifference' to the fate of civilians during its attacks.

These attacks included near-constant air and sea assaults on Beirut, Tripoli, Tyre, Qana, Srifa and Baalbeck. Roads, bridges and factories were targeted alongside civilian areas – like the large, impoverished, mainly Shi'a southern suburb of Beirut known as the Dahyeh – while the oil refinery at Jiyyeh was bombed, causing massive environmental damage along 150 km of the Lebanese coast.

As a consequence, as aircraft bombarded towns and cities and ground troops thrust into Southern Lebanon, refugees from across Lebanon, and particularly Southern Lebanon, abandoned their homes and villages and flooded into central Beirut. The refugees' requirements were immediate and substantial – food, accommodation and medical support had to be provided and a range of social, welfare and psychological needs had to be met. But the traditional suppliers of welfare in Beirut, the vast number of civil society organisations in the voluntary sector and the more limited state sector both removed their staff and closed down under the air assault.

Into this gap stepped a new, vibrant and democratic organisation – *Samidoun* – which became the main provider of basic needs for a large section of the refugee population in the city.

In January 2009 we arrived in Beirut with a vague awareness of the organisation and its role in providing 'humanitarian support' during the 33-Day War. Over 10 very intense days, we spoke to 15 key activists who were involved in every aspect of Samidoun's activities. Each recorded interview lasted for approximately 90 minutes. In addition, the activists provided us with written material and photographs relating to their activities during the war. We were quickly put right about one issue in particular: it was not solely 'humanitarian aid' but 'popular resistance' that the movement was engaged in. The organisation was consciously political and the activists saw themselves taking part in the war as part of what they termed the 'internal front'. The name Samidoun is itself important to understanding the organisation: in English, it translates as collective 'steadfastness', and it is a word imbued with notions of resistance.

In this chapter we intend to look at the development of Samidoun and the various initiatives it undertook in the context of the July war. We explore the politics behind the organisation and its links to the broader social movement against the invasion. Finally, we ask if there are any general lessons that can be drawn from the Samidoun experience for social workers and welfare providers in 'extreme' circumstances as well as more generally. In doing this, we draw on the words of the activists themselves. Due to the continuing political instability in the region, to protect individuals' security, we have not used actual names.

We start, however, with what we believe is a necessary, albeit brief, description of the background out of which Samidoun emerged – the modern Lebanese state and its (continuing) tense relationship with its Israeli neighbour.

The creation of modern Lebanon

The modern history of Lebanon is one that is shaped by the country's encounter with western imperialism. Although French interference in the Mount Lebanon region started at the end of the 19th century, an understanding of the problems of the modern Middle East has to begin by looking at the 'carve-up' of the region by the French and British colonial authorities on the collapse of the Ottoman Empire at the end of the First World War (Hourani, 1991).

During the war the British, in particular, courted various Arab nationalists with a vague promise of support for independence after the war if they would join allied forces against the Ottomans (encapsulated best in an exchange of letters between Sir Hugh McMahon, British High Commissioner in Egypt and Husayn Bin Ali, the Sharif of Mecca, known as the McMahon–Husayn correspondence of 1915–16 [Fromkin, 1989]). In June 1916 the Arab Revolt saw somewhere in the region of 70,000 Arabs rise up against the Ottoman sultan in a series of attacks that paved the way for the British capture of Palestine and Syria (Hourani, 1991).

Yet, despite the above-mentioned commitments, in May 1916 the Sykes–Picot Agreement between Britain and France set in play a process that divided the Middle East and the Maghrib into French and British spheres of influence, mandate areas and regions of more direct control. Britain took control over

Iraq, Iran, Egypt, Palestine and Jordan; France controlled Algeria, Tunisia, part of Morocco, Syria and Lebanon.

The present-day borders of Lebanon were drawn up by the authorities of the French colonial mandate over Syria and Lebanon in 1920. The French instigated a system that built sectarian divisions into the very fabric of Lebanese state and society: people were (and still are) given a religious affiliation at birth (Sunni, Shi'a, Christian, Maronite, and so on) and this then determines their engagement with society, including (today) where they can vote (Makdisi, 2008).

In 1943 the National Pact became the founding agreement of independent Lebanon – but it sanctioned 'the sectarian distribution of positions and seats in the Lebanese state according to a rule that gave a 6–11 majority to Christians' (Achar and Warschawski, 2007, p 12). The agreement built instability into the very fabric of Lebanese society.

A further important element in the politics of Lebanese society came with the arrival of a large number of Palestinian refugees in the aftermath of the Nakba of 1948. Today Lebanon contains 300,000 Palestinian refugees, about one-tenth of its population. The Palestinians are treated as second-class citizens (even the vast majority who were born in the country). They are restricted from access to certain jobs and 'most … have had little choice but to live in overcrowded and deteriorating camps and informal gatherings that lack basic infrastructure'; most have suffered 'systematic discrimination' at the hands of successive Lebanese governments (Amnesty International, 2007).

In 1958 the first cracks started to appear in post-war Lebanese society. For many Muslims in Lebanon, Nasser's Egypt and his vision of a United Arab Federation seemed attractive and a way to unite the Arab peoples and confront imperialism and Zionism in the region. For other segments of Lebanese society (mainly Christian), Nasser's vision was looked upon with horror. Into this divide US marines arrived in Lebanon at the request of the then President Chamoun and helped the Maronite Christian General Chehab to set up an increasingly authoritarian rule (Achar and Warschawski, 2007).

In the 1950s and 1960s Lebanon experienced a period of significant economic growth. This economic growth benefitted some communities over others, with the Shi'a community, in particular, being marginalised. It also had the effect of sucking people into Beirut – to the extent that today over half the population of the country lives in the greater Beirut conurbation (Traboulsi, 2007).

Sectarian, political and class differences created the context within which Lebanon entered a period of civil war, military intervention (from Syria and Israel) and occupation (Fisk, 1990). Lebanon was divided by civil war between 1975 and 1990. In 1978 Israel occupied Lebanon south of the Litani River. In response to UN resolution 425 it withdrew later in the year, to be replaced by the UN Interim Force in Lebanon (which remains there today). However, the Israelis retained control of the southern region of Lebanon by managing a 12-mile (19 km) wide 'security zone' along the border. To hold these positions, Israel installed the South Lebanese Army (SLA), a Christian/Shi'a proxy militia, which it supplied with arms and resources. Israel also intervened in the Lebanese civil war to support Christian militia and the Maronite Phalange.

Both the SLA and the Phalange were to play a role in the invasion of 1982. After years of border incursions and bombing, the Israelis invaded to create a northern 'buffer zone' and expel the Palestinians from the country. The Israelis drove towards Beirut, placed the city under siege, expelled the Palestine Liberation Organisation leadership from the city and oversaw the massacre of Palestinian refugees by the Phalange in the camps of Sabra and Shatila (al-Hout, 2004). The Israeli occupation was to last 18 years and saw further intervention from US forces, all with disastrous results for the Lebanese people (Fisk, 1990).

The civil war and occupation led, on the one hand, to the decline of the political left and pan-Arab nationalism as significant political currents within the country; the Iranian Revolution of 1979, on the other hand, seemed to offer an 'Islamist alternative', one that was taken up by the emergent organisation Hezbollah (Norton, 2007).

The Israeli occupation created the space for the growth of Hezbollah, and throughout the 1990s Hezbollah spearheaded the resistance to Israel. In the process, Hezbollah was transformed by its role in the resistance movement from a military organisation to one that looked to more 'traditional' forms of political engagement. Early indicators of a change in direction appeared after the publication of its letter to the 'Downtrodden in Lebanon and the World', published in February 1985, which combined strong anti-imperialist rhetoric with the outlines of a social and political programme to improve the lives of the poor and the dispossessed (see Harik, 2004; Norton, 2007). In the 1990s Hezbollah started to provide health, welfare and education programmes that took it beyond the limits of a narrow Islamist politics to one that appealed to a 'national movement' for liberation from occupation.

In May 2000 the Israelis abandoned Lebanon. Hezbollah took the credit for the liberation of the country and its support base grew as a result. Hezbollah stood in Lebanon's parliamentary elections and was drawn into the government. But its hopes of transition into a mainstay of Lebanese politics were dashed after the 11 September 2001 attacks on the US. Hezbollah was declared a terrorist organisation by the White House. The US and France authored UN resolution 1559, which called for Hezbollah to be disarmed and for the Lebanese army to protect Israel's northern border (Saad-Ghorayeb, 2002; Harik, 2004; Norton, 2007). The demonisation of Hezbollah also created an opportunity for Israel to deal with its intransigent opponents to the north of its borders.

The 'War on Terror' and the 33-Day War on Lebanon

The Israeli attack on Lebanon in 2006 can be fully understood only as part of the broader 'War on Terror' that was launched by the US in the aftermath of the 9/11 terror attacks on New York and Washington. The attacks on Afghanistan and then Iraq saw US and British troops – with smaller contingents from a range of other countries known as the 'coalition of the willing' – launch major ground and air assaults on Afghanistan (from October 2001) and Iraq (from March 2003). In both cases 'early victory' was declared (most infamously on 1 May 2003 when President Bush delivered his 'mission accomplished' speech from on board the USS *Abraham Lincoln*); but in both countries the Coalition forces found themselves drawn into a protracted war of occupation (German and Murray, 2005).

By 2006 US and British troops in Iraq found themselves increasingly isolated, casualties were increasing and large parts of the country were under the de facto control of the Iraqi resistance (Cockburn, 2008). In these circumstances there was increasing discussion in political and media circles about the supply routes to the resistance forces and the perceived forces at work supplying and supporting the resistance movement in Iraq. Increasingly this was identified as the 'problem of the Shi'a crescent': the notion that Iran (identified as a rogue state and part of the 'axis of evil') was funding various Shi'a organisations across the region (many of them identified as 'terror organisations' by the White House) to foster instability and increase its support base. As Bröning argues:

> [there is] a perception [in Western circles] … of a hegemonic Iran that is attempting to dominate the region through an array of Shiite proxies. This Iranian fifth column is believed to stretch from Beirut via Damascus, Gaza to Baghdad and finally from Iran to Saudi-Arabia to Yemen. (2008)

The links between, for example, Shi'a Iran and Sunni Hamas are not fully explained in this analysis, but in 2005/06 the notions of the 'Shi'a Crescent' offered some an appropriate 'enemy' to target and to explain their military failings. But the idea of the Shi'a Crescent is at best problematic. It is:

> ultimately based on generalizations that reveal more about its advocates than the actual reality on the ground.… Take Iraq … Iraqi Shiites do not form a homogenous block that opposes the supposedly unified Sunnis … These complexities are lost on many observers when matched up against the convenient and catchy rhetoric of the 'Shia Crescent.' (Bröning, 2008)

Journalist Jason Burke suggested:

> The 'Shia axis' depicted by Israeli, US and some European commentators and by Sunni regional powers links Syria, Hezbollah and finally Sunni Palestinian organisations such as Hamas. While rulers like King Abdullah of Jordan or Egypt's Hosni Mubarak have obvious reasons to fear a resurgent Shia bloc, the broad coalition of 'neo-conservative' analysts seek to minimise local social, economic and political factors

behind radical movements in favour of all-encompassing explanations that finger individual people or states. (Burke, 2006)

For the US, targeting Iran while being already involved in two costly interventions in Iraq and Afghanistan was risky. But Hezbollah offered an easier proxy to engage – especially as many Western analysts thought the popular mobilisation of 14 March in Lebanon (which forced the expulsion of Syria from Lebanon) had left Hezbollah weak, vulnerable and isolated (Achar and Warschawski, 2007).

The second factor at play was Israel's determination to deal with Hamas in Gaza. In January 2006 popular elections in Palestine saw the election of the Islamist movement Hamas to government (though the Presidency of the Occupied Territories remained in the hands of Mahmoud Abbas, leader of Fatah). In response, the US, Britain and Israel launched an economic blockade against Gaza and the West Bank. Israel argued that Hamas (another White House-identified 'terror organisation') was armed, trained and financed by Iran via Hezbollah – thus, dealing with Hamas meant dealing with the 'Shi'a Crescent' at its weak point: Hezbollah in Lebanon. Therefore, continuing a very traditional role as, in the words of Israeli newspaper *Ha'aretz*, America's 'watch-dog' in the Middle East (see Rose, 1986), Israel prepared to attack Hezbollah for its own strategic aims and in the wider interests of imperialism in the Middle East.

The creation of Samidoun

In June 2006 Israel attacked Hamas's stronghold in Gaza. In response, pro-Palestinian activists in Lebanon organised a sit-in protest at the Beirut sea-front. As they gathered, they received news of Israel's attack on Lebanon. Some left immediately to go back to their families, others (for example the few members of the Lebanese Communist Party who were present) left to join the resistance fighters in the south of the country, but the majority stayed to debate what they should do. BE described the scene:

> "It was very chaotic. People were angry, scared, excited – it was a strange feeling. But we had to decide what we were going to do. There was a lot of debate and argument but then G and B argued that we should use our skills and our knowledge to set up a popular resistance movement."

This was the starting point of a movement that grew from a handful of activists to a grassroots organisation with over a thousand volunteers in a matter of days. Not only was the growth of Samidoun remarkable, but the extent of its operations could be argued to exceed that of major NGOs in the field of disaster relief.

M was also present at the sea-front. He recalled:

"We decided we had to do something, but what we were doing only became clear over the following days. Initially we knew there would be people who would flee the fighting and come to the city – this is Lebanon, we know what happens in war. We knew they would need basic support. So we decided to form 'Samidoun' and see what we could do."

G told us:

"We argued that we should be part of the popular resistance – part of a united front with Hezbollah and the Communist Party who were taking up arms. We had shared goals with them: resistance to Israel. But as they fight they need to know that their family, friends and community are safe. The popular resistance interconnects with this and becomes an important part of the resistance movement. Our slogan was 'unconditional but critical support' for the armed resistance, but full support for popular resistance and being with the masses."

The roots of Samidoun can be traced to four sources. First, as G told us:

"It harked back to older traditions of solidarity in Lebanon that were apparent in the 1970s. There were strong activist and left currents in Lebanon at that time and strong traditions and established networks that could provide support and direction to working-class communities when Lebanon was going through one of its recurrent periods of crisis or war."

In other words, establishing such a solidarity network was part of what sociologists of social movements might term the Lebanese left's historic 'repertoire of contention' (Tarrow, 1994).

Second, there was the creation of a new left that was developing in Lebanon out of the Global Justice or anti-capitalist movement. As B relates:

"In Lebanon the protests at Seattle [in December 1999] and the creation of the World Social Forums was very important. They helped open a space for debate and acted as a mechanism to pull activists together in Beirut in particular. We had been so divided and so marginalised for such a long time – Seattle and the Forums were the inspiration for a new generation."

So B suggests that, after years of civil war and political isolation, the new global wave of protest that was initiated at Seattle acted as a magnet to draw activists together in the Beirut region.

Third, there was the impact of the imperial intervention into the Middle Eastern region, the second Palestinian Intifada and the Israeli attacks on Gaza and the West Bank on the growth of the pro-Palestinian and anti-war movement that developed in Lebanon in 2002 and 2003. Here L outlines the importance of the Palestinian question:

> "I started working in one of the Palestinian refugee camps in 2002 – as a worker with an NGO. The Palestinian issue has always been central to Lebanese politics and solidarity with the Palestinians a central concern for anyone who considers themselves as either an Arab nationalist or a leftist or an anti-imperialist. The Palestinian presence in Lebanon is a constant reminder of both the existence of the state of Israel and its links to imperialism in the region and to the unequal and divided nature of Lebanese society. Attacks on the Palestinians are close to us – geographically and politically."

In 2002, in response to the Second Intifada, Israel launched a series of major incursions into the Palestinian West Bank. Nablus was placed under curfew for 200 days (between 18 June and 31 December); in Jenin an estimated 100 Palestinians were killed during an eight-day incursion into the refugee camp – an event which earned the nomenclature 'Jeningrad' in Palestinian circles – and Ramallah was invaded and President Arafat's compound was seized (Baroud, 2003; Pratt, 2006).

In the face of this political crisis and attack on the Palestinians of the West Bank, activists staged an 'open sit-in protest' in Martyrs Square, close to the sea-front area of Beirut. The square became an open space where people could come and discuss a range of political questions and organise activities and demonstrations in support of Palestine. It was in this space in 2006 that Samidoun was formed.

Last, the large number of NGOs operating in the Beirut area provided a reservoir of young activists with relevant social welfare and social work skills. There are an estimated 4,000 registered NGOs in Lebanon (close to one for every 10 citizens), with half operating in the greater Beirut area. They vary in size, links with the Lebanese state and their links with international co-partners or parent organisations. The NGOs are contradictory institutions. The larger, international NGOs have often been used as the 'soft face' of welfare privatisation in much of the developing world under the suggestion that civil society (that is, non-state) organisations are more efficient and more democratic than state providers of services. But the NGO sector also includes smaller, more radical organisations, many of which have grown up in the vacuum left by the decline of the organised far Left in the 1980s and 1990s (Lavalette and Ferguson, 2007b). The NGO sector in Lebanon is also a major employment outlet for many young graduates. Further, working in NGO social welfare work in a society like Lebanon requires an engagement with significant political questions, as G suggests:

"You cannot be a social worker in Lebanon unless you are an activist. Every issue is political. How do you talk to a conservative woman about breast cancer, or young people about sexuality, without talking about politics? These are political issues which link into campaigning activities … The international NGOs want to de-politicise these things, but it's not possible."

The first task Samidoun faced was finding somewhere to operate from. H told us:

"In previous wars people have headed to the Sanaya Park. This started for the first time in 1982 – and later 40 people were massacred there – but it's now common knowledge, that's where you go. So we needed somewhere close to the park to operate out of."

Lebanon's history of war and civil strife meant that people knew where to go, where was safe and where they would find others in a similar position to themselves: there was an embedded historical knowledge of what to do in crisis situations.

Luckily for the Samidoun activists, the ideal venue to operate out of was close at hand. Many of the activists were involved in gay, lesbian and transgender politics and the Helem LGBT centre was next to the park. G runs the centre and was one of the volunteers. After a quick management committee meeting it was agreed to hand the Helem centre over to Samidoun for coordination of immediate relief work. Interestingly, given some of the perceptions in the West regarding attitudes to sexual politics, the LGBT centre is in the Sunni Muslim sector of Beirut; activists told us it would be much more difficult to run the centre in the Christian part of the city. Further, and again challenging preconceived notions about Islam and attitudes to sexuality, over the next few weeks leading Hezbollah figures met with Samidoun activists to coordinate their spheres of operation – and were happy to meet in the centre, replete with its posters and adverts for safe sex.

With their base established, activists had to institute some basic working rules. As G told us:

"Our aim was to get working. We didn't want to spend hours debating what to do, we wanted to do it! But at the same time we wanted everyone to feel that they had ownership over the organisation. So we decided we should strive for a flat organisation, one that was de-centralised and without any hierarchy. We wanted people to be able to take initiatives and get on with the job at hand – imagine if everything relied on the say of one person or a small group of people and they got killed or injured, the organisation would collapse. Similarly, what if everything had to be debated and voted on – we'd never actually do anything! So second, we wanted there to be as few obstacles as possible. If you have a job, go and do it. But third, this only works if there is complete democratic involvement. So we had an open meeting, an assembly, every night – once all the work of the day had been done – when we would reflect on our day's work and activities, discuss our needs – what we were short of, for example – and plan our activities for the following day. But importantly, we also discussed and debated the progress of the war because we weren't just a relief group, we were a political part of the resistance movement."

Samidoun's evening assemblies were held from 11pm onwards and often lasted for several hours. Figure 2.1 is a photograph of some of the activists at an early assembly.

Figure 2.1: Samidoun's daily assembly (photograph courtesy of Samidoun)

Perhaps not surprisingly, given its roots, Samidoun's activists interpreted their actions in very clear political terms:

Our strategy ... was to build Samidoun as a popular solidarity campaign, which supported the resistance against the aggression, through civil, popular and unarmed means ... [But] at the same time, the campaign called for unconditional but critical support for the resistance. (Chit, 2008)

Finally, this wasn't an exclusive club! The intention was to establish a popular resistance organisation that focused on meeting the basic material needs of the victims of the Israeli assa ult. Such a grand plan required people to volunteer and get involved. They managed to persuade Lebanese television to put out a call for volunteers. T told us:

> "Nobody told me in advance, but my mobile number was put out as the contact point. Suddenly my phone started ringing. That first day I got over 400 calls from people phoning to volunteer with our operation."

By the end of the 33-Day War just over 1,000 people had volunteered and been active within the Samidoun network.

Meeting human need in a time of crisis

During the first couple of days of the war the activists had organised themselves and found a base to work from, but there was still confusion over what was to be done. As F told us:

> "In the first two days of the war we were not sure what to do. But for that first week we were the only ones who were working and providing relief for the refugees. The state and the large voluntary sector in Beirut all pulled their staff out of front-line work."

Gradually, as increasing numbers of refugees came to Sanaya Park, the priorities became obvious: Samidoun had to turn towards meeting basic human needs. At the assembly on the evening of the third day of war the activists started to grapple with the scale of the issues they had to address. The most pressing issue was the provision of appropriate shelter. F and T were tasked with organising this for the people in the park. Historically, the Lebanese state had allowed people access to school buildings when they fled to Beirut. This time the schools had been locked and the refugees kept out. T and F told us what they decided to do:

> **F**: "We went to the schools. There were people outside but the schools were locked."
>
> **T**: "So we had no real choice, we decided we had to open the schools. We went to the nearest one with about a thousand people following us."
>
> **F**: "We approached the school janitor and he told us that he had been told he was not to open the schools. So I got on the phone and got through to the government and told them I was going to bring the

TV people down and show how our government was doing nothing. They told me that their decision was final. So T and I decided we would kick down the school doors and open the schools."

T: "I was nervous ... but there were all these people there. There were kids with no water; families were sleeping in the streets. These people had travelled for five or six hours to escape the bombing. So what could we do? We had no choice. We broke in, opened up the schools and provided shelter. After we had done the first school, the rest were easy. I'm glad we did this; it was the right thing to do."

F: "After the first one we just went from school to school. We opened 10 schools that first day – each time we had to break in. The next day the government relented. They opened the schools officially because we told them we would break in if necessary."

Eventually Samidoun was covering 30 schools with over 10,000 refugees in them at any one point.

The schools were opened and classrooms were allocated to families. But, as they realised at that evening's assembly, this success raised new 'demands': people had to be fed and watered; it was essential that families had something to sleep on, so mattresses and blankets were required, soap and shampoo were needed to maintain hygiene standards; cleaning equipment was necessary so that the schools could be kept clean; some of the refugees had injuries and some required prescription medicines, so there was a need for some medical support. As L told us:

"At first we were going to schools and writing down what people wanted, but it became clear very quickly that this was too chaotic. At our assemblies we started to talk about this. We decided we needed to specialise into teams – for medicines, food, hygiene etc. I headed up the medical team ... even though I had no medical experience. But I was able to do needs assessments of the immediate and chronic illnesses that people had. Then, as we got publicity, we had doctors and pharmacists who came to us and volunteered to work with us. Eventually we had a pharmacy run by pharmacy students; a mobile medical unit run by doctors who would travel to the schools and do check-ups and assessments of people."

Thus the assembly decided that the only way for the organisation to function appropriately was by specialising. The participants voted to divide themselves into specialised sections. Over the next few days the number of sections grew until there were 15 operating out of the Helem centre. These were Distribution (making sure that there was a match between demand and supply of goods), Call Centre, Stores (supply of materials and foods was irregular, so there had to be somewhere to store and retrieve goods – often this was in activists' homes), Assessment, Data Centre, Medical, Health and Prevention, Media Unit (which comprised two sections, one dealing with internal Lebanese media, the other with external media relations), Volunteer registration and allocation, Co-ordination Unit (to work with other NGOs), Finance, Purchasing, Psycho-Social Support, Hygiene and Public Health. The functions of some of these centres are obvious (Finance and Purchasing, for example) but the role of others is perhaps less familiar.

The Data Centre ran the website and was primarily concerned with plotting the military activities of the Israeli Defence Force. Hour by hour it plotted where bombs were landing and the extent of Israel's invasion of the south of the country. It then produced daily maps of areas that were being targeted and these were published on the website www.maps.samidoun.org (unfortunately the site is no longer active). As an example, one of the daily maps is reproduced here (Figure 2.2). Samidoun's maps were so precise that the BBC and other international media started to use them as the most accurate description of what was happening and where attacks were occurring. But the reason why Samidoun started plotting the attack sites was not to service international media outlets. There were two reasons for such work. First, through the website, it wanted to engage politically with other internet users about what was happening in Lebanon, the scale of the attack and the progress of the resistance. Second, the bombing maps helped to ascertain where refugees were coming from, where it was safer for Samidoun activists to travel to, where it was best to open up shelters and where cluster bombs were being dropped (the IDF dropped over a million cluster bombs on Lebanon during the war, as well as large numbers of phosphorous shells [Rappaport, 2006]). It soon became clear that Israel was bombing particular parts of Beirut, the poor, southern Shi'a quarters and the Palestinian camps, for example. This information affected where Samidoun opened up schools and shelters and where it would go on relief runs.

The Call Centre was the key organising hub of the network. It acted as the activists' main point of contact. It was where daily digests of what was happening and what was needed were fed to and sent out from. It was where other organisations could contact Samidoun. It was the Call Centre, for example, that took a call from a woman who was trapped with her children in a bombed house in the Dahyeh (the main Shi'a area in the southern suburbs of the city.) One of the activists, a young Palestinian, M, volunteered to go and get her. This was a dangerous mission, but the daily maps helped to give some idea of where the raids were happening that day. M takes up the story:

> "The woman phoned us and was desperate. She had been trapped for three days with her kids. They had no food or water. What could you do? What choice was there? We couldn't leave her. Of course it was dangerous, war is dangerous … but we had to help her."

Figure 2.2: Example of Samidoun daily map (this one was produced on 10 August)

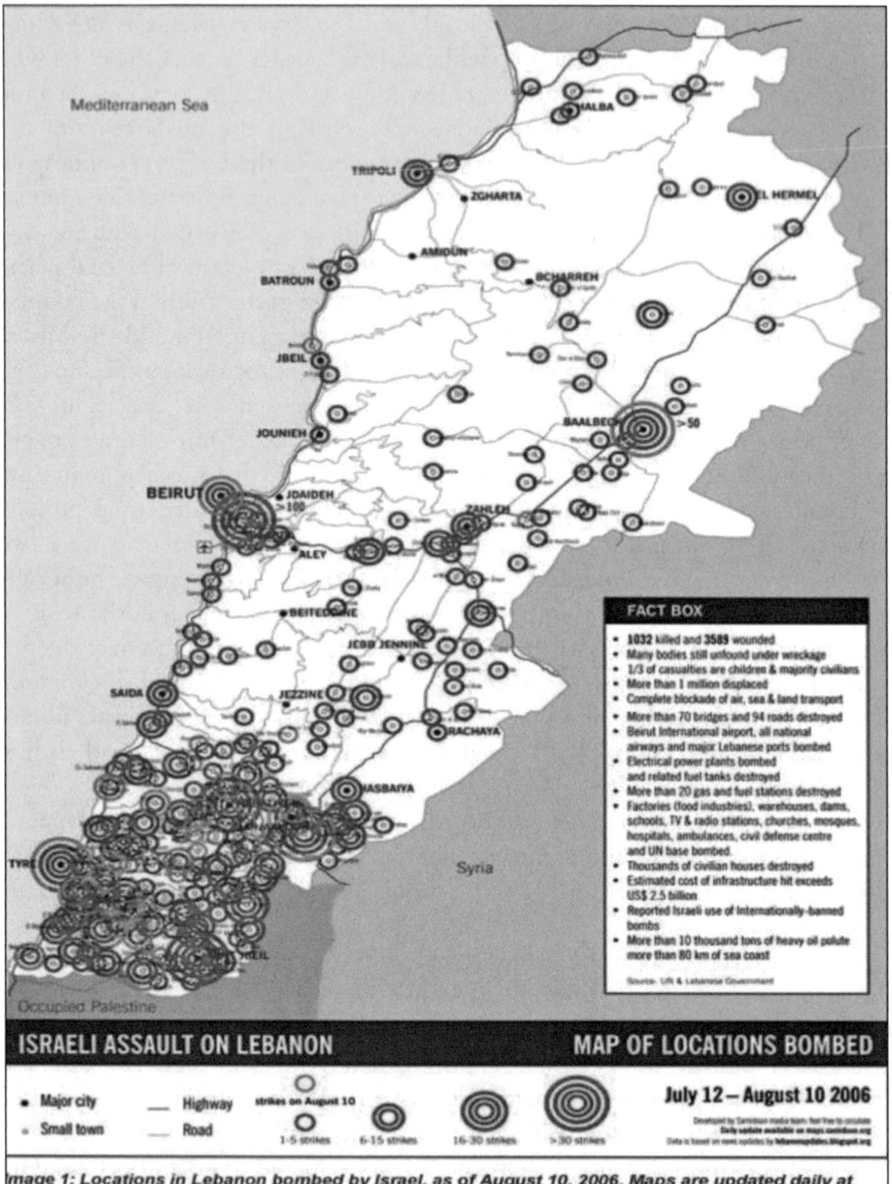

Mediterranean Sea

TRIPOLI
ZGHARTA
EL HERMEL
AMIDUN
BATROUN
BCHARREH
JBEIL
BAALBEC >50
JOUNIEH
BEIRUT
JDAIDEH >100
ALEY
ZAHLEH
BEITEDDINE
JEBB JENNINE
SAIDA
JEZZINE
RACHAYA
HASBAIYA
TYRE

Syria

Occupied Palestine

FACT BOX

- 1032 killed and 3589 wounded
- Many bodies still unfound under wreckage
- 1/3 of casualties are children & majority civilians
- More than 1 million displaced
- Complete blockade of air, sea & land transport
- More than 70 bridges and 94 roads destroyed
- Beirut International airport, all national airways and major Lebanese ports bombed
- Electrical power plants bombed and related fuel tanks destroyed
- More than 20 gas and fuel stations destroyed
- Factories (food industries), warehouses, dams, schools, TV & radio stations, churches, mosques, hospitals, ambulances, civil defense centre and UN base bombed.
- Thousands of civilian houses destroyed
- Estimated cost of infrastructure hit exceeds US$ 2.5 billion
- Reported Israeli use of internationally-banned bombs
- More than 10 thousand tons of heavy oil pollute more than 80 km of sea coast

Source: UN & Lebanese Government

ISRAELI ASSAULT ON LEBANON   **MAP OF LOCATIONS BOMBED**

- Major city   — Highway   strikes on August 10
- Small town   — Road   1-5 strikes   6-15 strikes   16-30 strikes   >30 strikes

July 12 – August 10 2006

Developed by Samidoun media team: feel free to circulate
Daily update available on maps.samidoun.org
Data is based on news updates by lebanonupdates.blogspot.org

Image 1: Locations in Lebanon bombed by Israel, as of August 10, 2006. Maps are updated daily at http://maps.samidoun.org/

This case made the activists aware that a number of refugees were trapped in the southern regions of the city and were not able to get to the safe shelters. L volunteered to drive through Dahyeh looking for those who had been left behind. She told us:

"I started to drive around and look for people and take them to the shelters and the schools. People from Dahyeh are the very poorest in Beirut. They have no credit cards or savings. So when they fled their homes they had nothing."

People telephoned the Call Centre because of the success Samidoun was having with its local media operation. As the only active and functioning network working with and for the refugees it started to get airspace on Lebanese television and radio. Its contact details were published widely. People started to access its website to get accurate information about what was happening. Donations started to roll in, both from within Lebanon and from the international community. This in turn allowed the network to purchase essential goods and get them out to the refugees on the ground. R remembers:

"Just after the fighting stopped we got a phone call from a woman in Egypt. She told us that she had arranged for a plane load of goods to be sent to the airport for Samidoun (the airport had only just re-opened). I rushed over with T to get the material – only to find that the government had appeared and requisitioned the materials. We never saw any of it."

Decisions on all these matters were raised and discussed at the evening assemblies. One slight regret that the activists expressed to us was that they did not take any money from the donations they received to cover the network's running costs. Every penny raised was used for immediate refugee relief. While this was very admirable it did mean that many of the activists ended up with considerable debts as a result of their involvement in Samidoun (telephone bills, car-running costs, purchase of foodstuffs in the early days, were all met out of the activists' own pockets).

The Finance section was crucial to the operation. D ran the section, kept detailed accounts and after the fighting stopped was central to various 'bid-writing' applications to the EU and various international NGOs for aid and support. But at the height of the fighting things were less organised. As she told us:

"Of course we couldn't open a bank account in the middle of a war! So we used our personal accounts to get money for the organisation. But for most things we needed cash. So people would come to me for money to buy food or medicines or whatever. Every day I was walking around the city, in the middle of a war, with $4,000–$5,000 in my handbag! Of course people might say 'this is not good', or 'this is not accountable' or whatever … but it was the middle of a war. We didn't have the luxury of formal financial procedures. But everything was accounted for, everything was open and everyone knew what was happening and what we were spending money on."

Perhaps the most important section was the Assessment Section. This was charged with keeping track of the numbers of refugees in each school and shelter and keeping in daily contact with the shelters to ascertain their needs for food, money, medicines, specialist help and so on. It was often the report from this section that would alert the activists to immediate shortfalls or failings in their operation. F and T played the central role in this part of the operation. They told us how they managed the liaison. F told us:

> "We discussed how we could keep in contact with so many schools and shelters and how we could manage to keep on top of what was happening and know about shortages, needs — in fact even the numbers involved. Before the war I would have thought that a refugee population like we had would be fairly static, that people would flee their homes, come to a shelter and stay until the fighting was over. But it wasn't like that. Some people stayed the entire time; others fled their homes, came to a shelter and then, after a few days, moved on to live with relatives in a safer part of the country or city."

At one of its assemblies it decided the solution was for each shelter to elect its own organising committee and for that committee to keep in regular daily contact with the Assessment Section. The democratic ideals of Samidoun made this solution seem obvious: it encouraged wider democratic involvement and engagement in the process of meeting community needs. However, the ideal came up against the harsh reality of Lebanese society in a time of conflict. T takes up the story:

> "We wanted each shelter to elect their own committee, but it became clear this wasn't going to work. The shelters were all over the city and the militias in each zone wanted to make sure that their people had a role running the shelter where they were. Some of these people are very dangerous and some were very suspicious of us and what we were doing. In the Christian areas the war of 2006 marked a break with the past in that the population supported the resistance and there were even signs of support for the Palestinians — but the organisations in these areas had to be handled with care! In the parts of the city run by Amal [a Shi'a militia with strong support from Syria that has historically fought against both the Palestinians during the 'War of the Camps' and Hezbollah] it was also difficult. Amal have a history of violent opposition to the Left — and they worked with us, but again wanted control of 'their' schools and shelters. Actually the easiest to work with were Hezbollah. They were mainly concerned with the military struggle against Israel and let us just get on with running the schools and shelters as we saw fit. But we decided in each shelter to be pragmatic, if there was an opportunity for the people in the shelter

to elect their own committee – great, if people were appointed by the organisations that was fine too."

Each shelter had a committee, therefore, and each day there would be a telephone conversation (at the very least) between the shelter and the Assessment Section to discuss what resources were needed. Each shelter committee was responsible for ensuring that the shelter was kept clean and swept, that there was space for the children and that inter-family disputes, should they arise, were managed appropriately.

However, as T suggested, precisely how this was managed in each shelter depended on the area where the shelter was located and the role of the local militias. This is something that D also commented on. She told us:

"As Samidoun activists we cut across the militias and their ways of organising. But we had to be careful. Some of the militias have some very rough thugs attached to them. I think I can speak for all the activists when I say that we preferred going to Hezbollah areas. You felt safer and they left us alone."

The relationship with Hezbollah emerged after the first few days. As the only active group on the ground providing relief and support in Beirut, Samidoun was approached for a formal meeting with Hezbollah's Beirut military commander. The meeting was arranged at the Helem Centre. B describes what happened:

"We met and discussed how we could work together. Of course we have many differences and disagreements with Hezbollah, but we told them that we saw ourselves as part of the popular resistance and that our task was to be with those behind the front lines making sure they are safe and they have the resources they need. He told us that Hezbollah supported our activities and if we had any trouble we should contact him. To get such official backing was very important for us. It made our movements and our activities across the city much easier. I think Hezbollah felt that if we did this kind of work, it meant they didn't have to, they could concentrate on fighting – and their fighters would know that their families were being looked after in Beirut."

More humorously T, who had organised the meeting, told us:

"During the meeting the Commander was looking at the posters on the wall. There was one advertising condoms, another of two gay men kissing. At the end of the meeting he said to me: 'What is this place?' and I told him it was the gay and lesbian centre. He then asked: 'Are they supporting you?' and I told him they were giving us their office and were very involved. He just said: 'God bless you all' and left!"

After the first few days a basic routine was established. The days were long (activists told us they had as little as four hours sleep a night) but each section knew what it had to do and got on with the tasks in hand. However, the Assessment Section soon started to report that the children in the shelters were getting bored, with little to do, and that there was concern that some of the children had been traumatised by the horrors that they had witnessed. The Psycho-Social Support Section developed its work to address these issues.

MI is a social worker and was working in the voluntary sector before the war. She played a leading role within the Psycho-Social Support Section, along with O and A. MI told us about their initial concerns:

> "We thought we should try to focus on issues of trauma among the displaced. We were particularly worried about the children and the sights they had seen. So we got volunteers who were social workers, psychologists, teachers and put together a programme to try and offer some form of psycho-social support."

O explained some of their thinking:

> "We tried to offer a space for individual sessions, if people wanted to come and talk to us. We thought they would perhaps want to come

Figure 2.3: Entertaining the kids (photograph courtesy of Samidoun)

and talk about what they had seen. But we also wanted to address the trauma in different ways. One of our members (M) was a clown and he moved from shelter to shelter. The kids loved it and he got lots of coverage in the news. It was strange to see a clown in the middle of bombed-out buildings! [Figure 2.3] A was a traditional story-teller and he used to put on sessions telling classic Lebanese stories. Then we had art classes and other organised activities for the children."

Originally the activists thought they were providing a service for the children, but they were surprised to find that many of the adults started coming to the events. In the conversations that took place and in some one-to-one sessions it was clear that the adults had been traumatised by their experiences and this had been compounded by anxieties over what was happening to their children.

The team used a variety of broadly social pedagogical approaches to engage with the refugees, to create the space for them to think and talk about what had happened to them, to express their fears and anxieties in a collective and non-threatening way and for the refugees (many of whom came from quite conservative parts of the country) to start to connect with each other and come to some form of collective understanding as to what had happened to them. Art and drama, singing and story-telling, juggling and work with clowns, football and other games were all used as a means of bringing the refugees together and allowing them individually and collectively to express themselves.

The psycho-social unit included some intensive work and some intensive relationship building in the midst of the war. Indeed A told us about the trauma he felt at the end of the war:

"You know for 33 days I was heavily involved in Samidoun. After the first week I was involved as a story-teller – doing what I like best. I spent time with the children. I told traditional stories – and if I got it wrong – and sometimes I would do so deliberately – they would all shout and laugh and tell me, tell it right! I had a great time … I know that sounds strange but I loved it, in the middle of a war, I loved it. But the war finished very abruptly. And when the bombing stopped the families left very quickly. I didn't get a chance to say cheerio to most of them and I felt a really deep loss. I still miss those children and those days."

A's story of loss was repeated by almost all the activists we spoke to. They had been involved in a very intense experience. When the war stopped, most of the activists found it difficult to adjust to the normal routine of life. In the middle of war they had forged a politically engaged 'popular resistance' and welfare organisation. It provided a glimpse, for many, of a different world, with different priorities and a different way of organising to meet people's needs. They had worked, debated, argued and thought about the war and its consequences, about the immediate needs of the refugee population, about how their organisation could develop in the future. They had been so successful that when the war stopped they were formally approached to deliver immediate relief to the south of the country – something they all agree was important. But moving away from Beirut took the key organisers out of the city and left the majority of volunteers without a functioning organisation.

Samidoun: social work and popular resistance

> War is … a political situation … and cannot be reduced to a humanitarian situation, since behind its tragedies lies an open struggle. … [H]umanitarianism sees the tragedy [of war] and its causes outside of its social and political context. [But] when people are killed, then we know that someone or something has killed them; when people are displaced, then someone or something has forced them to move…. In times of war … there are tanks that bombard and aircrafts that destroy, and there are those who confront the assault. The question is fairly simple: Who are you with? With the one who assaults and kills … or with the one who confronts the aggression? (Chit, 2008)

Forged in the midst of war, Samidoun stands out as a concrete example of a popular social work experiment that was democratic, non-hierarchical and focused on meeting human need at a time of crisis. It was a consciously political intervention – part of the popular resistance to Israeli aggression – that linked resistance, political struggle and social provision. It was able to organise 1,000 volunteers and support over 10,000 refugees. The initial needs of the refugee population were material needs. Samidoun had to establish safe and secure centres (and had to challenge the Lebanese state's priorities while doing so), it had to feed the population and ensure they had water for drinking and washing. But it also realised that this was not enough. In the midst of horror people need to feel part of a collective, to experience solidarity and to forge relationships which confirm their humanity. In the early 20th century, in a strike by textile workers in America (and the Lawrence factories), the strikers used a slogan that resonates with the activities of Samidoun: 'We want bread, but we want roses too.'

There are lessons here for humanitarian responses to war and other disasters, as well as for social work more generally. First, that grassroots responses can be hugely effective in mobilising local resources and can have real advantages over 'official' responses. Second, that ideology is a key element in developing such responses and the notion that 'aid' or 'social work' is somehow neutral needs to be constantly challenged. Last, and this is perhaps the key issue for social work as it redefines itself in the continuing economic, political and military turmoil of the 21st century, that there is a need to take sides; if social work is truly committed to social justice, then this means standing up for the poor, the dispossessed and the oppressed against the oppressor and, through this process, truly achieving liberation.

THREE

Grassroots community organising in a post-disaster context: lessons for social work education from Ilias, Greece

Maria Pentaraki[1]

Introduction

On the 24 August 2007, 67 people were killed and 5,392 people were affected by a forest fire in the province of Ilias, a predominantly rural and semi-rural area in the Peloponnesus region of Greece. The fire was considered the worst 'natural disaster' in Greece during the period 2001–10. The economic damage was calculated to be in the region of US$1,750,000,000 (International Disaster Database, 2010); the environmental degradation was enormous.

The governing party (New Democracy) argued that weather conditions had played an integral role in the spread of the fire. It tried to abdicate responsibility for its slow and insufficient response by suggesting that the fires were a 'natural disaster' and tried to strip away the political context of the disaster by relocating the blame from the structural to the 'natural' (see Wisner et al, 2004). The claim made by Mr Polidoras, the Minister of Public Order and the man in charge of the fire fighting efforts, that '*General Wind* is the one that is prohibiting the fire fighting efforts' was indicative of that attempt. Such statements were replicated over and over again in various media accounts (for example, Newsroom DOL, 2007).

Numerous accounts, though, have suggested that other forces were at play. For example, development projects created an incentive for the removal of forested areas and created opportunities for exploitation by corrupt public officials (Karamichas, 2007; NTUA, 2008; Zirogiannis, 2009). The suspicion is that the slow response of the state machine was not accidental (Pendaraki, 2010). As a member of the citizen's action group put it:

> The fires were not inevitable, as the New Democracy government kept claiming. The scale of the destruction wasn't inevitable and wouldn't have occurred if it hadn't been for the unprecedented deficiency, lack of coordination and operational planning of the government in responding to the fires. Instead of taking measures in order to solve the problem of fires, all the governments of recent decades moved in the opposite direction. In their actions (forest-killing laws, attempts

to amend Article No 24 of the Constitution2) or their omissions (National Land Register, Forest Register) and their tolerance they have left arsonists, intruders, and land-hungry persons undisturbed. We could also say that they have facilitated them. It is typical that from the year 2000 until today not a single euro has been absorbed from the 3rd Community Support Framework's funds amounting to 24 million euros for works dealing with fire prevention and protection of forests from fires. (Mpistas Kyriakos, member of Pan-Iliaki Action Committee for the Fire Affected Areas, personal correspondence)

In this chapter I want to explore the immediate aftermath of the 2007 fires, the government response and the development of a grassroots network of community activists who campaigned for both compensation and the defence of their own and public lands against property developers. In so doing I report testimony from farmers and activists, both from public meetings I attended and helped to organise and from interviews undertaken. I then go on to outline a social work student project that I initiated at my previous higher education institution, TEI Patras, which involved senior social work students working in fire-affected communities and organising with the community to raise awareness about its situation. I suggest that the educational project offers valuable insight for engaged social work in post-disaster situations, and, more broadly, for a community organising social work practice.

I start by looking at the immediate responses to the fires of 2007.

The government response

Despite the rush of government policy announcements that occurred immediately after the fires, the recovery process was not implemented in an efficient, holistic and sustainable way or, indeed, one that was relevant to the needs of the people affected. The restoration policies impacted on people differently, depending on their socio-economic status. Small farmers were excluded from the benefits of recovery policies, which were class biased and implemented via a top-down approach, reinforced by the government's indifference, due to its neoliberal concerns. Instead of the recovery process offering an opportunity for people to get back on their feet, to address and ameliorate previous injustices and to support a socially just development, it created a space wherein profiteering and corruption could flourish (Pendaraki, 2010). Unfortunately, this does not seem to be unique, as similar post-disaster accounts exist from different parts of the world (King, 2006; Klein, 2007a).

Furthermore, many people from the affected communities criticised the recovery policies because of the vast discrepancies between what was promised in the run-up to the September 2007 elections and the reality of aid spending once the election was over. In the immediate aftermath of the fire, ordinary people, national and international NGOs and associations and various governments donated money for people affected by the fires. The money was administered through the government's Eidiko Tameio Antimetopisis Ektakton Anagkon (ETAEA) (Special Fund for Emergency Responses) of the Ministry of Economics and Finances that was set up for these purposes. According to ETAEA (2010), the money that was gathered was €198,123,335.51, and with the accumulated interest it has reached €211,078,628.87. Up to 10 March 2010 the amount spent was €76,622,018.04 leaving €134,456,608.83 'unused'.

The affected communities were vocal in their criticism of the top-down, class-biased, highly centralised and bureaucratic procedures developed by the Greek authorities. There was little consultation prior to the announcement of the reconstruction policies. One of the criticisms levelled by farmers was that they had been used as part of the government's pre-election propaganda. Some of the farmers interviewed put it this way:

> **Farmer A**: "As soon as publicity lights were turned off, the government's caring face disappeared. All their mitigation efforts amounted to distributing the €3,000 in front of the TV cameras as a tool of the election campaign."

> **Farmer B**: "They [the politicians] implied that everyone could get the cash without doing a disaster background check. If that wasn't an election bribe, then what was it?" (Interview, January 2009)

Immediately after New Democracy were re-elected, things changed. The Greek tax revenue authorities started sending urgent notices demanding the return of the aid donations. In particular, notices were sent to households where two adult members had accessed aid. The government claimed that this was appropriate, that aid shouldn't be paid twice, but it ignored the local reality that in rural areas it is not uncommon for grandparents to live in the same house as their adult children and their families – a reflection of class and cultural traditions reinforced by poverty. In these circumstances both grandparents and their adult children had lost land, livestock and crops (which they cultivated to support three generations of family). Thus, it was appropriate that both the grandparents and their adult children should claim the emergency aid, for both had lost land and property. The government also ignored the fact that there were households where husbands and wives each had their own farm land. No matter, the government sent tax bills to them demanding the return of the emergency cash aid. Almost no one was able to comply, since they were struggling financially in the aftermath of the fires. The result is that many households that received two emergency cash aid payouts have now had their farm/house mortgaged by the government until they can repay the amount received (Personal interview, Mpistas Kyriakos, 2 May 2010).

The class nature of policies

One of the themes that emerged from the interviews with those directly affected by the fires was the class based nature of the post recovery policies. This is best summarised by the statements made by two grassroots activists. The first is from one of the founding members of the citizens' action committee from the village of Agia Anna, who, during one of the community forums organised in an affected community, 18 months after the fires, argued:

> "The recovery process does not apply equally to all people. In effect the recovery policies exclude people who do not have resources to complement the amount given for recovery, so the aid goes only to those with money. If the government didn't know what policies to implement why didn't they ask us? We've been trying to inform them about the necessity of revising the policies, so everyone could fully take advantage of them, but to no avail. It seems that they made a political choice. It's not that they don't know what's best for the people, it's that they don't care." (January 2009)

Mpistas Kyriakos, a founder member of the Pan-Iliaki Action Committee for the Fire Affected Areas, summarised it this way:

> "During the last months we had been witnesses to the intolerable policy on compensation for fire-stricken homeless people, farmers, shepherds, and self-employed farmers. After having granted €3,000 to each one of these persons as a tranquilliser they cleverly reclassified the burned houses from 'rebuildable' to 'repairable', under pressure from the Ministry of Environment, Town Planning and Public Works. This reduced the payments to just €750 and €142 respectively. Through a range of bureaucratic manoeuvres, they managed to reduce the number of eligible persons, farmers and stock-breeders as well as the level of compensations. The result is that thousands of small and medium farmers and stock-breeders can restore neither their lost income nor their vegetable growing and stock breeding capital. As a consequence, young people are seriously considering abandoning their properties in order to become internal migrants." (January 2009)

Furthermore, the compensation for lost agricultural income was ineffective, since the government did not take into account the specifics of the lost farm production. For example, most of those affected were olive growers. The compensation given to individuals per burnt olive tree correlated to three years of income, but an olive tree that has been burnt and replaced requires a 10-year growth period before it starts to produce olives, and thus income. The majority of people affected were small subsistence farmers. They now face a monumental period of time with no agricultural income. 'What will become of us?' was the agonising question heard over and over again in the open community forums.

Profiteering

The majority of small farmers found that the compensation regime worked against them. In contrast, however, there were numerous accounts that suggested that aid resources had been misappropriated and misused by sections of society for their own personal enrichment. There were other cases where the relief resources were appropriated by public officials engaged in administering aid. In one such instance it was reported that public officials took new electric appliances for their own use and gave away their old appliances to those affected by the fires. In another case, exposed by campaigning journalist Makis Nodaros, a local mayor and leading politicians attempted to build first a new city hall and then a cultural centre using aid money. The money had been donated by the Australian government and was administered by the Red Cross in order to help the fire-affected areas. But the mayor made plans to start building the cultural centre in order to find a way to present 'overcharged bills'. This case was exposed in the Greek media (Nodaros, 2008a; 2008b). Although the mayor filed a libel complaint, both the newspaper and the journalist were acquitted by the court. In the aftermath, the journalist who exposed the racket became the victim of a mafia-style attack (in 2008). He was targeted for his investigative reporting on corruption and the mismanagement of relief efforts for victims of the Greek forest fires (International Federation of Journalists, 2008).

There were numerous other newspaper accounts about how developers, in close cooperation with central and local government bodies, tried to indulge in profiteering and get hold of public land in the fire-affected areas. For example, in an agreement signed by the Ministry of Economics and the local government of Zacharo, a fire-affected coastline area that was officially protected by Natura 2000 was handed over to developers to put up tourist buildings and hotels. The agreement was rushed through and signed just four days before the national elections. The developers had been desperate to get their hands on the land for years before the fires, and now used the opportunity presented by the fires to pursue their agenda (Kostarelou, 2007). This example highlights one of the themes in Naomi Klein's (2007a) work, where she suggests that developers use the opportunities presented by 'social shocks' to instigate 'disaster capitalism' and grab public assets. In this case, however, a number of grassroots initiatives, working in close collaboration with nationally based environmental organisations, mobilised against the sale and were able to get the contract annulled.

In another example a grassroots organiser from the Lake Kaifa region talked to me about an attempt to destroy the protected area around the lake under the pretext of post-recovery development:

> "Luckily the community resisted, even though the developers, along with six mayors, threatened us. The interesting thing to note is that these six mayors made a joint appearance on TV in order to mobilise support for their profit making plans to commodify the protected nature area. These mayorstdidn't make a joint statement after the fire, in the interests of their communities, but now, all of a sudden, they decided to make a joint statement and a joint appearance regarding the need to destroy a protected public nature reserve, in the name of 'development of the area'. Their rhetoric presented the destruction of the Natura 2000 protected area of Lake Kaifa as the ultimate development solution; luckily the community, along with local environmental and citizens' action groups, such as the Environmental Committee of the town of Zacharo, the Pan-Iliaki Action Committee for the Fire-Affected Area, and the Greek chapter of WWF, were able to see through it all and put a stop to it ... There is power in the people, as long as they actively resist and organise." (Mpistas Kyriakos, personal interview)

Were these developments planned well before the fires, or did the developers act opportunistically after the disaster? However we answer that question, the conclusion is the same: some people and organisations tried to make a profit out of the disaster. The degree to which they were successful depended partly on the level of community resistance they encountered.

So, some sections of society saw the disaster as an opportunity to grab public land and enrich themselves, but in opposition to this we saw the affected people becoming organised and demanding a quicker response to their needs, as well as aid and support that met the requirement of 'justice for all'. As citizens realised that the government's efforts were too slow, action groups started to develop, holding meetings, consciousness-raising events, and demonstrations, in the hope of applying pressure on the government and stopping the profiteering.

Social work intervention

In real terms, after a year people had still not seen any of the government's promises materialise. They had been unable to start rebuilding their burnt homes. They had seen their income fall dramatically. They were struggling for their day-to-day survival. Thus, they started to organise and demonstrate. The demonstrations, along with the publicity they created, brought to my attention the vast social problems that people affected by the fires faced and the need to support their struggles. At this point I decided to engage a group of senior social work students to further their education by involving themselves in a struggle for social justice that offered a possibility for them to play a role as a 'community organiser' and that would enhance their learning of macro social work skills.

Even though community organising and community development is a compulsory third-year subject, involving 15 weeks of two-hour lectures, there is little, if any, community organising and development content in the accompanying direct practice subjects, such as working with individuals, working with groups and families, fieldwork skills, and so on. Overall, the subject of community organising seems to occupy a marginal place within the curriculum, the greatest amount of emphasis being placed on clinically related courses, both clinical social work and clinical psychology. Consequently, most of the social work graduates of the Social Work Department of TEI Patras think of themselves as psychotherapists training to work as clinical social workers (Teloni, Pendaraki et al, 2010). This marginalisation has been noted in other social work departments in different countries (Jones, 2007; Jones, 2009; Mendes, 2009; Strier, 2009) and is related to the historical domination of case-work as the main social work method. This is especially true in Greece, because the origins of social work have never been based in local and progressive traditions, but instead dominant Anglo American models of clinical social work have been transplanted from abroad (see Ioakimidis, 2009). I started teaching the community-related courses in 2004, having experience as a director of planning for community initiatives, funded by the European Union, to fight the social exclusion faced by various marginalised groups. This experience, along with my community organising experience with different social movements, confirmed my belief that community development interventions needed to be complemented by collective activism in order to be effective. Furthermore, they reaffirmed my belief that both were an integral part of social work practice.

Working in extreme post-disaster circumstances can provide insightful lessons for social work students, away from the dominant clinical approach, that they can carry with them in their professional career in order to enrich mainstream social work theory and practice. I wanted my students not only to get a glimpse of radical social work education, but to be actively involved in grassroots actions. I believe that the exposure of how post-recovery policies are related to structural inequalities allows students to comprehend the relationship between social political processes and individuals' conditions. Thus, I engaged a group of senior social work students as part of a class assignment within a senior seminar class during an academic semester (September 2008 to February 2009). My hope was that engagement in radical experiential learning would offer support to the community and provide appropriate learning opportunities in radical social work practice. Social work practice in a post-disaster context offers a unique site for social work students to grasp the socio-economic context that leads to social and personal problems, and an opportunity to start organising and working with the affected community. Loretta Pyles (2007), in a study of the post-Hurricane Katrina context (see also Chapter Ten) suggests that there are a number of reasons why social work too often fails to organise affected communities in post-disaster settings. First, most social workers have no experience in this type of work, due to social work's historical focus on micro-level issues. In this model, community organising is marginalised, at best. Second, social work education curricula rarely focus on community organising (Jones, 2007; Jones, 2009; Mendes, 2009; Strier, 2009). 'Social work education … needs to focus more of its resources and attention on communities and their needs, policy advocacy and the group work skills that are necessary to build grassroots organizations' (Pyles, 2007, p 330). Third, the predominant engagement of social workers with trauma and grief counselling is due to the availability of those state-funded and supported and large private and voluntary services. The interests of the powerful – in the state, voluntary and private sectors – are not in community organising, and this holds true especially in Greece. Thus, in taking my students to Ilias I had to move away from the dominant practice of social work (and social work education) and collaborate with grassroots action groups. This collaboration meant reclaiming the radical legacy of social work by reflecting on our value base and developing a corresponding knowledge base that provided the opportunity to present an alternative vision of an alternative social work – one that encapsulated what Mohan (2005, p 248) calls a 'practice of hope'. The social justice value base (Razack, 1999; Dominelli, 2002; Garrett, 2002; Ferguson and Lavalette, 2006; Solas, 2008; Mmatli, 2008; Morley, 2008; Anand, 2009; Chu et al, 2009; Ferguson and Woodward, 2009), as modelled by our code of ethics, can be our own inspired alternative vision, it can be our own social work-inspired utopia that can help us to keep trying to change the world. We can argue that our code of ethics requires that we keep preparing our social workers for work towards social change, among other things. To hope for and to imagine an alternative vision in the context of glaring inequalities requires strong adherence to the social work values of social justice. It requires the assertion that change is possible and that thus another world is possible. It requires an assertion that the social work profession can play an important role in solving inequalities.

With this remit, the students and I engaged in a number of social work encounters.

First, we organised a 'process of critical consciousness dialogue in the context of promoting collectivization' (Mullaly, cited in Cabrera, 2009, p 41). The process of consciousness raising was mainly facilitated in open community forums where affected people could air their personal concerns, but at the same time see how they were linked to the wider socio-political context. The open community forums were organised in close collaboration with the elected community leaders and, wherever possible, with the collaboration of the grassroots citizens' groups. Our aim was to draw the affected people's attention (mostly farmers) to the links between:

- their personal difficulties after the fire and similar problems they had encountered before the fire, due to the EU Common Agricultural Policy, that resulted in a sharp drop in their agricultural income;
- their personal difficulties/harsh social conditions and the similar problems encountered in similar situations in other parts of the world;
- the profiteering that was taking place, how similar situations had occurred in post-disaster situations in other parts of the world and how grassroots networks had mobilised to stop them. The students had developed a flier with relevant case examples within the context of disaster capitalism which they distributed to the communities. They had also developed a banner with relevant slogans,

and the goal was to empower the community to believe in themselves in order to become active.

In forums the social work students helped to develop a brochure that included the details of citizens' action groups and information about relevant social services for any socio-psychological needs they might have. These were distributed to the communities. In these forums we also talked about the value of collective organising and the need to join forces with other, similar groups.

The underlying idea informing all the discussions was the simple point that individuals affected by an issue have more power to create change by coming together than by acting individually. The underlying theme was that social change is possible through collective action.

Second, we set out to engage with the media. This meant encouraging the students to talk to the press and television along with the affected people and the grassroots activists. Using the media can be a form of community organising, a way of gaining a hearing for an alternative reality. After the TV interviews the affected people told us that they felt that their voice had been strengthened by our bringing 'academic credibility' to their campaign.

Third, we undertook a community needs assessment in order to gather relevant information for use in the campaigning process.

Fourth, we attempted to mobilise support from the general public by campaigning and fund-raising. The goal was to raise awareness about the issues among the general population. The students prepared two exhibitions, one relating to the political context pertaining to the disaster, the profiteering that was occurring, the government's responsibilities and the need to hold it accountable; and the other relating to the environmental degradation that had resulted from the fires and the need to implement a reforestation process. In both these exhibitions the public were invited to make donations that would be used to buy, mostly, school supplies for the affected children and trees for reforestation. Those who attended the exhibition were also asked to write messages of support to be taken to the affected communities. The majority of the messages that were written wished people strength in their struggles, reflecting a political connection with those who had suffered so much.

Fifth, we engaged in an analysis of service resources, which involved an evaluation of the human service agencies within the province of Ilias. This analysis took the form of a human services directory. The information compiled was included in a brochure that was distributed for self-referral purposes. Even though my main goal as an academic was to focus on macro social work skills and the necessity of community organising, the goal of the intervention was for the students to also grasp the need for a generalist social work approach, one that addresses both personal and social needs, because, even when we practise community organising, we also encounter people with personal problems that may need to be referred to appropriate services.

This engagement was based on my overall pedagogical approach, the aim of which is to inspire hope in my students that an alternative vision of our future is possible, a vision that is worth fighting for. This belief that change is possible can be visualised and actualised when we engage in collaboration with grassroots organisations in such social work educational encounters. This collaboration with grassroots organisations in a post-disaster context provided an opportunity to facilitate an educational process through which students were able to:

- recognise the value of social justice within social work encounters
- increase their awareness of the potential for change, as opposed to merely reflecting existing dominant ideologies (Collins, 2009, p 338)
- develop a capacity for questioning the existing order (Collins, 2009, p 338)
- learn to speak for the social justice-minded profession in solidarity with oppressed populations
- unmask the socio-economic roots of social problems
- learn the value of coalition building
- learn to identify the causes of injustices, attribute blame and suggest solutions in close collaboration with oppressed groups of people
- learn to facilitate appropriate arguments for policy change by listening and giving a voice to those from below.

Evaluation of the social work involvement

On the one hand, the engagement of the students empowered the people in the affected communities. A comment made over and over again by the affected people was how important our involvement had been to them, since they felt that they had not been forgotten by the outside community. They said that in the beginning politicians had been happy to visit them for public relations reasons, but now, after the public lights had gone off, no one paid any attention to their needs. But working with the students they felt that they were not alone in their struggles.

On the other hand, comments made by the students at the end of the semester were equally encouraging about the process they had gone through. It seemed that this process had entailed a transformative experience. The students reported a new confidence in community work skills as a necessary model for instigating social change. They expressed a new belief in the power of collective action. A number of students who had expressed a strong interest in doing graduate work in a clinical social work specialisation were now considering a community post-graduate specialisation. They expressed a strong respect for the grassroots community leaders who had given their time to organise collaborative community forums and answer their questions. It was this social work educational experience that led the students to 'know the relevancy and power of macro practice, to become believers and do-ers, thus creating the community organizers of tomorrow' (Carey, 2007).

Concluding discussion

As Pyles (2007, p 326) has observed, 'one must ask who is holding government officials accountable for doing the right thing' in a post-disaster context. To this I will add: Who will stop the neoliberal development agenda? Who will stop profiteering? Who will challenge the glaring socio-economic inequalities and work towards the redistribution of power? Who will promote a people's agenda? This is where social workers and grassroots action groups come in. Are social workers, though, equipped to be agents of change? The answer, based on the tradition of radical social work, is: yes, we can be. Social workers can be part of that resistance and struggle in collaboration with the affected community in order to change governmental indifference and halt business interests. We should be collaborating with grassroots citizens' action groups. These grassroots citizens' action groups are part of grassroots struggles all over the world to improve livelihoods, for instance, after a disaster or in the face of public land grabs, land deals and projects conceived by outsiders. 'Such locally organized pressure groups proliferated rapidly during the 1980s and early 1990s. They are now recognized as a major force for social change in general and disaster mitigation in particular' (see Blaikie et al, 1994, p 8).

In the case of Ilias, they may not have been able to change governmental negligence, but they were able to stop crass profiteering. The majority of the grassroots responses that started after the fire are still active and it is surely of the utmost importance that social workers in that area join forces and support the grassroots resistance. In Greece today the need for a social work of resistance has never been greater. The debt crisis is being addressed by a commitment to neoliberal economic restructuring imposed by the International Monetary Fund (IMF). If the government succeeds, socio-economic inequalities will grow and people will be much more vulnerable to the dictates of international bankers. If the IMF agenda is imposed – as numerous examples from around the world testify – it will mean mass unemployment, the unequal distribution of wealth and privatisation of public resources, all of which will make life for the vast majority much more severe. Now, more than ever, there is a need to build coalitions across both local/national and international lines. As Ferguson and Lavalette argue (2006, p 315), we, as social workers, can actively make the connections between the neoliberal global agenda and the day-to-day experiences of people all over the world. Neoliberal globalisation cannot be combined with issues of social and economic justice. Thus, within this framework, there is an urgent need for social work practice to become both global and local. This, according to Ife:

> requires the capacity to see local problems also as global problems, to see that they can only be adequately addressed by action at both global and local levels and to find ways to link the two. This, of course, cannot be done simply by a worker acting alone, it requires him/her to work cooperatively at two levels: first by working dialogically with the

people most affected (client, community, etc) and second by forming partnerships with other workers and clients or communities elsewhere that work towards the same issues. (2008, pp 186–7)

Social workers whose practice is informed by human rights, community development and a critical approach can play an important role in supporting the work of grassroots citizens' action groups to address their needs effectively and promote social justice. This is due to a number of reasons:

1 We are able to identify injustices, attribute blame, suggest solutions and work towards implementing them.
2 We can connect through our critical social work value base to the anti-capitalist movement slogan that the world is not a commodity, and work towards that vision (Ferguson and Lavalette, 2006, p 315).
3 We 'avoid the conservatising and disempowering construction of individualism (which is usually part of the problem rather than part of the solution)' by seeking more 'collective forms of action, working in solidarity with … colleagues, activists and other professionals' (Ife, 2008, p 184).
4 As social work academics, we recognise that we 'have a responsibility not only to teach social justice but to take a leadership role in actualizing social justice objectives in the public realm' (MacKinnon, 2009, p 519).
5 We can implement class-competent social work practice in order to be able to assist our clients in challenging class oppression (Strier, 2009), as well as any other form of oppression.
6 We can challenge existing social and economic structures, since the market creates, exacerbates and perpetuates inequality (MacKinnon, 2009, p 519).
7 We have to take sides. This means actualising the social work values of social justice. We need to side with the needs of people and resist business interests. We need to be inspired and informed by community, grassroots resistance and begin to practise social work as resistance (Pendaraki, 2010).

All of the above, practised in a post-disaster context, enable community members' voices to become stronger and 'demand the survival of their community'. Social workers, along with grassroots activists, need to be vigilant in order to make sure that the community affected accepts a leadership role in all stages of the recovery relief efforts, making true the meaning of citizen involvement as described by Sherry Arnstein in *Citizen Participation* (1969, cited in Gardner, 2005). The point Arnstein makes is still a very powerful one, and one that we need to remember in terms of ensuring citizen involvement not in a shallow way that reflects token participation, but in a serious way, one leading to citizen control of the decision-making process. After all, who is best placed to decide for the affected communities if not the communities themselves? As Saul Alinsky (1971) argued in *Rules for radicals*, the answer is political engagement, and empowerment of the people to take action themselves.

Notes

[1] Also known as Pendaraki.

[2] Article 24 of the Greek Constitution is the Forest Protection Article. Some interesting points have been made about how the last two serious forest fires, in 2000 and 2007, coincided with planned government attempts to amend Article 24 by the PASOK (social democrats or socialists, according to their claims) and the New Democracy (right-wing) government parties respectively. 'Both attempts to amend the most important institutional guarantee of environmental protection in Greece were seen as a disguised attempt to facilitate the plans of some insidious developers who had been targeting the real estate potential of areas in or close to the countryside for a long time. Both attempts were opposed by the parliamentary left parties and the environmental movement' (Karamichas, 2007, p 525), as well as by local citizens' action groups. By 'placing the 2007 forest fires in the context of attempts to revise constitutional Article 24 in conjunction with the absence of a partially completed land and forest register, a much more inclusive exploration of cause and effect was offered' (Karamichas, 2007, p 531).

FOUR

Grassroots community social work with the 'unwanted': the case of Kinisi and the rights of refugees and migrants in Patras, Greece

Dora Teloni

Introduction

In this chapter I reflect upon my engagement – as both a social worker and an activist – in the Kinisi movement, which has worked with refugees and migrants in Patras both to meet their needs and to campaign for political change in the way migrants and refugees are treated within the European Union (EU). I start by outlining the situation facing refugees in Greece, then proceed to look at the development of Kinisi, before reflecting on the role of social work in the campaign.

But before I proceed I want to highlight one 'linguistic' issue. In political debate a distinction is drawn between refugees, asylum seekers and migrants. Migrants are viewed as people who move for a job. Refugees are those who flee their home country because of political, religious or cultural oppression. An asylum seeker is someone who seeks formal recognition for their refugee status. But in reality, these distinctions are quite unhelpful and based on old and legalistic definitions. For example, if someone flees Afghanistan because they are a Communist facing persecution they would count as a legitimate 'refugee', but someone from the same country who left home because their village had been destroyed by imperialist intervention and they could no longer support themselves would be a migrant! Our view is that these distinctions are not helpful. The people with whom Kinisi works have fled countries destroyed by war and military intervention – we consider them all people who should have the right to free movement and the same human rights as everyone else. In what follows I refer to refugees, migrants and asylum seekers without distinction.

The EU's anti-immigration policy

The motto on the official website of the European Agency for the Management of Operational Cooperation at the External Border (Frontex) is 'Libertas Securitas Justitia' (Frontex, 2010). It has replaced one of the core demands of the French

Revolution (equality) with one related to modern concerns (security). The three elements of the slogan, 'freedom, equality, justice', were seen for many years as interconnected. Interestingly, in contemporary Europe 'equality' has been sacrificed in the name of 'safety'. This issue is in line with the dominant policies of the EU and the US, by which, in the name of 'safety', wars in Iraq and Afghanistan have produced massive waves of displaced people. The consequences of the wars are more than apparent in the Mediterranean, where thousands of refugees regularly attempt to cross borders and try to enter Europe.

However, the EU's policy is to coordinate the control of immigration by stopping refugees at Europe's borders. In the Mediterranean area, the actions of Frontex are known as the Poseidon project, and its declared aim is to prevent refugees from reaching the coasts of Europe. But, from the refugees' perspective, the 'paradise' of Europe is viewed as their only hope of survival after escaping the destruction of their countries.

Their 'journey' is a struggle for survival. The refugees usually walk for thousands of miles, putting their lives in danger, before they continue, in poorly constructed plastic or wooden boats (after paying money to smugglers), in the hope that they will be treated with respect and compassion.

As a young Afghan boy living in the Patras camp in 2007 told me:

> "I had no idea that I would come to Greece. I just wanted to live somewhere that is safe, where I can have a job and be respectable.... You say that you have democracy, this isn't democracy."

This young Afghan boy was one of the 'lucky ones' who managed to reach Greece safely. It is estimated that between 1988 and 2006 somewhere in the region of 14,714 people lost their lives struggling to travel to 'Democratic Europe'. In the Aegean Sea, between Turkey and Greece, an estimated 1,315 people lost their lives (Fortress Europe, 2010). In 2009 alone, according to the Greek Ministry of Protection of Citizens, 24 refugees lost their lives and 54 went missing (UNHCR, 2010).

Occasionally, the EU accuses Greece (and other Mediterranean countries) of violation of refugees' human rights. However, in practice the EU uses these countries as 'scapegoats' who, in effect, are merely applying EU policy. Although it is undeniable that Greece violates the rights of refugees, using detention centres and exposing them to inhuman conditions (see below), this needs to be examined within the general context of EU policy.

The EU has funded a €1.2 million programme to facilitate cooperation between Greece and Turkey to create 'removal centres' – following a UK model where 11 centres are run by private companies. The aim of these 'removal centres', which will be based in six cities (Gaziantep, Erzurum, Van, Istanbul, İzmir and Ankara), will be to detain refugees, expedite their claims for asylum and deport the 'unwanted' back to their countries. This strategy is based on the concept of 'out of Europe' (UNHCR, 2008). As the Deputy Director of EU Strategy of the UK Border

Agency put it in an interview in *Hürriyet Daily News & Economic Review*: 'The question is whether they [asylum seekers] are making a well-founded claim or not. Even if Turkey has a geographical limitation, it can still decide whether the claim is well-founded' (Ozerkan, 2010).

However, the concept of a 'well-founded' claim for asylum is hypocritical, given the fact that asylum seekers overwhelmingly come from countries where EU and US military intervention has devastated society and often destroyed documents that could support their claims. The above expectation, therefore, aims solely to justify deporting asylum seekers, but aims to do so in a formalised, methodical and 'clinical' way.

What is not said is that the EU has started another, more covert, war against immigration. The operation of Frontex and the development of 'removal centres' is only one aspect of the EU's policy. The member states of the EU follow a general directive whose intention is to stop refugees reaching and living in Europe. The Greek Helsinki Monitor (2008) believes that EU policy is based on two main objectives. One is the protection of the EU's borders and the encouragement of countries such as Libya to prevent refugees from entering the EU. The other is the creation of a 'common asylum system' that will be followed by all EU members (Greek Helsinki Monitor, 2008).

This 'Common European Asylum System' was agreed in 1999 (Kumin, 2007). In theory it is based on the 1951 Convention for the Rights of Refugees, while in reality it has created the basis for a 'Fortress Europe' where aspects of immigration control clearly violate the rights of refugees. The Eurodac Regulations and Dublin II Convention provide the foundation of the above system.

The Eurodac is a database system that

> enables Member States to identify asylum applicants and persons who have been apprehended while unlawfully crossing an external frontier of the Community. By comparing fingerprints, Member States can determine whether an asylum applicant or a foreign national found illegally present within a Member State has previously claimed asylum in another Member State, or whether an asylum applicant entered the Union territory unlawfully. (Europa, 2010)

Consequently, refugees' fingerprints are available to all security authorities across Europe. This regulation is linked with the Dublin II Convention. According to this Convention, refugees should seek asylum in the first country within the EU in which they land. This means that refugee travel is curtailed. Even if they successfully travel to another European country, they will be sent back to their point of entry. As the report of the European Council on Refugees and Exiles highlighted:

> The application of the Dublin rules causes additional, unnecessary suffering to already traumatised refugees. (European Council on Refugees and Exiles, 2008, p 5)

Practically, this leads refugees to become trapped in the first European country in which they arrive (in effect, the southern European countries). For example, if refugees manage to get into mainland Europe through Greece but are then identified elsewhere in the EU, they will be returned to Greece. A number of anti-racist organisations in Greece, as well as NGOs, have campaigned for the cancellation of the Dublin II Convention. Although Norway stopped returning people to Greece in the spring of 2008, it was forced to overturn that decision later that year, under EU pressure (NOAS, Aitima and Norwegian Helsinki Committee, 2009a).

The treatment of refugees in Greece

In Greece, refugees are held in detention centres, live in inhuman conditions and are subject to harassment and attack by the police. These are, perhaps, just some of the reasons why refugees do not want to seek asylum in Greece. The detention centres on Samos, Lesbos and Evros are notorious for their harsh treatment of refugees. Prisoners are held for months, packed into small rooms with little water and food and with limited access to lawyers and translators.

A young man interviewed in Patras by the Migreurop organisation described his experiences in the detention centre in Orestiada:

> I was locked up for three months upon arriving in the country, then again a few months later. I've had enough: since I left my country, Iraq, I have spent more time in prisons than outside them, without committing any offence. (Migreurop, 2009, p 23)

Of course, the refugees' 'crime' is that they are travelling in order to survive.

The Greek state also engages in illegal deportations. A number of organisations have highlighted 'the experiences of asylum seekers who have been deported across the border to Turkey under the cover of night, and who have not been given a chance to have their need for protection assessed in any European country. In Turkey, they run a considerable risk of being sent onwards, to their home country' (NOAS, Aitima and Norwegian Helsinki Committee, 2009b). Illegal deportations, of course, are not the sole preserve of the Greek state. Similar practices are also followed in other EU countries, including the UK.

In the Greek case, access to asylum procedures is particularly problematic, as the applications are made to police departments, where there is usually a lack of training and of translators. According to Vasileiou, a member of the Legal Department of Greek Council for Refugees, 'the Greek system acts as a "trap" for the asylum seekers' (cited in NOAS, Aitima and Norwegian Helsinki Committee,

2009a, p 16). The asylum seekers face a number of problems, due to the authorities' illegal practices. The most common malpractices relate to minimal access to lawyers; lack of translators in police departments; and a failure to map the reasons that lead people to seek asylum. Furthermore, even when asylum seekers succeed in completing their application, their statistical chances of getting asylum are grim. According to data from the Greek department of the UNHCR, in 2007, of 25,113 refugees who applied for asylum, only 0.04% were accepted. In 2008 only 0.05% of the 25,113 applicants were accepted, and for 2009 only 0.04% of those that applied gained asylum (UNHCR, 2009).

Refugees are perfectly aware that even if they make an application for asylum their living conditions will not improve. In 2010 a Sudanese refugee in Patras told me:

> "Why should I make an application for asylum? I live on the streets, under the trains, just like my brother who has a red card [that proves he is an official asylum seeker]. What difference does it make?"

In Patras, violations of the human rights of refugees are common. Traditionally, refugees (Kurds in the past and Afghans, Sudanese and Somalis today) use the city's port as a gateway to Europe. They hope that they will stay in Patras for a short time and most of the refugees try to leave hidden under or inside trucks. Yet this does not alter the brutal response of the authorities, who try to stop them leaving while at the same time making their lives in Patras as difficult as possible.

In Patras the Afghan refugees created a makeshift camp, a replica of an Afghan village, where they live under plastic sheets and have limited access to toilets, water and food. By the middle of 2007 the number of refugees living in the camp was estimated to be 800–1,500. Most of them were young men, the majority aged less than 30, and some were children as young as 5 years. In response, a group of local residents organised a demonstration in the port, with the participation of the mayor and head of the county, under the xenophobic slogan: 'We won't permit the dream of the migrant to become our town's nightmare'. In a radio interview the mayor baited the refugees' supporters by telling them to 'take them into your home', while the local councillor responsible for welfare services declared, 'not even one euro for the refugees'.

A number of organisations, for example the Greek Ombudsman (Sinigoros tou politi), in his report of 5 February 2008, described the living conditions of Patras's refugees as a 'humanitarian crisis' (Greek Ombudsman, 2008, p 4) and called the local authorities and government to intervene immediately. The local authorities ignored these calls and failed to provide any kind of support to the refugees, arguing that this was a problem to be solved by the government. In turn, the government (both New Democracy and PASOK) presents the opposition of the local authorities as the main obstacle to providing support for the refugees.

It was within this atmosphere that the organisation 'Kinisi' was established. Its aim was to provide grassroots welfare support for Patras's refugees.

The creation of Kinisi

Kinisi is one of tens of similar organisations that are active within the anti-racist movement in Greece. Similar organisations exist where there are large concentrations of refugees and asylum seekers, such as in Athens, Crete (Hania), Thessalonica, Volos, Mitilini and Samos. This network is vibrant and organises various creative interventions such as web pages, meetings, demonstrations and anti-racist festivals. The example of Patras is not unique and should be examined as part of this broader movement that shares knowledge and experience, reflecting the collective experience from across the networks.

However, Patras's example is important. In November 2007, in a negative and hostile atmosphere fuelled by the media and politicians, a number of people attempted to come together, to consult with one another and act for the rights of refugees. The initial meetings involved people from all walks of life (workers, unemployed, teachers, activists, lawyers, social workers, students, academics, doctors and psychologists) who came together in order to 'do something about the situation'.

One of the first steps in building a grassroots organisation is to analyse the situation and draw up a minimum shared agreement that provides a basis for action. The first steps were not easy. There were many political disagreements between the participants. However, gradually differences were overcome because of our collective concern and commitment to defending the rights of refugees. The basic elements of the 'contract' that the members of the organisation had were:

- *No political party is leading our organisation. All of us are equal and decide through open meetings (assemblies) every Monday evening.*
  Many of us had been involved in other campaigns where political parties had colonised initiatives; we were committed to remaining 'equal and independent', yet highly political. Moreover, it was a priority that the 'voice' of the refugees needed to be heard. So 'equality' meant equality for all; refugees were included as full participants.
- *It's a political and social organisation.*
  Our main aim is to defend the rights of refugees and immigrants. In our collective view, migrants are among the most oppressed section of the population and an attack on their rights is an attack on us all. Immigration was a political issue in our analysis: 'Imperialist wars, poverty and climate change produce more and more refugees. Western societies should give back what they stole. Refugees in Europe take a small amount of resources compared to what was stolen from their countries, they have equal rights, we need to fight together.'
- *Independence of the organisation.*
  In Europe one of the easiest and most effortless ways to gain instant recognition and status is to register as an NGO. However, Kinisi rejected this option. The independence and freedom of grassroots activism within

the social and political sphere is one of the core characteristics of Kinisi. We all share the costs of our centre, while no one earns any money from their participation in the organisation. The resources of the organisation are based solely on regular donations from the members, as well as on contributions from the local people in terms of money, food or clothes. Expert knowledge from professionals (doctors, lawyers, social workers, psychologists) is 'donated' to the movement. This issue is particularly important when practitioners, as well as academics, try to find effective and creative ways to contribute. Formal knowledge of theory, methods and techniques, along with practical knowledge regarding the available welfare and educational services, were valuable resources. Such knowledge helped to inform the creation of our welfare structures (see below) as well as our initial approach to migrants. For example, two practitioners (a social worker and a psychologist) who had worked with migrants before were the key people to make connections with them and to help in the creation of 'welfare' activists.

- *Acting politically requires multi-level action.*
  Acting politically includes action on the social level as well as solidarity in practice. Our political analysis of immigration offered enough 'tools' to respond to the complex issues of immigration and their immediate needs. Moreover, political action for the rights of the most oppressed in society needs to be shaped by solidarity and humanitarianism.

Community work on multiple levels

Ferguson and Woodward, discussing the importance of community work, have suggested that

> the fact that they are concerned with collective responses to collective problems often means that it is easier to make the links to wider political and structural issues than is the case with individual approaches. (2009, p 134)

In many ways the path that we followed was the reverse. We started with an analysis of the political and structural causes of refugee problems and then attempted to create appropriate responses that could act on different levels: the individual, the social, the political and so on.

However, working with the migrants and trying to act on a political level with them was not easy. On the one hand, the majority of refugees in Patras wanted to leave the country and move to northern Europe, and on the other, some of them had little or no experience of acting collectively.

The media had repeatedly demonised refugees, and as a result the majority of local people had mixed feelings. They felt sympathy for refugees but at the same time were concerned about the impact on their own living conditions. The growing number of refugees living in extremely bad living conditions was portrayed by the media as a threat to the 'harmony' of the local community. Such propaganda by media and local authorities gradually fostered hostility towards the refugees. Consequently, given the general political context as well as the particularities of Patras, there was a need to organise our actions step by step and on different levels.

New forms of collective action had to be found that included the direct involvement of the refugees. This involved us all in an ongoing process of reflexive thinking. We had to consider and reflect upon the political and socio-economic situation and its global and local impacts. We had to analyse the particularities of the area and we needed to come up with practical suggestions for activity. So we established thematic groups to consider these issues. One of the groups studied Greek legislation, human rights conventions and looked at the experience of other anti-racist organisations in Greece and abroad. We needed to become well informed about the refugees' plight and the legal and political context in order to engage effectively within society and in the media. These issues are particularly important for community and social workers. Jones refers to the need for social workers who are 'thinkers' and not only 'doers' (Jones, 2007), committed to a social work that fights for social change and social justice. Obtaining knowledge and an analysis of the general context and the particularities of the community are important factors in being able to act in and with the community.

These values are not exclusive to social work: they are also part of the praxis and analysis of political organisations that act for a just world.

The demands of Kinisi were written and published in the local and national media, presented at press conferences and sent to local authorities. They combined the general demands of the anti-racist movement, adapted to fit the case of Patras. From this, we established open centres for the refugees and set about meeting their immediate human needs (food, clothing, health and social services), organised to stop attacks by the police and campaigned on the general demands of the anti-racist movement, such as immediate provision of asylum and legalisation of refugees.

We focused on recommendations not only at a 'philosophical' level. The broad task was to press for political change, and also to create networks of solidarity for refugees in the community. This meant that members of Kinisi began acting on the following levels:

- Greek society, engaging with labour and social movements
- building relationships and trust with the refugees
- pressing for political change (local authorities and government)
- creating grassroots 'welfare' structures as an expression of solidarity in practice.

These 'levels' of activity were all interconnected, but for the purposes of this chapter my analysis is divided into different sections looking at the social, political and practical spheres.

Acting on the social level: the creation of grassroots networks

Given the hostility of the local media and the local authorities to the refugees, it was crucial that we challenged and changed the atmosphere of refugee demonisation in the city. Our organisation started campaigning for the rights of refugees (using leaflets and posters), making announcements, organising press releases and articles and intervening in the mass media (TV channels, radio, newspapers). In addition, open discussions and meetings were (and are) encouraged in the central areas of the city, discussing the specific issues and inviting the people of Patras to express their anger not against refugees but against the policies responsible for this situation.

Kinisi also attempted to make broader coalitions and connections with unions, social and political organisations, parties and academic departments – all of which proved invaluable when the police attacked the refugees' shelters. These coalitions strengthened and broadened the voice demanding respect for refugees' rights. In particular, the involvement of the social work department at the Technological Institute of Patras was important and engaged a number of social work students in work with refugees.

Through teaching sessions, day seminars and open discussions, social work students had the opportunity to listen to and understand in more depth the situation of the refugees and to connect these issues with general policy. The media hysteria about the refugees suggested that the only solution to the 'problem' was their forceful deportation. To confront this we regularly invited refugees to describe their situation, their experiences, their feelings and their hopes. This proved to be an extremely powerful tool for changing attitudes and raising awareness within the student group. As a result, some of the students joined Kinisi, while others became involved in different ways: campaigning for the rights of refugees, collecting food and clothing and so on.

In addition, the everyday activity of Kinisi gradually led to a coalition with practitioners: social workers, doctors, translators and lawyers. This was useful because it meant that we could send refugees to them when they needed services. It was also fruitful when some professionals who worked for the state informed us of plans for the police to attack the camp. This cooperation turned gradually into 'deep trust' and led to the sharing of information that literally, in some cases, saved the lives of refugees. For example, some practitioners informed us about refugees who were trapped inside trucks and were suffocating. We immediately intervened and put pressure on the port authority to save them. The practitioners faced restrictions on what it was possible for them to do in their working life, but the build-up of trust meant that when they could not intervene directly the information they provided allowed Kinisi to step in and act.

We also used every opportunity to highlight the refugees' case internationally. International media often visited the camp, as did international NGOs, political organisations and researchers. They came in order to get access to the refugees or to learn about the situation in Patras. The organisation of the first anti-racist festival of Patras in October 2008 was another important intervention into the social and political field. This was not only because it was the first time that such an event had been organised in the city but also because we succeeded in hosting it in one of the central squares with the active participation of 1,000 refugees. (The refugees were normally kept on the outskirts of the city.) The fact that the 'unwanted' came to the centre to participate in this cultural and political event alongside locals sent a clear message that the 'unwanted' existed and had substantial support.

Acting on the political level

As well as intervening on the social level we also campaigned to promote policy change locally, nationally and internationally. A crucial moment was at the end of January 2008, after a brutal police attack on the makeshift refugees' camp. In the aftermath, about 1,000 refugees, together with approximately 600 Greeks, demonstrated in the centre of Patras, demanding asylum, respect and freedom. It was the first time that the refugees had demonstrated in such numbers and marched in the centre of the city. This demonstration gained support from a variety of political groups, organisations and individuals and helped us to raise the campaign's profile and highlight the fact of the police brutality.

After this we held a number of demonstrations that, taken together, made a difference to citizens' and media views on the problems of the refugees. This encouraged us to intervene in local authority council meetings and raise refugee issues. This reached a high point in March 2010 (as this chapter was being completed), when a delegation of Sudanese refugees accompanied by members of Kinisi visited the head of the regional authorities demanding immediate support to cover their basic needs (housing, food and healthcare).

After January 2008 we ensured that whenever the police attacked the camp we had the means to publicise the event and offer legal support to the victims. However, on 12 July 2009 the camp was broken up on one of the 'darkest days' in the history of Patras. If living conditions had been bad in the camps, after their destruction they deteriorated significantly.

Solidarity in practice, or creating grassroots 'welfare' structures

The humanitarian crisis in Patras is obvious. Homeless refugees and asylum seekers (some of whom are unaccompanied minors) have been left with little food and water and no access to toilets. Following the demolition of the camp, the refugees now live on the streets or in the fields on the outskirts of the city. From its inception, Kinisi has been committed to providing humanitarian help for the refugees, expressing its solidarity in practice. Its perspective is that even small-scale humanitarian help should be part of the agenda of any organisation that acts for the rights of the oppressed. Its declared intention was not to substitute for the state's responsibilities but to highlight the refugees' needs and force the state to meet its obligations, as defined by international treaties. Our welfare activities included:

- *Provision of food.* Once a week members of Kinisi visited the camp with food. The food was bought using money donated by the citizens of Patras or via stalls outside the supermarkets in town. Kinisi members leafleted the stores every Saturday morning. This activity had two aims: to gather food and to raise awareness.
- *Health care.* Throughout 2007 volunteer doctors supported by the union of doctors and health professionals visited the camp to meet the urgent health needs of the refugees. By 2008 'Doctors Without Borders' had taken over this activity. It is important to note that no local hospital ever denied access to any of the refugees and asylum seekers.
- *Legal support and representation.* A group of lawyers provided free services in the aftermath of the police attacks and arrests. Moreover, with the support of lawyers, Kinis systematically challenged state brutality against the refugees.
- *Greek lessons.* Learning the language proved to be an invaluable tool for the integration of migrants. This was necessary for activities of everyday life such as job seeking, communication and the creation of social and personal relations. Teaching Greek was a transformative experience for all. Some of the refugees had to work with people from different 'enemy' nations, while others found space to challenge oppressions and stereotypes brought from their countries (for example regarding aspects of women's oppression). Interestingly, even the educators changed their attitudes as we came to challenge our own prejudices. We came to realise that we needed an 'alternative' school that permitted access to the 'invisible people'. So we established an educational institution based on the needs of the camp. Even though we did not have a specific theoretical approach when we created the school we broadly followed the Freirian approach of emancipatory pedagogy (Freire, 2009). The emancipation of refugees is one of the basic aims of the school, while we also aim to think with them about their situation and consider ways in which it can be challenged.
- *Information help desk.* The help desk ran for a year. It opened once a week and was staffed with a one social worker, an immigration officer, a psychologist and a doctor (all volunteers). Its aim was to provide free information for the refugees about their rights and the immigration process. The staff also tried to help them find jobs and referred them to other services.
- *The social centre (steki).* This centre is open four days a week for the school, but on Fridays it is open to everyone. The centre is a safe place where refugees can have a coffee and a chat with others. They can use electricity to charge their mobiles and surf the internet. Gradually the centre has become the place where the refugees hold their meetings and take decisions about their campaign. This is an extremely important site. It provides an opportunity for the refugees – from many different cultures and backgrounds – to meet up in

a non-threatening and non-confrontational setting. It helped them to build relations of trust with us and with each other.

The above 'welfare' structures were totally independent of the state. We did not accept or expect government support or funding. The services were all run by volunteers. The development of these structures needed to be well planned and organised. They were run by committees which decided what needed to be done. For example, the school committee was responsible for organising the practical issues, managing the number of students and holding monthly meetings where both students and teachers exchanged their experience and planned ahead.

The 'gains'

In 2007, a group of people decided to stand up for the rights of refugees, open their eyes to a big (yet hidden) humanitarian crisis and act. Three years later Kinisi has become one of the most important projects in Patras and the main channel for the refugees to make their voice heard. Local, national and international media frequently refer to Kinisi and a number of documentaries have been made about its activities. Kinisi has now been invited to participate in meetings with the secretary of state, members of parliament, the head of the municipality, county and periphery as well as big NGOs. Furthermore, on the social and political level, Kinisi is recognised as one of the main actors in supporting the rights of migrants. This was even recognised by the authorities when, finally, in February 2010 members of Kinisi gained access to local prisons where refugees were being detained, with a view to providing some services for them.

This shows how an organisation that is neither registered as an NGO nor has any official recognition can gain legitimacy from those it works with and, via its campaigning activities, force the authorities to recognise it and its influence. In addition, Kinisi was able to force a change in the terms of the debate about refugees and the required solutions. In summary, the gradual change in attitudes towards refugees, the help in practical issues, the delay we achieved before the camp was broken up, the confidence that the refugees gained to act more collectively and politically can all be seen as some of the gains of the movement.

Implications for social work

All of the above actions and interventions offer a paradigm of how social work can engage with a social movement that attempts to act creatively, democratically and 'from below'. The campaign offers an example of how we can act on the social and political level within the community. Kinisi established networks inside the community that were based on meeting the immediate needs of the refugees. This can be seen as community social work that aims to develop local networks and action by users and activists. As Smith argues, 'Community work needs resources that will enable local networks of workers and activists to flourish so that people can learn from each other and from shared experiences' (Smith, 1989, p 277).

'Learning from each other and sharing experiences' was central to the Kinisi experience. Kinisi members brought their own ideological and political experience with them and we gradually learned to listen and work together for the general good. But the day-to-day relationship with the refugees led to changing attitudes among refugees and volunteers. Learning from each other, challenging and changing attitudes and perspectives, finding new ways of thinking about problems and reflecting critically on what we are doing are all important issues that can impact on social work practice in general. Acting together provided us with relevant and challenging experiences and gave us the opportunity to work with service users as equals in ways that challenged hierarchies, and we were able to work collectively to challenge the trauma and despair of refugee life and channel it into collective action of various forms: we learned how to turn the despair into action.

There are some additional points that are of interest to social work. They relate to what I call 'lost in the personal'. In many cases the members of Kinisi had to focus on refugees' personal problems, such as unaccompanied minors, mental health and health problems, separated families, problems with accommodation. Working with individuals was very important. There were periods when the 'personal' problems were so intense that we focused almost exclusively on solving practical issues and supporting the individual,[1] rather than acting on the societal and political level. However, the fact that the group had an opportunity once a week to discuss its actions and its targets ensured that we did not become 'lost' in the 'personal' and forget that the main target was to struggle to change the policies that had led people into such despair, poverty and deprivation in the first place.

Thus, the broader structural causes that lead people to seek social services support need to be taken into consideration and not be forgotten in the everyday routine related to the needs of our users. The support and trust generated within Kinisi gave us the freedom to discuss, to reflect upon and to criticise our actions and to acknowledge the limitations we faced in trying to meet the immediate needs of the migrants.

Further, we also recognised that working every day with people who face multiple problems can lead to high levels of stress. Thus, we had to protect ourselves. The sense of belonging to a group that supported each other and could provide help whenever it was needed helped to protect us from the stresses of constant exposure to human suffering. This led to the realisation that roles and duties can always be negotiated and changed, in an effort to support activists and practitioners interacting in the 'front line' of social and political problems.

Although social work, according to the IFSW definition, is committed to human rights and challenging oppression, social work practitioners found that many of their agencies put barriers in the way of their attempts to work with refugees. Agency structures posed a great number of obstacles to many practitioners who tried to challenge the structural causes of social problems. To be more specific, in Patras's case, practitioners who worked with migrants and wanted to do more than 'just doing the everyday job' faced restrictions from their organisations, who attempted to prevent them from getting involved in any political action.

Participation in the movement appears to have been an 'emergency exit' for the practitioners who wanted to act in a more holistic way – not only because it helped them to address the structural restrictions that affected service users, but also because it involved them at the political level, campaigning for change. In a slightly different context, Ferguson and Woodward (2009, pp 7–8) have argued that:

> if the business agenda in social work is to be effectively challenged, then building links with these broader movements of resistance and participating in their forums and debates is essential.

In the case of Kinisi, the link between practitioners and the movement was essential. It helped to create 'channels of information' (Popay and Dhooge, 1989, p 161) between agencies and Kinisi that facilitated action and help during emergency situations. Furthermore, the connection of social workers (as either academics, practitioners or students) with the movement has informed practice and thinking both inside and outside the agencies and the academic departments: it helped us to rethink what we do, how we do it and why. In this way social workers have been important bridges between service users, agencies and movement activists. Social workers have played four key roles. First, listening to the refugees about their needs and problems and taking their issues seriously. Second, negotiating with agencies and demanding service provision for the refugees. Third, accessing 'activist expertise', learning from the movement and bringing new ways of thinking about problems back into social work. Fourth, engaging in community-based models of social work has enriched our practice and meant that we have been able to bring insight and our skills to the movement to work with and defend refugees and their rights in Patras.

In some cases, the values of social work have affected our actions, such as our commitment to confidentiality and respect of the refugees' free will. These values were our 'guide' in order to avoid the exposure of vulnerable people to the will of journalists or politicians. Moreover, we constantly had to be aware of the possibility of unintentional and implicit manipulation on our part. For example, we always attempted to fully inform the refugees about the implications of their actions within the broader movement.

Social work can offer many things to movements and sometimes its values can also be a 'guide' for activists. But movements can make a great contribution to social work. Fighting for social change and social justice is not an exclusive privilege of social work but it is certainly one of its responsibilities or, as Pendaraki and Skandamis (2009) argue, social action is one of the duties of social work. Although social work appears to be limited within specific organisations and workplaces, if we want to be consistent with the values of social work and the struggle for social change and social justice, we need to find more collective and creative ways of acting.

I am confident that the analysis of our actions in Patras can offer a contribution to the broader discussion about social work and activism. It clearly offers an example of this link within the Kinisi movement, but I think it could provide some ideas for acting in the 'here and now' as a response to extreme circumstances. Finally, in this chapter I have explained why social work cannot and should not be silent when the rights of service users are violated and social injustice prevails. All that we need is our vision for an equal society and our commitment to work 'from below', collectively and democratically.

Note

[1] Although the practitioners might do their best in 'micro-practice' that could be seen as 'good social work', on the other hand, as Jones argues, this cannot be perceived as radical social work: 'Social work is replete with subversive practices, whether it's accepting that clients have to subvert the benefits systems if they are to survive, or using one's own money to help people out, or looking away as fuel meters are bypassed … I have met so many practitioners who recognize that the hardships facing their clients have everything to do with the nature of contemporary neo-liberalism and nothing to with character or morality. To my mind, we make a mistake to regard these kinds of micro-practices as radical social work' (Jones, 2007, p 193).

FIVE

In search of emancipatory social work practice in contemporary Colombia: working with the *despalzados* in Bogota

Carmen Hinestroza and Vasilios Ioakimidis[1]

Washing one's hands of the conflict between the powerful and the powerless means to side with the powerful, not to be neutral.
Paulo Freire

Introduction

In this chapter we explore the issue of internal displacement in Colombia through a 'social work lens'. In recent years this humanitarian crisis has reached a climax as millions of Afro-Colombians, indigenous people and peasants have been forced off their land and moved into urban areas where they face further oppression, violence and lack of opportunities. The issue of displacement cannot be seen in isolation from broader political and social struggles in Colombia nor from the ongoing civil war that has raged for almost 50 years. In these circumstances it is our contention that social work practice cannot rely on individualistic North American and Eurocentric approaches to working with oppressed groups. Building grassroots alliances and encouraging 'conscientisation' have been some of the main approaches of Latin American welfare work for decades (see Alayon et al, 2005) and their use in the case of the *despalzados* (the displaced) in Colombia is explored here. We suggest that Western social work could benefit from exploring the popular and emancipatory approaches that have developed in Latin America and integrating these into social work practice in the West.

This chapter draws upon our work in the field. We draw information from and reflect upon our direct work with the *despalzados* communities in Colombia (Carmen Hinestroza) and interviews with a number of Colombian social workers and social activists over recent years (Vasilios Ioakimidis).

Liberation from historical and social amnesia

When Silvana Paternostro, a New York journalist, returned to her native Colombia after many years one of the first things she noticed was the dire situation of the internally displaced Colombians. What came as an even bigger surprise to her, however, was the fact that this issue received little attention from the state and local middle classes. In her own words, 'When people read the morning paper they skip the news about the *despalzados*, and go straight to the Sociales to see what kind of clothes the carnival queen wore' (Paternostro, 2007, p 81). Such an observation captures the 'invisibility' of the *despalzados* in Colombian society, but this is only part of the problem: behind the displacement of millions of Colombians from rural areas lies a history of fierce exploitation, unimaginable violence and massive poverty and inequality.

Colombian President Alvaro Uribe boasts that he has brought security and development to the country, but a visit to the impoverished areas and the central parks of the capital city exposes the extent of the mounting humanitarian, social and political crisis. In order to better understand the issue of displacement we need to look at the modern history of Colombia, a history that encapsulates both the grim destiny of most Latin American countries under the heel of colonialism and the sense of dignity, solidarity and determination that flourished in many communities fighting for emancipation.

Colombia's blessing and curse is the diversity and richness of its natural resources. Lying in the northern part of the subcontinent, the country is bordered by two oceans, the Pacific and the Atlantic. Its fertile valleys reach down to the Amazon (in the south and south-east) and the country is also home to the Andes mountain range. Such geographical and environmental diversity means that Colombia is considered one of the richest countries for natural resources in the world. The Spanish *conquistadores* in the 16th century discovered Colombia's wealth and set up the 'mechanisms' for its exploitation. Bananas, sugar, coffee, flowers, tobacco, cocoa were systematically exported to Europe. During this period Colombia became one of the main destinations for the African slave trade, as the indigenous population was considered 'dangerous' and 'undisciplined' by the Spanish conquerors (see Oliver and Fernando, 2006).

After a long period of rebellion against Spanish rule (led by Simon Bolivar), Colombia gained its independence in 1819. The slave trade was abolished in 1851, and this was followed by a period of state-induced 'miscegenation' aimed at the elimination of the 'African element' in the newly independent country (Murillo, 2001).

Despite the radical republicanism of the 19th century, multinational business interests were protected by the Colombian state throughout the 19th and 20th centuries. The extraction of emeralds, gold, petroleum, silver and natural gas by multinational companies tied Columbia into American imperialist interests. In 1903 Panama (part of Grand Colombia) was ceded, after the open intervention of the US, which later constructed and controlled the Panama Canal (Posada-Carb, 1998).

The history of modern Colombia is marked by repeated episodes of violence by the state, multinational corporations and big landowners against the poor and the exploited. It became common practice for multinational companies and big landowners to violently suppress trade unionists and communities living in resource-rich areas. These practices are well documented and have led several international human rights organisations to produce reports critical of human rights abuses in Colombia (see American Center for International Labor Solidarity, 2006).

State violence is fuelled by the ongoing civil war, as several armed groups (paramilitaries and insurgents) have been operating over a large part of Colombia for almost 50 years. Historically, the period of political instability and power struggles between the two major parties (liberals and conservatives) from 1948–58 and the increasing inequalities and poverty among the peasants, Afro-Colombians and indigenous communities led to the creation of 'autonomous' communities influenced by the Colombian Communist Party. A decision by the state to crush these communities in 1964, under the pressure and supervision of the US, resulted in the creation of guerrilla armies (most notably the FARC and ELN) and the launch of the civil war. Nowadays, the involvement of the US army in promoting free market and US business interests in the area is enshrined in the US's Plan Colombia. The intensification of US involvement and support to the Colombian State Forces has led to the FARC's military retreat. The guerrillas have long abandoned their aim to seize power and have little support from the local population, who are exhausted by the conflict. Today the FARC's strategy is to focus on its physical, financial and political survival through the control of limited territories and communities (strongholds) – allegedly, these areas are linked to coca cultivation and processing.

Narco-trafficking appears to be the main activity of the right-wing paramilitary groups that have developed as part of the counter-insurgency. In its effort to defeat the insurgents, who in most cases were backed by local peasants, the state turned a blind eye to the creation of these paramilitary 'self-defence' groups organised by the big landowners. Eventually the Autodefensas Unidas de Colombia (AUC), an umbrella paramilitary organisation, grew so much in size and power that the links between the Colombian political elites and the paramilitaries became inseparable. The demobilisation of the paramilitaries in 2005, under the Law of Justice and Peace, made little difference, as fragmented military groups continued to operate. As Human Rights Watch observed in a recent report:

> The successor groups regularly commit massacres, killings, forced displacement, rape, and extortion, and create a threatening atmosphere in the communities they control. Often, they target human rights defenders, trade unionists, victims of the paramilitaries who are seeking justice, and community members who do not follow their orders. (Human Rights Watch, 2010)

The main victims of this endless conflict are the communities who, historically, reside close to war zones. Statistically, these communities are indigenous people, Afro-Colombians and *campesinos* (peasants) whose land is rich in natural resources.

According to Amnesty International (2008), in 2008, 380,000 people were targeted and forced off their land. The number of internally displaced Colombians is estimated at around 4.9 million people: internationally only Sudan has more internally displaced people (IDMC, 2010).

The number of kidnappings and murders targeted at communities who persist in staying on their land or those who are human rights activists and trade unionists has increased significantly in recent years. According to Amnesty International (2008), more than 70,000 people have been kidnapped or killed over the last 20 years. Despite the fact that FARC is not without blame for the killings, there is evidence that clearly demonstrates that paramilitary groups are mostly responsible for the majority of the killings and large-scale massacres (Hylton, 2006). Such massacres and kidnappings are 'justified' on the grounds that the victims – trade unionists, human rights activists, rural communities – have collaborated with the insurgents. Yet there is little evidence to support this claim. Further recent evidence confirms the link between the paramilitaries and the multinational companies active in the country. In a period when Alvaro Uribe has re-affirmed Colombia's commitment to free markets and the further entrenchment of neoliberal policies, a number of well-known multinational corporations have been forced to admit their ties with the paramilitary groups (see Martin-Ortega, 2008). The services of the paramilitaries have proved invaluable to the companies, as they have helped to suppress trade unionism and clear out areas rich in natural resources. It is estimated that more than 2,000 indigenous activists and trade unionists have been assassinated since the 1990s (see Martin-Ortega, 2008). This wave of violence, intimidation and oppression has uprooted whole communities and brought indigenous cultures close to extinction. Masses of people have been forced to 'surrender' their land to either armed groups or businesses. Ultimately, these communities have headed to the urban areas, hoping at least for survival. As we mentioned at the beginning of this chapter, within the middle- and upper-class areas of the developed urban cities, the phenomenon of displacement appears to be nothing more than 'collateral damage'. The complex and systemic issues behind this humanitarian tragedy are often hidden under the carpet of amnesia; an amnesia that was institutionalised by the 2005 Law of Justice and Peace and led even the UN commissioner in Colombia to demand its revocation, as 'this law violates the right of victims of human rights abuse to truth, justice and reparation' (Amnesty International, 2009).

Working with the *despalzados*

The intimidated, exhausted and traumatised groups of *despalzados* head towards the urban areas, and in particular the capital city of Bogota, hoping to find some means of survival. Despite the recent increase in numbers, internal displacement in Colombia is not a new phenomenon. Previous waves of displaced communities moved to the big cities and formed 'makeshift settlements' which eventually became permanent residential slums (UN-Habitat, 2003). These slums can be found, for example, on the periphery of 'down town' Bogota. It is not known how many people live in these peri-urban areas – a large number of the *despalzados* do not possess papers and this makes them invisible in state statistics. Reports from international organisations estimate that there are 'hundreds of thousands' of people living in these areas, in inhuman conditions (Meertens, 2002).

Despite paramilitary aggression against human rights activists, some of the experiences of the people living in the slums have been recorded and documented by international and regional NGOs. In a recent report the organisation Doctors Without Borders (2005) drew a grim picture of the living conditions in the slums. They suggested that the *despalzados* live in unacceptable conditions, without documents, jobs, access to electricity or medical care.

> These families have borne witness to massacres, detentions, and the disappearance of family members or their neighbours. They have been harassed by armed groups, 'taxed' for money and property, and in some cases they have been forced to flee to save their children from forced recruitment. (Doctors Without Borders, 2005)

Yet despite this, for the *despalzados*, the main enemy is no longer the armed groups but malnutrition and deadly diseases. Despite the dire conditions in the slums, these areas have provided some basic shelter for displaced people who moved to Bogota. But now the slums have physically reached their capacity to absorb any more people. As a result, new displaced communities have moved into 'public spaces' in the centre of Bogota, including the large national park, which has been occupied by thousands of *despalzados*. The occupation of the parks has two main purposes. The first one is, of course, the practical need to find space for temporary residence. The second objective, however, is more political. The leaders of these communities, angered by the indifference of the state, decided to avoid moving into the centre to be closer to the developed down-town area, and thereby to force the political elites and middle classes to confront their existence and address their needs.

The response of the central and local governments was predictable and punitive. Police were soon called in, in order to contain the expansion of camps within the public parks. The image of displaced and impoverished people so close to the business district did not really fit with the notion of Bogota as a developed 'modern' city which could attract investment and tourists. By and large, the leaders of the *despalzados* avoided engaging in violent resistance against the powerful and heavily militarised state. Nevertheless, the links between the paramilitaries and the state meant that violence was visited upon the poor. The revelation that Colombian army officers had murdered hundreds of poor and displaced young people, whose bodies were later found dressed in guerrilla gear, shocked Colombia. The scandal of 'false positives' referred to innocent civilians who had been killed and presented as insurgents in order to meet the 'security targets' and demonstrate the determination of the army to deal with 'insurgents' (see Wood, 2009).

Mounting international pressure on Colombia, following a string of revelations, forced the state to begin to recognise the problem of displacement and poverty. Unsurprisingly, the state's interpretation of the problem ignored the broader political context and instead presented the issue as a series of minor problems with regard to hygiene, malnutrition and criminality. In fact the concepts of crime and violence have been used extensively by the state to justify repression operations against the *despalzados* and to push them away from the visible areas of the city. However, the publicity created pressure and opened up space for grassroots social work and 'reframing' of the problem. The fact that the state was forced into recognising the existence of the problem meant that social services were directed to the national parks in order to work with the *despalzados*. This created a 'critical space' that allowed social workers to work with and alongside the *despalzados*.

However, the social workers were forced to confront a number of ethical issues. These issues and dilemmas are related to the character of their work, their identity as state social workers, the mistrust they faced from the *despalzados* and their own (in many cases) Afro-Colombian or indigenous background. Working under these circumstances demanded a clear understanding of the context and the issues facing the *despalzados*, and the ability to work creatively to address the needs of this marginalised community. Below we describe the main activities that direct work has so far involved. In particular, we look at how some of the social workers have been able to make use of this new social space in order to explore emancipatory dimensions in their practice.

Meeting urgent needs/mediation

The main priority for the workers is to address the poverty and deprivation that the *despalzados* face. Conditions in the shelters are precarious; international observers often report severe malnutrition and epidemic disease in the slum areas (IDMC, 2010). Nevertheless, the state has maintained an ambivalent stance towards the *despalzados*, hoping that delay would 'peacefully' force them from the parks.

The social workers focused on charting the urgent needs of the community and making use of all available resources, no matter where they came from, in order to get basic support in place. In pressing and extreme situations it is vital for social workers to act quickly and avoid delays, bureaucracy and lapses of communication. In practice, this has had two consequences. First, 'politically' it put pressure on the local and central administrations to fulfil their constitutional obligations. According to existing laws in Colombia, the *despalzados* are entitled to basic help in the form of cash benefits, food stamps, shelter and medical care. Part of the social work engagement, therefore, was political in the sense that it exposed the state's dereliction of duty and failure to meet its statutory obligations.

Of course the social workers' expectation was that the state would be unwilling to provide resources for the *despalzados*. Therefore the second strand of their initial intervention was to identify urgent health and nutritional needs and to address them. This involved cooperation with international organisations operating in Bogota in order to increase the resources at the social workers' disposal. But this also had a 'political dimension' insofar as it highlighted the humanitarian crisis and the state's failure to act, in both the local and international media, and this meant that the government was constantly under pressure to provide some material support for the *despalzados*, despite its hostility to the 'occupation of public space'.

At first sight, there is nothing necessarily emancipatory in working alongside statutory services and international NGOs in order to coordinate support for displaced communities. However, reality dictates that, in order to engage with forms of liberatory and political practice, a necessary prerequisite is to make sure that these communities can survive physically and that their basic needs are met. In many parts of the world basic human rights to life and shelter are breached. Consequently, in order to allow grassroots innovation to flourish, these basic needs must be met. But once this has been achieved it can open a space that allows other forms of engagement that can help to identify the social and political roots of the problem and look towards structural solutions.

A further issue that lies within this initial stage of intervention is to ensure the safety of the *despalzados*. Two main issues have arisen regarding the safety of these communities. The first one is related to the desire of the state to push the communities away from the city centre – their mere presence is an embarrassment to the administration. The constant threat of attack from riot police, of harassment and arrest is ever present. But here social workers have to be very careful. The space for social workers to operate openly in defence of the communities is limited – even an unfounded claim that one's actions oppose the security forces and betray 'sympathy for insurgent ideology' can prove literally fatal. Consequently, the main objective focuses on the process of 'mediation and conciliation'. Even though these terms have long been associated with social and political neutrality, in Bogota's case these techniques provide valuable space and time for the social workers to ensure basic protection of the *despalzados*.

State and media propaganda against the 'polluting and looting criminals' who reside in the parks leads to tensions between the *despalzados* and those who reside in the middle-class residential areas close to the parks. On many occasions this has led to violence; it has also led many middle-class residents to demand greater intervention from the state, leading to more controlling and punitive policies and approaches from the state and its regulatory and enforcement bodies. On several occasions social workers working inside the national parks have tried to intervene when tension has threatened to spill over into confrontation (with either the police or local residents). It is important to bear in mind that any confrontation between the security forces and the *despalzados* would lead to further repression against the latter.

Trust building/participation and democracy

Addressing the needs of the *despalzados* for food, shelter and safety does not automatically mean that these communities will be moved to trust and accept social workers. The process of creating trusting relationships does not come mechanistically, as part of a transaction based on the assumption 'I provide for you, therefore you trust me'. What the Colombian case clearly shows is that social workers working with oppressed and impoverished communities have to work hard and methodically in order to earn genuine respect and trust. The *despalzados* have been uprooted from their homes, they have experienced intimidation and violence from the state and the paramilitaries (associated with the state, the drug traffickers, the multinationals and the insurgents), they have witnessed family members and friends being injured, killed or 'disappeared'. And all of this is located within a long history of oppression, inequality and violence that has its roots in the struggle for control over the rich resources of the country and the continuation of the power of the elites. The white middle classes, the state and even the insurgents (despite their declarations towards social justice) have historically failed the *despalzados*. Displaced communities, composed of indigenous people, Afro-Colombians and small peasants, are deeply suspicious of the state and the armed groups that surround them. In this context it comes as no surprise that social workers are also looked upon with suspicion.

Thus, meeting basic needs provides the workers with only an initial point of contact. The process of building trusting relationships with the *despalzados* demands that social workers identify the political dimension of their work and make sense of the dynamics of hierarchy. The *despalzados*, despite their ordeal and ongoing tragedy, have maintained a great sense of community. Large groups of people and families live close to each other, creating small networks of solidarity and self-help (psychological and practical). This starts with information sharing about existing resources, safety measures from external threats and collective decisions. Moreover, such a sense of community allows them to recognise and choose their local leaders according to their rituals, traditions and knowledge. Despite their difficulties, the *despalzados* often share common cultures and experiences. In theory this had been recognised in the constitution of Colombia, which provides for the autonomy of certain groups of indigenous and Afro-Colombians. The reality, however, is rather different.

The existence of different cultures, traditions and experiences is one of the first things that need to be recognised by social workers. Decision making and the selection of local leaders often take place outside the official procedures of the state. They are more related to local needs and rituals rather than to statutory directives and laws. This appears to be a critical point. Traditional statutory social work is usually heavily bureaucratic and restricted by formalities, risk assessments and official prescriptions; such an approach cannot be followed by social workers who aim to establish trusting relations with the *despalzados*. Practitioners need to be flexible and create the necessary space to enable them to recognise, understand

and respect the internal procedures of these communities, even when they are not formally defined. It is not uncommon for social workers in Colombia to work with people who are not even registered as citizens; who do not even exist as far as the state is concerned. Strictly following the statutory bureaucracy means, at best, that social workers will always be estranged from the communities, and at worst, that these people will remain isolated and victimised.

Recognising the internal functions and traditions of the community is complex, but it is only an initial step. The main challenge remains to build strong bridges and links. On the one hand, social workers attempting to establish these links struggle with the label that follows them as 'statutory workers'. On the other hand, as we explained above, it is exactly this identity that, in many cases, helps them to find the space and resources essential to working with and meeting the needs of the *despalzados*. An important element of direct work with the *despalzados* is the establishment of a democratic and participatory decision-making 'mechanism' that respects the traditions, functions and voices of the displaced. Such mechanisms offer the space where social workers and local communities interact. They provide a guarantee that social workers will not slip into manipulatory methods and that the *despalzados* will demonstrate a sense of control over their situation.

Participatory processes include the organisation of open assemblies in the parks attended by the displaced and, in some cases, where trusting relationships have been built, by representatives of local residential areas. During this process social workers function as organisers who attempt to make full use of their institutional capabilities (access to facilities, funds and so on) for the benefit of the communities. On several occasions this has been followed by small cultural and sports events co-organised by the practitioners in direct collaboration with the communities. These events were 'owned' by the communities, but would not have been organised, had the social workers not made use of their influence within the state system in order to obtain approval for the events. Through these activities, the *despalzados* have enhanced their collective structures and found themselves in a context where they have received respect and understanding. However, what pushed us, as workers, towards emancipatory dimensions in our practice was not only establishing empathetic relationships with the *despalzados* but entering a process of building active and conscious solidarity with them.

Conscientisation and emancipation in social work practice

In the last two sections we have described how direct social work practice with displaced communities in Bogota has attempted to meet people's survival needs, tackle violent attacks against them and encourage democratic participation and empowerment. These actions target the urgent needs of people in the 'here and now'; an important element of social work under extreme circumstances, but one that does little to address problems in the longer term. As we have shown above, it would have been impossible to engage in political social work praxis, had social workers and communities not succeeded in addressing, at least temporarily, the issues of community and individual survival. We stress the word 'temporarily', because it is our conviction that the problem of the *despalzados* in Colombia is structural and deeply rooted in the social inequalities and oppression that characterise the country. Consequently, this issue cannot be permanently resolved unless the systemic and historical causes of the problem are recognised and structurally addressed. The only solution that can do justice to the *despalzados* is the creation of conditions that will allow them to return to their lands to live in dignity and prosperity. This will not happen unless the drug lords, armed groups and multinational companies stop exploiting the natural resources of the country for their own ends of accumulation.

Social workers who engage in trusting political and social relations with the displaced cannot pretend that the solution can be found in magical tricks or through the circulation of 'food stamps'. Equally, the adoption of the punitive and controlling approach of the state cannot be considered even as a valid social work practice. Finally, Eurocentric and North American clinical and individualistic approaches can offer no remedies in this case, and simply look out of place. Social workers need to break free from these dominant models and seek alternatives in the rich traditions of liberation social movements of Latin America.

The recognition that social workers have no 'magic wands' or easy answers leads to another question: 'Who then has the solution?' This question has long been at the heart of Latin American grassroots welfare work, whether it is inspired by liberation theology or by the praxis of critical social pedagogy. The centrality of the right of the oppressed to control their lives and seek emancipation is fundamental. During this process social workers attempt to make sense of the complex political realities of situations, while working in a 'dialectic relationship' with the *despalzados*. In other words, social workers do not pretend that they possess expertise and status to help the *despalzados*; they accept that they constantly learn from their interaction with the displaced communities, creating 're-humanising' opportunities for both groups.

Through dialogue, mutual respect, democratic processes and cultural activities, both social workers and displaced communities work towards understanding the structural causes of social problems. In doing so, a very important stage in this process is the building of broader social alliances. Oppression and social inequalities affect not only the groups of people occupying the national parks. All sections of Colombia's peasantry and working class have been affected by the violent conflicts, social inequalities, privatisations and neoliberal policies of recent decades. A number of activities within the parks and the public spaces have attempted to bring together all these groups in an effort to challenge alienation, indifference and individualism. Such active demonstrations of solidarity can have a two-fold effect: restoring trusting relationships and creating the basis for future structural solutions. The creation of trusting and equal relationships between different sections of the working classes in Latin America has historically helped the most vulnerable and oppressed sections of society to deal with the effects of collective trauma, while making sense of history and politics. Class solidarity, rather than elitist philanthropy, has offered examples of emancipatory action. Moreover, class solidarity acts as an agent of active learning through practice. A combination of learning through critical–conscious solidarity actions and participation in organic social alliances has often directed communities towards the struggle for broader social changes. Watkins and Shulman, inspired by Latin American emancipatory work, have described these practices:

> like wellsprings erupting out of the ground [...]. We recognise these practices when they focus on the wellbeing and self organisation of people and their communities, when they promote critical reflection and transformation in local arenas and when their goal is not the imposition of a prescribed yardstick of development but an opening toward greater freedom in imaging the goals of life. (Watkins and Shulman, 2008, p 5)

Contemplating the future

We decided to avoid using the word 'conclusion' for the final section of this chapter. One reason is related to the fact that direct work with the *despalzados* is still ongoing. Even though for the purposes of this chapter we have 'codified' some of the practices involved in this work, we strongly believe that there is still a long way to go before social work efforts can be considered 'successful'. The mission and objectives of popular and emancipatory forms of social work cannot be considered accomplished unless it leads to the transformation of structural injustices.

In the case of the *despalzados*, the return of their rightful land, under conditions of social justice, safety and equality, does not seem to be imminent. Nevertheless, as leading liberation theologians Camilo Torres and Gustavo Gutierrez have argued, humbly accepting the present oppressive and unjust status while hoping for redemption in another life is an unacceptable condition for the people who work with the most vulnerable and poor in society.

> Only authentic solidarity with the poor and real protest against the poverty of our time can provide the concrete, vital context necessary for a theological discussion of poverty.... For the Latin American Church especially, this witness [of poverty] is an inescapable and much-needed sign of the authenticity of its mission. (Gutierrez, 1971, p 176)

Paraphrasing from Gutierrez's classic text, we can conclude that, for Latin American popular social work, seeking the conscientisation and emancipation of the oppressed is the necessary 'sign of the authenticity of its mission'.

Note

[1] We are indebted to Natalia Barrera for her support while writing this chapter. Her comments and suggestions have been invaluable.

SIX

Addressing social conflicts in Sri Lanka: social development interventions by a people's organisation

Ashok Gladston Xavier

Introduction

This chapter looks at three projects that are being run by social workers in Sri Lanka to build community robustness, women's engagement and post-conflict cross-community engagement. By focusing on grassroots community building shaped by values of non-violent resistance and social justice, I argue that community social work models have had a significant impact in building cross-community support networks and tackling issues of inbuilt suspicion and rivalry between the different communities.

To start the chapter, however, it is necessary to paint a picture of the background to Sri Lankan society and the roots of the conflicts that have shaped the island since independence in 1948.

Historical background

Sri Lanka has occupied the centre of South Asian conflicts for the last three decades – a consequence of the way in which the colonial authorities planted the seeds of ethnic divide and rule when the country (then known as Ceylon) was part of the British Empire. The post-colonial history of the country has been filled with structural inequality and oppression, punctuated by moments of extreme violence directed primarily against the Tamil minority. Although there has been a long history to Sri Lanka's troubles, I will concentrate on the recent past, beginning with Sri Lankan independence in 1948.

Sri Lanka is home to Sinhalese, Tamils, Burgers, Veddhas and a few other communities. The Sinhalese constitute 70% of the population. They live mainly in the southern part of the island. The Sinhalese are overwhelmingly Buddhist, though there is a smaller Christian community (Clarence, 2007). The Tamils inhabit mainly the northern and eastern parts of Sri Lanka; they are the second-largest community on the island and constitute about 18% of the population. They are overwhelmingly Hindu, but again there is a smaller Christian community. There is also a significant Muslim community on the island (about 8% of the population). In addition, there are communities of Burgers, Veddhas and Malays, all with different heritages.

By and large, the communities have learnt to coexist in harmony in the urban areas, where there is much interaction. However, in the rural areas the interaction between communities is limited. Nevertheless, during common meetings, festivals and celebrations it has been customary to meet and greet friends of different ethnic groups, religions and cultures. It is against this social background that the present divisions need to be viewed. Decolonisation left Sri Lanka with a great deal of disparity (Richardson, 2005). Historically, the Tamil minority included a section that was better off than the majority of Sinhalese. The establishment of the missionary schools in the north brought English education to some Tamils and facilitated their ability to occupy some of the coveted positions in the government. This hang-over from Empire was used by some nationalist politicians to stoke resentments.

In addition, the Tamils and Muslims together potentially accounted for about a quarter of the voting population. In the first post-independence elections the Tamils and Muslims together won about one-third of the seats. Nationalist Sinhalese politicians saw this as a threat and used it to rally support within the Sinhalese community (Uyangoda, 2007). They thought that the only way they could deal with this threat was to disenfranchise the up-country Tamils, who were of Indian origin (about 900,000 people who worked in the tea and rubber plantations had been taken to Sri Lanka from the poorest districts of Tamil Nadu during the early to mid 19th century [Richardson, 2005]). Since they clearly formed a decisive element in the 'vote bank' of politics they were the easiest to get rid of. The Tamil leadership treated the up-country Tamils as second-class citizens and their class prejudice strengthened the hand of the Sinhalese nationalists, thus playing a facilitative role in the oppression of the Tamils of Indian origin (Somasundaram et al, 1992). Once this was done, the next step was to come up with a system to deal with the Sri Lankan Tamils of the northern and eastern parts of the country. In the meantime, the state began discriminating against Tamils and Muslims (for example, by blocking their education).

Tamils who wanted to get government jobs were forced to learn Sinhala. The Sinhala Only Act of 1956 and the Standardisation of Education Act of 1957 were some of the obvious examples of institutionalised oppression (Bandarage, 2009). Tamil interests were led by S.J.V. Chelvanayagam. Chelvanayagam, an eminent lawyer, also known as the Gandhi of Eelam, fought in non-violent ways, along with his party, to promote Tamil rights. Two landmark agreements, the Banda-Chelva Pact of 1957 and the Senanayake Chelva Pact of 1965, were signed to restore the rights of the Tamils. But both collapsed when the Sinhalese government refused to keep its promise. These failings increased the disenchantment of the Tamil-speaking population. The Tamils harnessed all their support, contested the 1977 elections and won all the 17 seats that they had contested. They became the single largest party in the opposition and, for the first time, Amithalingam, a Tamil, became the leader of the opposition.

There were several reasons for this political breakthrough, such as lack of Sinhalese unity, lack of vision on the part of the Sinhalese politicians and growing divisions between left and right within the Sinhalese community. But the fact that a Tamil was the leader of the opposition was simply not acceptable to many of the Sinhalese politicians. The treatment given to the opposition leader was shabby. Open threats were made against him on the floor of parliament. The marginalisation and mistreatment of Amithalingam fuelled the bitterness within the Tamil community, and sections of the Tamil youth who were dissatisfied with the entire state of affairs began to group together and take up arms against the government. In the middle of the 1970s several armed groups were formed (Uyangoda, 2007). The objective of these armed groups was to fight for the rights of the Tamils by militant means. Many of the groups consisted of a just a few youths. They were involved in minor crimes and issued threats to the administration. But the activities of the armed groups grew in response to the increase in oppression of the Tamils. The groups were gaining members from all sections of society. They were preparing for the worst and started to campaign for a separate country for the Tamils, taking their cues from the Vaddukottai Declaration of 1976.

The Declaration was supported by all Tamil-speaking groups, who concluded that the only option left to them was a separate homeland for the Tamils. The driving force behind this radical announcement was the continuous betrayal by the Sinhalese regime in dishonouring its own promises to find an appropriate answer to the Tamil question. There was a sharp increase in violence against the Tamils in all areas. In 1984 planned attacks against the Tamils were carried out nationwide, in a genocidal fashion. Business establishments, journalists and anything to do with Tamil people were attacked. This systematic attack resulted in the further polarisation of the groups.

In response to these incidents, India started to support the armed struggle. Tamils in Sri Lanka were seen as family to the Tamils of Tamil Nadu. Most of the armed groups were brought to India, where they were trained in several parts of the country. The objective of the training was to combat the oppression of the Sri Lankan state. But this move by India didn't improve things. From 1984 to 2002 war ravaged the island nation and, though there were short moments of respite, continued relentlessly.

During this time the LTTE (commonly known as the Tamil Tigers) became the most prominent force fighting against the Sri Lankan state. The LTTE controlled the northern and eastern parts of Sri Lanka and ran a parallel administration in those areas. In 2002 a truce was signed between the government of Sri Lanka and the LTTE to end the conflict (Fair, 2004). Six rounds of peace talks were held between February 2002 and March 2006. But little progress was made. In 2007 the government launched a major offensive, the aim of which was to eliminate the LTTE. The war came to an end on 17 May 2009 with the killing of the LTTE leader, Prabakaran.

Issues confronting peace-building initiatives

According to reports, the conflict displaced about 700,000 Tamils, who sought refuge in over 51 countries. Although most of them settled in the developed world, about 150,000 moved to India, of whom about 75,000 live in camps in Tamil Nadu. Currently about 350,000 people from the war zone are living in internment camps with very few facilities (Darby, 2001; Johnson 2005; Richarson, 2005).

Being a small country, Sri Lanka does not have many resources; control over the sea is one of the major sources of conflict, and since the Tamils live in the northern and eastern parts of the country they have increased access to the sea. During the days of the LTTE they controlled almost 45% of the fertile seas. Though the Sinhalese fishermen controlled the southern and eastern seas they had very limited access to the east coast. The competition over the waters, to a great extent, remains one of the sites of tension and conflict between the communities. The north and east were seen as thriving agricultural lands, and this resulted in the Sinhalese settling in the Tamil areas. In many instances the government deliberately settled Sinhalese peasants or labourers in the Tamil areas so as to create an imbalance in the population and gain a share of the land resources. This can be seen in parts of Trincomalee, where several former Tamil villages have been taken over by Sinhalese farmers. When the Tamils return they are given alternative land that in no way matches the area or fertility of their original land. There have been measures to counter the deprivation and insecurity that dominate in Tamil areas. The difference between the Tamil and Sinhalese areas, especially in the east, is obvious. Lack of adequate teachers in Tamil schools, unmaintained buildings and inaccessible institutions of higher education systematically deprive the Tamils of educational opportunities. Although much of this is attributed to the war, there is a general lack of interest in developing these areas of Tamil life.

Within this mix, the state and the guerrilla armies have conducted their actions, killed adversaries, threatened civilians and demanded support from impoverished civilians. All this is done with impunity. All these acts of violence cause a great deal of anxiety among the people.

Over the years, the conflict has assumed several dimensions, such as ethnic, linguistic and religious. The ethnic angle is based on belief in the improbable fact that the Sinhalese were of an Indo–Aryan race and the Tamils were of a Dravidian race. This has been proved wrong by several anthropologists. With the help of legends and myths, the ideas continue to be propagated so as to fuel the differences. The introduction of the Sinhala letter 'Sri' into every car number plate in the year 1958 brought the linguistic dimension of the conflict to light. The Sinhala Only Act of 1956 gave the language supremacy over Tamil. It became the only official language of Sri Lanka, Sinhala being a prerequisite for getting a government job even in entirely Tamil-speaking areas. The religious dimension becomes evident from the composition of the country. A majority of the Sinhalese are Buddhist, a majority of the Tamils are Hindu. A relative minority from both linguistic groups are Christian. The Muslims generally speak Tamil. The conflict is essentially seen as one between Sinhala and Tamil, Buddhist and Hindu and, above all, Aryan and Dravidian. Most of this is baseless, as the divisions were created to support the vested interests of political factions.

There are deep-seated grievances about the overall perceptions of the community. Remarks are often heard such as, 'The Sinhalese are very warm and friendly people, but collectively they can be dangerous', 'My Muslim friends will give their life for me but I can't trust them as a community', 'The Tamils are known for their friendship, yet they are all ardent Tiger supporters'. The conflict has created a deep-rooted intolerance within communities, passed on from one generation to the next.

Poverty and under-development are easy to identify in the country. A random visit to the rural areas will put things into perspective. In the Tamil north and east of the country it can be seen that very little development has taken place in the last two decades. Many of the national development schemes have simply not been implemented in the north and east of the island.

A whole range of violent groups operated in the north and east – many of them simply criminal organisations. Their main targets were civilians who lived outside or adjacent to the conflict zone. They would terrorise and extort the little that these people had and claim that they were fighting for the restoration of rights. Government-appointed paramilitary forces such as the 'home guards' took the law into their own hands and began to punish those whom they suspected. The infamous 'white van' that was used by groups to abduct people, the masked man who came to identify the so-called 'miscreants', the deep penetration units and other covert groups often surfaced to cause insecurity in the minds of ordinary civilians.

These groups have left deep-rooted scars in the minds of the people. It is in this context that any peace building has had to take place. As a social worker working in this area, my work is shaped by themes.

Philosophical foundations of social work interventions

Based on the non-violent traditions of the subcontinent, there was a need to take a fresh look at the causes and effects of the conflict. Since the area of our work was in places that bordered the actual scenes of violent conflict or in areas where the violence had just come to an end, special attention was paid to the affected communities. The following contextual foundations were adopted in the interventions:

- building community confidence/social capital
- restoring democracy/people's participation
- gender balance/inclusion of the excluded
- restorative justice and peace building
- building community confidence.

Building community confidence/social capital

First, communities that have been deprived of basic rights and subjected to deprivation appear to remain helpless. Their ability to engage creatively in the process of development is hindered by their lack of confidence in themselves and in their community. Further, this strengthens their perceptions of their inability to recover from severe loss. Second, the community feel betrayed by the breaching of every single agreement and promise on the part of the state and its structures. Third, a feeling of mistrust has taken deep root in the minds of the minorities. An analysis of the situation reveals that the vulnerable have developed strong positions against the majority communities. In turn, the majority communities have developed misconceptions with regard to the minorities and see the minorities as the exploiters who want to divide the country and make them homeless. These perceptions make it all the more difficult to build confidence among the warring groups. The first initiative in terms of working with the communities was to restore trust. For this, there was a need to establish points of contact. At the grassroots level community leaders who had proved their concern for the vulnerable were engaged in the process.

Restoring democracy and encouraging people's participation

Thanks to the conflict, the community structures had collapsed. The village-level committees had been replaced by informers and ring leaders. Decisions were being made on the basis of power. The community leaders had been either eliminated, or intimidated into remaining silent. New, undemocratic structures had been created to facilitate the exploitation. People were strongly discouraged from participating in any common activities and, if they did participate, they were further labelled as the stooges of the government and would be treated as traitors of the liberation cause. Since the rule of the law had been replaced by the rule of the gun, the foremost imperative for peace building was to create community leadership. This was carried forward with a view to rebuilding the war-torn nation. The major challenge was to get people to trust each other and believe in the process of participation beyond the threats.

Gender balance

The war has shifted the gender equation. In the Tamil areas there are more women than men. Many families have lost a father, brother, son–in–law, husband or uncle. The situation has produced many widows. Despite this fact, very few women have assumed community responsibilities or participate in any processes. The role of women continues to be submissive and subjugated. In order to rectify this situation, special attention is paid to women. The idea is to enable them to participate actively in all levels of work related to them.

Inclusive approach

In the context of Sri Lanka several groups of people have been excluded from the process of development. The disabled, women, children, the aged and the displaced communities have been constantly ignored in terms of involvement in the implementation of programmes. In order to repair a conflict-ridden system, it becomes primarily important to include the excluded in the process of empowerment.

Restorative justice and peace building

Restorative justice principles are used to heal the wounds and nurture inter-ethnic, interfaith and inter-cultural relationships. Conscious efforts are being made in the direction of conflict transformation and peace building, in order to work for human rights and justice.

Interventions

Given the background of the conflict, our interventions started during the peace process in the year 2003. In order to put things in perspective, three case studies are presented. The first deals with a comprehensive peace-building strategy beginning from pre-school and moving on to inter-community dialogue. The second case study deals with economic interventions where inter-community self-help groups were formed so as to facilitate development along with peace. The third case study deals with the evolution of community leadership for peace building.

Case 1

Vavuniya district is the gateway to the northern part of Sri Lanka. This is also the border district for entry into the former LTTE-controlled areas. It has been the scene of conflict for the past 30 years. The town of Vavuniya has a majority of Tamils, Muslims constitute a significant minority and the Sinhalese a small minority. Due to its strategic location a huge army camp was set up just outside the town. It later became the head quarters for the government's Northern Command. The inhabitants around the camp were of mixed ethnic origins. Many Sinhalese settled outside the camps to provide essential services to the soldiers. These settlers eventually became permanent residents of the area. They had very little interaction with the Tamil community even though they were neighbours. The Tamils, in turn, showed their hostility towards the Sinhalese. The Muslims had very little interaction with either of the two communities outside their business in the town. Small, insignificant incidents were given communal colour and sparked violence.

The army would regularly raid the villages. Anyone with the remotest connection with the LTTE was arrested. Amidst this disturbed atmosphere there was very little interaction between communities. In a street where both Tamils and Sinhalese lived, they would not be able to tell even their names. The worst part was that the Sinhalese children would not be allowed to play with the Tamil children. When a Sinhalese parent met a Tamil child the immediate reaction was, 'he is a little tiger'. As it stood, there were more points of divergence than points of convergence. There were too many things over which they assumed to have differences. They thought that there was very little in common with each other. Further, the factors of demonising a community and entrusting collective responsibility were common.

Since the Tamils were in the LTTE, or since the Sinhalese were in the army, the entire community was branded as sympathisers. It was under these circumstances the first intervention began. The objective was to reach out to each community and build inter-community confidence. In an assessment, it was found that parents from all the communities had expressed the need for a pre-school. This was seen as the primary point of convergence. There were several concerns before starting the pre-school. Parents were concerned about the security of their children. They feared that they would be abducted by one side or another. The location of the school had to be in a neutral, violence-free place. While we were looking at the options, the local Buddhist Monastery was contacted. This place had a very understanding abbot who spoke the two languages and had the confidence of the community. He readily agreed to the plan and gave space for the pre-school. A shed was constructed and the pre-school began.

The pre-school started with six children and currently has 50. It teaches Tamil, Sinhala and English. Prayers of all four religions are recited. Children now have friends from all the three communities. In the beginning the parents were a bit uneasy to see their children coming home and speaking different languages. With the passage of time, the parents began to say, 'at least let our children learn the language that we were not able to learn'. Within three months there was a visible difference in the community. The parents were asked to attend a parent–teachers meeting, and an association was formed. It was the first time in several years that neighbours had sat close to one another, setting aside their prejudices. In the first few meetings the needs and welfare of the children were discussed exclusively. After three months common social needs were being discussed. The parents came up with several social issues that needed to be addressed, such as security, livelihood, housing, infrastructure and so on.

In response to the needs, specific programmes were developed to train the parents. They were first formed into self-help groups. A small savings scheme was initiated. Once they knew that they could save money and spend it on personal and common causes there was a steady rise in levels of trust. The parents began to trust one another. When they evaluated their personal situations, they found that there was very little difference between the Tamils and the Sinhalese. They were even heard to say that the politicians had manufactured the entire conflict for their own benefit. This marked a critical breakthrough in the peace-building work. While this was happening, the violence around the area escalated. The LTTE attacked the army camp outside the village. A curfew was called immediately. Usually when an attack of this nature occurs, the army rushes into a Tamil settlement and takes the youths on suspicion; or there is random firing at the Tamil areas. This time, as soon as the villagers learned of the attack, the Sinhalese, invited the Tamils to their homes to protect them. When the army round-up happened the Sinhalese stood up and supported the Tamils and prevented anyone from being taken on suspicion. Similarly, when a militant group took a Sinhalese man hostage, the elders of the Tamil community rushed to his help. They negotiated with the group and released him with a minimal ransom. Though the state remains oppressive and discriminatory towards the Tamils, the close inter-community trust that was built has taken the community a long way. They are now able to advocate and lobby for their rights collectively.

This was seen as a good beginning for community progress amid the warring climate.

Case 2

This case is set in the eastern part of Sri Lanka, in the Trincomalee district. Following the ceasefire agreement of 2002, the displaced people were being resettled in their home towns. The village in question is located in the Tamil–Sinhalese border area. Several violent incidents have taken place in the area. Most recently, Sinhalese have been settled in the area. In reaction to this and a few other issues, a Sinhalese family was massacred, allegedly by the LTTE. Following this incident several army camps were set up in the area. Now, when the Tamils were being resettled in their village they were met with suspicion. They were called informers and traitors. During the regular army round-ups, the army planted bombs and weapons on people and took youths whom they thought to be 'suspicious'. A village community leadership was formed in the Tamil areas and met with the elders in the Sinhalese villages. To their surprise, they realised that they needed each other in order to survive the difficult situation. For instance, when the Sinhalese village was attacked, the Tamil village would feel the repercussions; if a Tamil village was attacked there would be repercussions on the Sinhalese village. Hence there was a need to help each other in terms of safety. The villagers agreed on a mechanism for mutual protection. The Sinhalese villagers would go to the army headquarters and introduce the Tamil village leaders, and in turn the Tamil village leaders would lobby with the militants not to attack the innocent Sinhalese villagers. Once the primary security issues had been taken care of, the villagers began to interact.

Since there were very few points of interaction, the two communities were still strangers. A programme was created to establish 'common space' for the villagers to meet. A needs assessment revealed that there was much willingness to cooperate in terms of economic benefits. Further exploration outlined three vital issues to address. First, being agricultural workers, they harvested considerable amounts of paddy every season, but they had to take the paddy for long distances to be threshed. Lacking their own means of transport, they ended up paying a lot of money for private transportation. The second issue was related to the fact that, prior to the war, the women and men had been engaged in cattle rearing. They had made good profits, especially from dairy products, so they needed to re-establish an income source. Third, a common savings groups was a possibility.

First, they were brought together for about six months and given the necessary training to hold together as a group. They maintained joint bank accounts and proved that they were sincere about working together. Once they had established their interest in sticking together, their proposal to set up a rice mill was considered. They were helped to set up the mill. Currently the women of the two villages maintain the mill and make a profit from it. They get a concession for their own rice and are able to help dozens of small farmers to process their rice also. Since they make sufficient money to be able save some of it, they plan to reinvest the profits to expand the business. Because of their experience with raising cattle, cows were distributed to the women in need. They had to commit to rearing the cows for one year before they actually produced any milk. Once they had given this assurance, special arrangements were made with the local cooperative dairies. Soon their labour was rewarded. Currently the women have formed a semi-cooperative among themselves and are in the process of setting up a processing plant.

While this was going on, the war was raging at its peak. A Buddhist monk who was a sympathiser of the Tamils was shot by a Sinhalese youth. This created a lot of disturbances in the area. At the same time the village agricultural consultant, along with three other people, was brutally murdered in broad daylight, allegedly by the army. In order to blame the Tamils, the army planted bombs in the Tamil areas. A few youths were summoned for investigation and later arrested. The villagers got together, went to the local army commander and argued the case of the youths. The army eventually released the boys. During several such crises the people from the two villages have come together and dealt with the issues. Now there is bonding and inter-dependence between them for economic and security reasons. The milk collection centre and the rice mill have become identified with the women of the two villages. They are planning to replicate this model in the neighbouring district.

Case 3

The village in this case is located outside the Trincomalee district. This place is known for the frequent round-ups conducted by the military to identify youth who, they claim, are supporters of the LTTE and other militants. A majority of the residents in this village are Muslim. About 20% are Hindus and 10% are Sinhalese. During the early 1990s the village received housing grants from Iraq, hence it was named Saddam Nagar. Owing to its remote location and lack of leadership, there has been very little progress there in the last 15 years. The housing project was one of the last projects in the village. For drinking water the villagers had to walk 3 km, to go to school the children had to trek about 4 km, and in emergencies people had to be taken at least 10 km. With no roads, transport would refuse to come to the village. Amidst all this, the conflict among the three communities continued to grow.

In this context, the women of the three communities were brought together in a self-help group. The objective of the group was to meet regularly and to save a minimal amount every week. The women began to meet every week. In their meetings they were introduced to the concepts of gender equality, ethnic conflict and peace building through development. Ongoing efforts were made to build their leadership skills. Specialised programmes on leadership and communication were conducted. While this was going on the village had to choose a leader. The villagers got together and considered who was the best person to take the role. They unanimously selected Vimalavathy. She was a widow with four children. She showed remarkable interest in the village's development. Surprisingly, she was a Sinhalese who could speak fluent Tamil. With their new leadership the villagers were now encouraged to apply to development organisations for projects, but they were not very successful. They persevered and finally organisations began to respect the leadership and the needs of the villagers and started to support them. The first project was for 25 houses. The task was to identify the 25 poorest families who did not have proper housing. It was difficult to choose 25 out of about 50 really poor people. The village committee decided to entrust the responsibility to Vimalavathy. She visited every house with a team and made a personal assessment and then decided on the beneficiaries. The entire village approved of her decision. Similar construction projects soon followed. The toilet construction project and well construction followed the same approach.

The leadership were put to the test when three village youths were taken by the military on account of conniving with the militants. The villagers knew that the youths had been wrongly accused. They went and represented the youths' case to the local army commander. They pleaded the case of one youth who had elderly parents and whose wife was pregnant. He had to be with her. The commander asked someone to remain as a guarantor for the youth. A guarantor has to stay in the army camp until the accused person either returns or is proved innocent. Normally if the army takes someone it is several weeks before they return home. In this situation Vimalavathy stepped in as the youth's guarantor. This sent shock waves through the village and the military. The army had to keep a woman in custody and release the youth. After much negotiation they agreed to keep her and let the youth go. In the meantime, the villagers got together and started to make representations to the authorities for the release of Vimalavathy and the other youths. She argued the case of the other youths and they were released in four days. The villagers supported her in her courage and sacrifice and today they continue to take their work forward. This case study demonstrates the extraordinary efforts made by ordinary women, especially Vimalavathy, who risked her life to save a fellow villager. It also demonstrates the human aspect of peace and justice. The community's level of confidence grew so that it was able to engage with forces that it might otherwise have feared. It is important to recognise the small interventions by social workers that made it possible to empower the community to transform adverse situations into opportunities for growth.

Conclusion

The foregoing case studies demonstrate that social work can succeed in extreme circumstances of social and military conflict. The context of application of the approaches described above contributed to the success of each venture. Many times conflict transformation patterns do not result in immediate changes. But they do produce immediate impressions that may lead to change in the long run. In dealing with social conflict, philosophical foundations were particularly useful. They were localised, and drawn from examples of peace building in the area. Many of them came from prevailing religious and social ideologies. An inclusive approach, built upon human values, was the key to the interventions. It developed mutual respect and restored dignity to the community. In moving away from conflict-based behaviour between communities that relies on values based on past glory, it is important to remember to strive for the traditions of peace. This must be done without ignoring the issues of justice, especially social justice. As the saying goes, if you want peace, work for justice.

SEVEN

International organisations, social work and war: a 'frog's perspective' reflection on the bird's eye view

Reima Ana Maglajlic

In this chapter, I offer a reflection on several 'critical incidences' from the past 20 years of my social work experience, initially as a social work student and then as a practitioner, activist and a researcher in the region that I come from, which is most commonly labelled South-East Europe. I studied social work in my home town of Zagreb, Croatia during the 1991–95 war. Following five years of study and work in England, I then lived and worked in Bosnia and Herzegovina from 1999 to 2007, a country that was 'recovering' from a war that lasted from 1992 to the end of 1996. During these war and post-war periods, I worked for a number of local and international organisations or initiatives – from initiating or taking part in small-scale community activities to working as a consultant for organisations such as UNICEF, Save the Children, USAID and the EC.

The critical incidences that I shall reflect on are all related to the manner in which international and supranational organisations get involved in countries that experience extreme political conflicts and/or war. These are not, nor do I claim them to be, the *only* legitimate examples of these organisations' possible roles and actions. However, the reasons why I am focusing on these incidents in this book are two-fold. First, these organisations were not so active in my region prior to the war. Yet, over the past 20 years, they have become powerful stakeholders who define, at least on paper, how social work is to be implemented and practised. In a sense, the war provided these organisations an opportunity to implement a particular type of social work engagement. Second, international organisations within social work (such as the International Federation of Social Workers, IFSW) seem to be developing a new relationship with the area of work that is frequently referred to as 'social development', one which is promptly added to contexts that have experienced political conflict.[1] Hence, our profession is rethinking its past, current and possible future roles in this sphere of our practice and in contexts to which such labels are applied. It is also an additional field of work where international organisations play an active and important role worldwide (such as through the implementation of the UN Millennium Development Goals).

This brief exploration will be divided into three sections, focusing on an example from the war period, the immediate post-war period and the period where 'social development' and 'transition' labels are frequently applied to the post-war contexts. Few people reading this book will (hopefully) have direct experience of violent political conflicts or wars, but it is worthwhile noting the impact that war has on people, whether they are civilians or soldiers. Apart from the immediate threat to life and limb, people, regardless of who they are – but also at times due to their age, gender, ethnicity, race or other aspects of their identity – are exposed to death, purposeful disablement and rape, either as targets of or as witnesses to such activities inflicted on their family, friends or neighbours. They can also be made to leave their homes, sometimes with little or no warning or opportunity to take any possessions with them. These actions are not only carried out by unknown persons – at times, they are carried out by persons whom they considered to be friends, neighbours or even family members. People may also choose to flee their homes in an attempt to prevent exile or harm befalling them or their families. If they do become refugees or displaced persons, people may not know where they are going, can become separated from their family or friends and can end up in a country where they don't understand the language or have any familiarity with the culture and context in which they now find themselves. Further, there is no clear sense of when such experiences will end. The initial hope is that such experiences will be temporary. But trauma, stress and anxiety can be compounded by months or even years of waiting, by news of further atrocities (received either from other people in a similar situation, friends or family still directly exposed to the conflict, through the media or by other means) or by further experiences of violence, particularly if they take refuge within an area that is likely to experience the same or related violence. Men can be drafted to join armed forces against their will, or to join the armies willingly, only to witness or partake in events that can affect them for many years to come, with limited or no access to appropriate support.

Social workers living and working in countries affected by extreme political conflicts don't just have to deal with such situations in their professional capacity. They, too, will often experience all or some of the events taking place. But professionally, it is also possible for them to show resilience and draw strength through the situations they face. In a small-scale study entitled 'Wounded healers' (Muminović and Mustafovski, 2000), a social worker said something that captures the views of many practitioners:

> I think we needed help as well. Some initiatives offered support by specialised doctors and counsellors. I was a refugee, too, I experienced different traumas and I needed to be involved somewhere, to receive support and help. I think we accumulated strength out of a need to work and our wish to help others. I wouldn't go to work, trust me, I wouldn't expose my life to everyday danger if I wouldn't have a need to help other people. In a way, probably that work was therapeutic, too – you didn't have time to think about yourself.

The war period

In late 1993, I was offered an opportunity to work for UNICEF in Croatia on a project related to the so-called 'Week of Tranquillity'. This was a week-long ceasefire in Sarajevo (1–7 November), negotiated in conjunction with UNICEF, in order to get necessary winter supplies to the civilians in the besieged city. In order to support this activity, UNICEF Croatia organised a set of visits to the schools and refugee camps across the country – from those on the front line and in 'no man's lands' to those that weren't directly affected by the war. Children in these schools and camps were to draw pictures about their experiences (for example, about what they dreamed of for their future, their houses or places they came from during the war and how they hoped they would be in the future) and/or write brief pieces on themes such as 'What I would do if I was president'.

I was one of two people who visited the schools and camps, collating the children's drawings and writings, which were to be used to raise awareness of the war and its impact on children. For some reason, I had always wanted to work for the UN and this was my 'big break' into this magical world. When a colleague and I were briefed about what we were to do, we were told by the foreign UN staff member in charge of this activity that a similar initiative had worked really well in an African country where she had worked earlier, and hence it should work here, too. In return for the drawings, we were to take colouring pens and pencils to the camps and schools, together with other bits of art kit and school supplies. A selection of schools and camps was made, depending on how exposed they were to war.

Travelling to a school in a no man's land near Sisak, an hour and a half from where I lived, was the first time I'd really seen what the war was doing to life in my country. Abandoned ghost villages crumbled into the ground; destroyed buildings seemed to defy gravity, and there were army check-points which I had to pass. At the school, which was literally next door to the UN no man's land check-point, the children undertook their task. One of the boys skipped happily to the front of the classroom and handed in his drawing. In black pen it carefully documented the massacre he had seen in his village just down the road, with dead bodies, and soldiers busy at slaughter. He stood in front of me, smiling and waiting for a reaction. Truly not knowing what on earth I was doing, I asked him why he hadn't used any colours. 'Yes,' he said. He took the drawing back, skipped back to his desk and got busy drawing again. Minutes later, he returned. Red streams of blood had been carefully added to the picture.

On one occasion I was preparing a visit to a school and a camp on the north-western part of the Adriatic coast (which was free of fighting, but where many refugees were placed). I wanted to go there on my own. I knew how to drive and had access to a car but I was informed that this was not possible, due to insurance purposes. I suggested using the organisation's own vehicles, as there were some 10 vehicles belonging to the organisation parked in front of the office. I was told that was not a possibility either. Finally, in order to conduct the work, I was told that UNICEF would rent a car and a driver for me. At the time I was 20 and penniless, as the majority of us were during these first few years of war. But, due to such circumstances, I also found myself being chauffeur-driven around the safe parts of my own country. Accommodation was arranged in what remained of an empty five-star hotel, which was, at the time, frequented only by the ex-pats working in Croatia or people who worked for foreign organisations.

The whole experience seemed surreal and wasteful – even more so as I sat on the bed in the five-star suite of a hotel that was struggling to stay open during a war, surrounded by all the drawings by the refugee and local children, all of which were very similar to the drawing I have described above. One of them particularly stood out. It was by Zana, aged 12, and entitled 'Rodjena sam da patim' (I was born to suffer): it looked like Münch's *The Scream*. The discrepancy between the highly regulated and, from my perspective, opulent treatment I was receiving as a staff member and the drawn and written experiences of the children presented me with my first big ethical challenge; it also opened my eyes to what work in international organisations can be like. This became even more apparent when I visited the Savudrija refugee camp, where activities and daily life revolved around the tents, while I took bits of art kit from the back of a big rented car, 'extracted' the artwork from the children and drove off. I felt I was doing something that was wrong, that simply wasn't me, and so I quit after three weeks. Years later, again in a UNICEF office, I saw a book entitled *I dream of peace*. It contained a selection of the children's drawings from the camps and schools that I had collected. Later on, I heard that the 'Week of Tranquillity' had been only a partial success, as the supplies that were taken into Sarajevo had been bought in Serbia and people refused to take them. However, the records of the week indicate that '600,000 children were helped by the activity'.[2]

Subsequently, I arranged to have my social work course practice placement in the same organisation that I had visited in Savudrija, called 'Suncokret'. During the war it was the only organisation where those who worked with the refugees and displaced persons also volunteered to live in the camp, in the same accommodation as the refugees and displaced persons. It was founded by Nina Pecnik, who was, at the time, an assistant lecturer on the Social Work Programme in Zagreb. The principle of the work within the organisation was brilliant in its simplicity – in the majority of camps, volunteers initially started by organising activities for children. These were open not just to the children living in the camps, but also to the local children, aiming to break the barriers between the local population and the refugees and displaced persons. Through the children, they got to know the mothers and grandmothers and started organising support for them – depending on what they needed and wanted to do and the resources available. Links were made with the local Centres for Social Work (the statutory social work providers), local health services and any organisations aiming to provide support to the refugees and displaced persons (such as programmes for unaccompanied children; for further details see Pecnik and Stubbs, 1994). Volunteers came from Croatia, Bosnia (where the refugees and displaced persons came from) and the rest of the world, and they came for free. While very little had prepared me and my peers to cope with the distress of the refugees and displaced persons living in the camp, the manner in which it was run – despite much messiness and occasional disorganisation – seemed much more in line with my personal and professional values.

While truly international, it was created and led by the local professionals for the local people. It remains an exemplary case of how to organise support for people who are experiencing war. What works is simple; grassroots organisations that start with the people, where they live, and based on what they need. They grow based on those needs and wants. Not all needs can be met – most importantly, people's need to resume their lives where they came from – but such programmes don't waste resources and don't cost a lot to run. They work with individuals, as well as families, groups and communities, founded on respect for their experiences and offering support where they currently are.

The immediate post-war period

Although it may not be immediately obvious, wars can lead to future social policy and social work developments that are positive for civilian populations. For example, the post-Second World War period was marked in many European countries by significant welfare developments.

In general, while the destruction of large industries in Bosnia and Herzegovina (BiH) resulted in job losses, it has also contributed to positive environmental changes in many parts of the country. Long-stay mental health hospitals were bombed during the war, with patients in some institutions being sent out to march into towns as a warning to other inhabitants (for example, in Tuzla, Eastern Bosnia), but this also started a process that led to the reform of mental health services in this country.

The promotion of community-based psychiatry was a key objective of the bi-annual regional plan drawn up by the World Health Organisation (WHO) in spring 1994. Focusing on global healthcare reform, the WHO developed a strategic plan in cooperation with health authorities in both BiH entities[3] (Ceric and Jensen, 1996; WHO, 1997a, 1977b). The crux of the health reform consisted in the establishment of:

> family medicine practice, and introduction of the Community Based
> Rehabilitation Centres for Physical and Psychosocial Rehabilitation
> (CBRs). (World Bank, 2000b)

In plain English, what happened was that the right foreign and local professionals managed to collaborate at the right place and at the right time. On the one hand, the WHO office in BiH was run by Italian medics who were familiar with the work of Franco Basaglia on deinstitutionalisation and community-based mental health service development in Italy. On the other hand, the key psychiatrists in charge of the local mental health service development were educated abroad, particularly in the UK and also knew about and valued community-based provision. Hence, rather than considering the rebuilding of large long-stay hospitals, these professionals collaborated to initiate community-based mental health provision.

This led to the development of 38 planned CBRs, which started in August 1996 and lasted two years. They were to be staffed by a multidisciplinary team consisting of a psychiatrist, psychologist, social worker and two nurses. In some places both physical and mental rehabilitation centres were to merge into one centre, while in others they were kept separate. The aim was to provide community-based support to people with mental health problems and physical disabilities. In 1998, the CBRs for mental health were transformed into Community Mental Health Centres (CMHCs). Additional training for the staff was provided from 1996 until 2002. Several international organisations collaborated with the variety of statutory health structures, from the ministries, to the actual CMHCs, in order to coordinate and complement their activities. These, for example, included the Swedish Psychiatric, Social and Rehabilitation Project for Bosnia and Herzegovina (SweBiH), HealthNet International (HNI; a sister organisation to Médecins Sans Frontières) and the Harvard University Medical Centre project. I initiated a collaboration with the UK-based charity Hamlet Trust, which supported the development of mental health system survivor-run organisations across South and Eastern Europe and worked with the mental health system survivor representatives and local practitioners to help establish five survivor-run organisations across the country.

Until the early 2000s, this seemed to be an exemplar of the manner in which international organisations can collaborate with local decision makers, practitioners and service users to help support a truly relevant reform process. But by the early 2000s the interest in Bosnia and Herzegovina had withered. The war had ended some five years previously, and Afghanistan and Iraq were the new, 'sexy', war-torn countries. International organisations started to pull out and established their so-called exit strategies. Exits were quick and ill prepared, and the money withered. At times, the local management that was selected to lead the transition towards the creation of local organisations did not support the ethos of the activities that the international organisations had established. At the time, I was working for HNI. While HNI was renowned for supporting the development of community-based mental health systems, in the early 2000s it stopped doing that. Instead, the new projects included strengthening and supporting the transformation of institutional provision for children without parental care. Adults were no longer 'in'; there was money only to work with children. And transition from supporting the development of community-based mental health provision to strengthening children's institutions didn't raise too many eyebrows within the organisation itself. The important thing was for the organisation to survive, while the donors themselves promoted and funded only specific interests and perceptions, unrelated to the needs of BiH citizens or work conducted to date (Deacon, 1995; Gagnon, 2002).

The 'transitional' period

This new era was also marked by the dominance of two major international organisations – the World Bank and the EU. From 2003 to 2007 I worked as a freelance consultant, including work for UNICEF. In addition, I did volunteering work for a variety of initiatives. However, I stopped doing freelance work, as I felt it started to compromise me and left me taking money to carry out a job that was undermining local initiatives and grassroots engagement. I worked for a daily fee, on short-term contracts, and on activities specified and led exclusively by those who employed me. In 2007 I coordinated an assessment of child welfare reform in South East Europe from the early 1990s, funded and initiated by the UNICEF Regional Office for Central and Eastern Europe and Commonwealth of Independent States in Geneva. The assessment, based on case studies from Albania, Bulgaria, the former Yugoslav Republic of Macedonia and Serbia, aimed to explore the systemic changes in child protection reform.

The analysis seemed very clear. Across the region, child and social protection planning had been under the influence of country-wide strategic planning, promoted primarily through the efforts of the World Bank. This mainly related to poverty-reduction processes, with the related references to UN Millennium Development Goals. However, numerous other strategies followed, including national strategies and action plans in relation to children's rights or the rights and needs of specific target groups of children. The Social Protection Strategies had been the last to emerge, during the course of the previous two years. In Bulgaria, there was also a separate strategy for child protection.

These built on the experiences of the World Bank in regard to poverty assessments undertaken in other parts of the world, mainly in Africa, Latin America and Eastern Europe (including the former Soviet Union) in the mid 1990s.

> As of July 1998, 49 participatory poverty assessments had been undertaken – 28 in Africa, 6 in Latin America, 11 in Eastern Europe, and 2 each in South and East Asia ... [Eastern Europe includes the former Soviet Union, or, more precisely, Soviet countries] which are part of the Europe and Central Asia Region at the Bank. (World Bank, 1999, pp 40–1)

The Bank promoted a process that relied heavily on participatory methodology, which, in its view, ensured local ownership. It also emphasised cooperation between the World Bank and the IMF:

> There is a strong belief, backed by empirical evidence, that more progress in poverty reduction has been made in countries where the

strategies pursued were fully owned by the government and by society at large … This decision has three major implications: countries, not donors, would lead the process, assuming management and ownership; the formulation of strategies would be broadly participatory and the Bank and the Fund [IMF] would work much more closely together and with other development partners in support of country-owned strategies. (World Bank, 2000a, 36)

Since these strategies had been developed in the region from 1999 onwards, the EU accession processes also had a major impact in terms of their content. This was mainly reflected in the promotion of the following issues:

- decentralised governance and the related/subsequent bottom-up policy planning (not just in social protection);
- pluralism of service providers (promotion of the role of non-governmental and private service providers) and the related community-based care (and the related deinstitutionalisation of the current provision);
- improved targeting of material assistance.

The level of cross-over in terms of content and approaches was interesting, to say the least. Despite their geographical proximity, each of these countries had different historical, economic, social and political developments and traditions that were simply ignored. The Social Inclusion strategies that were subsequently developed seem to follow the same cut-and-paste logic and matrix. The lack of grassroots leadership in the creation of government-level policies is staggering and highlights the pervasive, top-down influence of major international organisations on social welfare.

What next?

Unfortunately, these types of experience jade the valued role international collaborations can have both in raising awareness about the experiences of the socially excluded in war and post-war countries and in coordinating relevant actions to address their needs. Western European and US models seem to be exported uncritically, driven mainly through the knowledge of English. Knowledge of this powerful medium of communication seemed to be more important when employing local staff than any actual expertise they might have regarding the local context or relevant professions. Lack of a translation for some relevant terms – including, for example, 'case management' – highlights the myriad difficulties involved in simple import–export practices.

What do seem to work are initiatives that grow from the grassroots, are led by the local people, are based on the needs of local populations and that focus on working with whole communities rather than solely with individuals. Respect for local traditions, understanding of local culture, social, economic and political situations cannot and should not be underestimated. No matter how much we know about our own countries, regardless of how rich our experiences are and how many similarities we seem to identify when working in a new country – they should not be mistaken for a green light to 'cut and paste' what we know into a foreign context. It is a shame that such thinking and actions remain labelled in our profession as radical rather than mainstream and common sense.

Notes

[1] An example is the recent IFSW/IASSW conference, which focused not only on social work but also on social development, www.swsd2010.org/en/about.html.

[2] www.greenstone.org/greenstone3/nzdl;jsessionid=123E473679C462685881FF01147E 5BF1?a=d&c=edudev&d=HASHb54cbd4d73632f10a3bafa.26&sib=1&p.a=b&p.sa=&p. s=ClassifierBrowse&p.c=edudev [accessed 6 September 2010].

[3] BiH has a complex administrative structure. It is comprised of two entities, Republika Srpska and Federation of Bosnia and Herzegovina. The latter is further split into ten cantons. There is also a district, Brcko District, based on the US administrative model. It is these levels of government that are responsible for the regulation and organisation of health and social care provision, making a total of 13 ministries responsible, for example, for social welfare.

EIGHT

Welfare under warfare: the Greek struggle for emancipatory social welfare (1940–44)

Vasilios Ioakimidis

Introduction

Critical social policy and social work studies regularly offer critiques on mainstream welfare systems, institutions and attitudes. But these approaches often leave little space for discussion about what alternative social work and welfare might look like. In the history of social work internationally there have been examples of collective and grassroots alternatives – forms of popular social work. In most cases, however, these have been written out of history and excluded from dominant definitions of social work.

The focus of this chapter is on a specific period of modern Greek history when an organic and democratic welfare network developed as part of a broader movement for liberation and social change. I explore the legacy, influence and vision of this welfare movement, which flourished in Greece during the politically and socially turbulent 1940s. I argue that this experience can inform modern social work practices and demonstrate that alternative social welfare models are not only desirable but possible.

In exploring the welfare and social work developments of this period there are two main points that need to be clarified. The first is related to the use of the term 'social work' and the second concerns the boundaries of social welfare during a period of military occupation and popular resistance.

My definition of social work is not restricted to the increasingly narrow perspectives of Anglo-American social work that dominate the literature of international social work. I suggest that social work as an activity can be much wider and organic than those activities shaped by 'professional' and 'legal' boundaries in the Anglo-American world. Definitions of social work need to embrace various local traditions, collective and democratic processes and grassroots creativity. In Greece the history of social work is split between the emergence of 'official' social work in 1946, which was imported by the Americans as part of a multi-dimensional (military, political, cultural and social) intervention into the country during and after the civil war, and the 'popular' social work that flourished out of grassroots welfare activities and networks that developed as part of the popular liberation movement first against the Nazi occupation and then within the context of the civil war. The experience of these networks and activities highlighted one of the most creative and inclusive welfare systems in modern Greek history, yet it has been systematically suppressed and ignored within official social work literature.

Moreover, the development of this welfare tradition has had an indirect yet extremely significant impact on the function and character of 'official social work'. The Greek state created the first social work programme in 1946, in the midst of the civil war. One cannot ignore the political significance and the hidden agenda of such a decision. Despite the professional declarations regarding social work's political neutrality and democratic values, it soon became clear that 'official social work' could not – and did not want to – escape the suffocating context designed by its founders (see Ioakimidis, 2009). A peculiar mixture of Anglo-American social work theory and Hellenic-Orthodox nationalist ideology became the knowledge base of the profession. The first social workers were placed chiefly in children's institutions, mainly located in 'leftist areas' of the country. One of the objectives of social work was, on the one hand, to control the marginalised local communities, with an emphasis on 'rehabilitating red children', and, on the other hand, to reinstate patriarchal and moralistic family ideologies (in contrast to the 'immoral and atheist' ethos of the Greek Left [Ioakimidis, 2009]). The relationship between the grassroots welfare developed (from below) in the 1940s and the creation of 'official social work' (top-down) needs to be examined within the socio-political dynamics of the period.

There is a second issue that needs to be clarified: how do we categorise the activities undertaken within the popular movement? In this chapter I focus on welfare developments as part of a set of broader political changes that were introduced by the resistance and liberation movement that followed the Nazi invasion and consequent occupation in 1941. The movement soon gained the characteristics of a social revolution that demanded liberation not only from the Nazis but from all forms of oppression. It thus posed questions about the nature of Greek society and the prevalent social order.

The military achievements of the Liberation Army (ELAS) led to the liberation of large parts of continental Greece before the official defeat of the Nazis. In the liberated regions the National Liberation Front (EAM) introduced embryonic forms of popular administration and justice that soon took the form of a democratically elected partisan government – known as the 'Government of the Mountains'. In this region there were a range of political, cultural, military and welfare developments. By focusing solely on the welfare dimension there is a danger of fragmenting and isolating an activity that was inextricably linked to a broad social movement and a range of other activities. For example, the emergence of the 'theatre of the mountains', a grassroots artistic movement developed by experienced actors and thousands of young people who joined the resistance, cannot be classified solely as cultural activity. It had a clear political character, as well as an educational one, but it was also intended to provide emotional and psychological relief and support to those affected by the war. Thus it was also partly 'popular' social work that had a clear welfare element. Therefore, in this study social welfare and social work are examined within the political and historical context of the Greek resistance and civil war.

A 'social welfare' dimension to the liberation struggle

On Sunday, 27 April 1941, German troops entered the deserted and silent streets of Athens. Before them, the Greek monarch, King George II, and his government fled to Egypt. Greece was divided into three zones of occupation: German, Italian and Bulgarian, though the Nazis maintained the general command. A collaborationist government was appointed by General Tsolakoglou with the support of some leading figures from the traditional mainstream parties. The main organs of the state remained in place and the Orthodox Church provided tacit support for the new arrangements. Findings from research relating to members of the Greek establishment of the period have revealed that most of them were supportive of the Fascist 'achievements' in Italy in the 1930s (see Linardatos, 1975).

The Greek people, frustrated by defeat and abandoned by the traditional political parties, soon realised that there was one more factor that would dramatically affect their lives: famine.

The occupation forces 'bought' and requisitioned vast stores of food, leaving most Greeks facing starvation. For the wealthy, life went on much as before, but this was not the case for the popular classes (the working class and the peasantry), who faced immense hardships. Within the first month the occupation forces:

> Seized or bought … all available stocks of olive oil, olives, raisins, figs, tobacco, cotton, leather, and the majority of the pack animals. The appropriation of all means of transport and fuel essentially prevented any transfer of supplies or population after the occupation. (Hionidou, 2004, p 83)

The situation deteriorated further after the Nazis placed a prohibition on fishing, and it became critical when the Allies imposed a naval blockade on Greece. The infrastructure of the country was paralysed. The occupation forces took the lion's share of taxation income and, when the first signs of stagnation appeared, they ordered the Bank of Greece to increase the circulation of bank notes and devalue the currency. The consequence was an immediate, astronomical increase in inflation, which led to the price of a loaf of bread rising to a million drachmas. The Greek people suddenly faced catastrophe and devastation. In this atmosphere the black market flourished.

One of the darkest chapters in the occupation was the famine of the first winter, 1941/42. It is difficult to be precise, but most researchers agree that approximately 300,000 people died during that winter (see Mazower, 1993; Hionidou, 2004). Mazower puts the number of deaths in the Athens–Piraeus region at between

49,188 (modest official data) and 500,000 (British Broadcasting Corporation estimates at the time) (Mazower, 1993, p 38).

Against this backdrop and in this context the resistance movement started. At first, acts of resistance were small and isolated, but they did indicate a spirit of rebellion and that 'something' needed to be done.

On 27 September 1941, the EAM was formed at a secret meeting in Athens. The key initiating role was played by the Communist Party (KKE), which approached politicians from across the political spectrum, academics, intellectuals and trade unionists and invited them to join EAM. Not all responded positively (see KKE, 1995). Most politicians from the mainstream parties distanced themselves from EAM throughout the occupation, and by the end of the war their hostility to the popular movement was palpable. So the founding declaration of EAM was signed only by KKE, the Agrarian Party and some prominent individuals. The founding statement of EAM was based on two fundamental conditions: the overthrow of the occupation forces and a post-war regime characterised by social justice and equality. After its launch, EAM members circulated a booklet called *What EAM is and what does it want*, written by one of the most eminent pedagogues in the modern Greek academy, Demetrios Glinos:

> Just as there can be no national struggle without unity in leadership, so there can be no national struggle without unity in organization. The struggle must include all social strata, from the worker to the bourgeois and from poor peasant to the landowner [...] The struggle must go on at all times and in all places ... in the market place, the café, the factory, the streets the estates, and in all work. Because everywhere and at all times we must affirm our rights, show our solidarity, and stand one beside the other against the foreign invader and the Greek traitor [...] otherwise it [the struggle] will be dissipated by futile acts ... and our misery will increase under the blows of the enemy. (EAM cited in Stavrianos, 1952, p 43)

EAM's manifesto declared its focus on 'national unity', a commitment that later on proved to be very costly.

However, the foundation of EAM was not simply the spark that lit the fire of resistance; it was the harbinger of a social revolution. Within a few months thousands of people had joined the resistance. Fraternal organisations were founded across the country. The most important was the Popular Liberation Army (ELAS), the armed wing of the resistance movement, which became a very effective *andartes* (guerrilla) army, capable of launching large-scale attacks (Witner, 1982). It is estimated that ELAS had 50,000–75,000 fighters within a formal military structure and a military school (Stavrianos, 1952, p 44). Alongside ELAS, there were EPON (United Pan-Hellenic Youth organisation), EA (the resistance 'red cross'), EEAM (workers' EAM) and a Women's Union.

By the beginning of 1944, ELAS had been so successful that it had managed to restrict the Germans to some urban areas, leaving the largest part of continental Greece liberated. In fact, within occupied Greece a functioning 'Free State' was created. In the Free State area the Liberation Movement even managed to organise democratic elections and establish self-administration. It was these radical developments which later were to provoke a fierce counter-attack from the ruling class backed by Britain and the US. In late 1944 Britain invaded Greece in an attempt to return the king to power and reassert the pre-war political order in Greece. This intervention led to a bitter, armed class struggle, better known as the Greek civil war. As Ralph Miliband observed:

> Greece [...] posed problems demanding rather more than merely political and ideological struggles. In Greece it was Britain which initially assumed responsibility for the task. This required that the Greek liberation forces (largely but not exclusively under communist control) should be crushed. [...] Thus was a traditional ruling class, remarkable for its ferociously reactionary character, deeply tainted by collaboration with the Germans, and also by its earlier support for dictatorship, enabled to reassert its domination by virtue of the decisive and indispensable help given to it, first by Britain under both the Churchill Coalition and then by the Labour Government, and from 1947 onwards by the United States. (Miliband, 1989, p 191)

The civil war ended in 1949 with the defeat of ELAS/EAM. During the next 35 years Greece went through a period of authoritarian rule. Hundreds of thousands of people who had participated in the resistance and the democratic front either fled the country or were subjected to long periods of imprisonment, to torture and even political assassination.

In the middle of the repression 'official' social work was formed in Greece. It used Anglo-American expertise to introduce case-work and intervene in the lives of 'problem' red families (Ioakimidis, 2009). The alternative tradition of collective welfare, used to deal with a range of needs of the Greek popular classes during the Second World War and civil war, was marginalised, dismissed and 'forgotten'.

It is my contention that the welfare initiatives of this period provide a glimpse of an alternative social work and an alternative approach to dealing with social welfare problems.

But while considering the 'welfare activity' of EAM it is necessary to bear in mind the conditions within which it developed. Considering the extreme socio-political circumstances of the time, it would be a mistake to compare EAM's welfare provisions to a modern Western concept of 'welfare'. EAM emerged from the ashes of a war – a time of severe hardship – and functioned for a limited period, primarily outside the large urban areas of the country. But, rather than see all this as a weakness, we should see its welfare achievements as remarkable, given the enforced limitations of the war.

For analytical purposes it is possible to classify EAM's welfare activities into three strands: the fight for survival, popular administration and 'holistic development'. Thus, while confronting the occupation was central, EAM nevertheless undertook relief work as well as attempting to provide for universal cultural and educational development.

The fight for survival

As I noted earlier, the occupation brought devastation and famine. The need for immediate relief from the famine was clear, and dealing with this became the first, basic activity of the resistance movement. It tested the movement's will, its ability to meet people's needs and its organisational capabilities to provide relief across the whole country. It was a challenge to which the movement was able to rise, but meeting the need required different approaches in rural and urban areas. In urban areas the struggle took the form of food distribution, while in rural areas the main priority was the protection of agricultural production from the occupiers, known as the 'Battle for the Crops'. Additionally, EAM took a hard line towards collaborators and black marketeers, whose activities made life for the vast majority much harder.

Urban Greece

The famine bit hardest in the towns and cities. Despite the general turbulence and confusion, people looked towards their traditional organisations to deal with the situation. Trade unionists, mainly in the public sector, had significant pre-war experience of organising under conditions of persecution. Using this 'expertise', and committed to meeting the immediate needs of the working class, socialist trade unionists formed Labour EAM (E-EAM) in June 1941. E-EAM was formed three months before EAM and was the organisational spine of the liberation movement (Mavrikos, 2004). Some of E-EAM's objectives were:

- to organise the struggle of the working class in defence of their working conditions and social and political rights
- to fight against the systematic robbery of the country by the occupation forces
- to fight against the black market
- to work towards the foundation of a Pan-Hellenic National Liberation Front, accessible to all parties and organisations, that would fight for the liberation of the country from the occupation (KKE, 1981, p 174).

The survival of the starving population was a priority. E-EAM tried to deal with the situation by developing a tripartite plan: redistribution of food, tackling the black market and organised protests against the collaborationist government (Livieratos, 2006).

The first attempt to distribute food was a combined effort by the Regional Labour Centres and some professional associations. The latter focused mainly on food distribution to the families of their registered members. A representative example of this process is provided by the Association of Banking Employees, which, after a 15-day strike, won the right to distribute food within the banks. It also organised relief services for orphans (SYTE, 2006). The Central Public Sector Workers Committee (KPE) organised similar activities and demanded official permission to develop partnerships for more efficient distribution. Given the scale of the humanitarian crisis, the government conceded to their demands (Ntona, 2004). Within a few months, most regional trade union committees had organised fund-raising activities almost everywhere, in universities, schools, banks, even in the streets (Papageorgakakis, 2006). Again, given the scale of the famine crisis, the occupying authorities assented to the demand to let the labour committees function. These committees became the core of organisations of the people and, as well as providing immediate welfare relief, helped to shape a sense of solidarity, collectivism and even optimism (in the sense of a hope for a better future).

E-EAM local committees encouraged participation and collective activity in the face of the occupation. One of their documents argued:

> What should you do? Here is what you should do. First of all you should not – for any reason or on any occasion – stay alone, away from the rest, an isolated person. Unite with others. Unite with your colleagues, in your Union, your partnership, your guild, your association, become an active member. Participate in all struggles, debates about everyday issues; protect your rights to life, to ensure your life, the survival of you and your relatives. After that, look for friends and relatives who can help you to set up an EAM team. Organise yourselves in this team and elect a secretary and a local committee. [...] fulfil your duty and do not let a day pass without asking yourself: what have I done for the liberation struggle today? How did I harm the enemies? How did I help our people? (Glinos, 1941, p 4)

The E-EAM committees thus did more than food distribution: they prepared the labour movement for the more aggressive mobilisations to come.

If E-EAM were to promote and defend basic human rights to life, it would have to fight. In April 1942 the first large-scale strike occurred. The main demands were inextricably linked to the immediate material needs of physical survival, but the strike demands also included an end to redundancies and intimidation by the occupying authorities. In August and September a second wave of strikes took place in Athens and Piraeus. Hundreds of thousands of workers ignored the curfews imposed in the big cities and demonstrated against the occupation forces and the collaborationist government (Mavrikos, 2004; Papageorgakakis, 2006, p 12).

The demonstrations forced the authorities to accept most of the trade unions' demands. They doubled the food vouchers, released arrested trade unionists and increased salaries. This victory had a great impact on the morale of the people and emphasised the importance of collective struggle and solidarity against the occupation.

The strikes also brought an end to the policy of 'labour recruitment for the Reich'. Labour transfers occurred across the Nazi-occupied territories. The 1942 strikes put a stop to such recruitment in Greece for the rest of the year. However, on 23 February 1943 the German High Command issued an order calling for the compulsory recruitment of Greek workers and demanded that it be published in 'the Government's daily documents'. The order 'Concerning the General Compulsory Work of the Greek Population' stated that:

> Every single inhabitant of Greece aged between 16 and 45 is subjected to compulsory work under the command and instruction of the German and Italian authorities ...Those who will not comply with the order will be penalized with 1. Unlimited penalty fine, 2. Detention, 3. Imprisonment in a military camp. (Vournas, 2000, pp 264–5)

Workers in the Central National Printing Services, which was printing the order, immediately informed EAM and KKE. Overnight the two organisations agreed to call for a popular uprising. The day after the news was circulated (23 February 1943), the demonstrations and protests began. During the first days of the uprising workers, students and pupils gathered in the city centre and occupied state buildings – most notably the Ministry of Labour. Protests reached a climax on 5 March, when approximately 300,000 workers clashed with the occupying forces (see Petropoulos, 2004). More than 17 protesters were killed and hundreds were injured. As the newspaper of EAM, *Eleftheri Ellada* (Free Greece), reported:

> The streets of Athens and Piraeus were painted with the blood of the workers who were murdered. 17 dead and 160 injured defined once again the right to life and freedom. (*Eleftheri Ellada*, 1943)

Despite the losses, the Athenians remained on the streets and their example was taken up by workers in the other major Greek cities. As a consequence, the occupying forces were forced to abandon their plan. Thus, on 7 March 1943 it was announced in the press:

> The communist organisation, EAM, unfortunately managed to influence a lot of students and workers who did not listen to my stern warnings. EAM organised anarchist gatherings all over the city aiming at disrupting free transportation and the function of public services. As a result these terrorist groups clashed with the police, [though] the latter finally managed to restore order.... The excuse for these insane terrorist provocations was the so-called labour recruitment. We already have declared to the population of Greece in the most official way, that

labour recruitment will not take place and whoever works currently
under the command of the occupying administration will not be sent
abroad. (Cited in Petropoulos, 2004, p 11)

Such an achievement can be understood only as being a result of E–EAM's efforts
and its commitment to the fight for survival. In 1943 the labour movement was
even able to force the collaborationist government to resign. Gradually E–EAM
implemented more militant methods in its operations and focused on 'looting'
the Nazis' supplies (lorries, silos, camps) and distributing goods, or selling them
at extremely low prices, to the population.

E–EAM's 'welfare' impact on urban areas was crucial. First, its contribution to
food provision was significant and 'the fact that the famine of 1941–42 stopped was
partially a result of the massive united struggle of the workers' (Papageorgakakis,
2006, p 12). Additionally, the demonstrations forced the occupying forces to
make significant concessions. However, perhaps the most important was that
E–EAM's actions and activities maintained an ethos of collective steadfastness in
the cities. Despite the devastation, Athens did not become a deserted city or a
ghost city where anarchy, disorganisation and 'looting' prevailed. Working people
demonstrated resilience and responded to the new environment with a sense of
social solidarity. The link between collectivism, social solidarity and social welfare
provided a new perspective on welfare and relief 'services' based on principles
of need and mutuality.

Rural areas

In the rural areas the fight for survival had a different character, but was also based
on tight community relations and solidarity. The peasants did not face the threat of
starvation during the famine because they had direct access to the land. However,
a combination of factors led to the gradual decline of agricultural production –
and this was made worse by the fact that the occupying forces constantly tried
to seize food and grain stocks in order to supply their troops and send resources
back to Germany.

Under these circumstances farmers were forced to hide their crops and try
to sell them locally (in contrast to the pre-war system, which involved peasants
selling to the state, which acted as a mediator to the market). Also, the breakdown
of transportation affected agriculture, as the peasants couldn't transport their
produce. Thus, in some rural areas there were large, hidden stocks of food, and
yet in urban areas people were starving to death. In these circumstances the
government sent officials to requisition the agricultural produce – but this wasn't
always successful either.

The Tsolakoglou government tried sending demobilised army officers
out to help collect produce. But these officers often sided with the
farmers as they did not believe that the crops would go to feed their

fellow countrymen and suspected that they would be shipped to North Africa for Axis troops instead. (Mazower, 1993, p 27)

In these circumstances EAM decided to act. In the autumn of 1943 the people of the Thessaly region and EAM members decided to increase agricultural production (Karavasilis, 2006, p 24). The resistance would then distribute the produce across the country. Farmers cultivated the land in secret, even working during the night. However, this activity could not remain a secret for long and so EAM organised the military defence of the agricultural region. ELAS dedicated several units, supported by armed farmers and their families, to defend the cultivation of the land. Numerous battles were fought in different parts of the country. Most of them were fierce and lasted several days. For example, in the Stymfalia Valley German troops had orders to take control of the land or burn the crops. But after three days of fighting the Nazis retreated, after suffering heavy casualties (420 troops killed, 56 captured, while 16 andartes were killed). The crops were protected and starvation was averted (Karavasilis, 1996, p 34).

Farmers worked the fields using any available tools and the partisans pumped petrol from sunken ships in Volos port to fuel all available tractors. A disciplined, well-organised and broad mobilisation ensured the success of the operation. The 'Battle for the Crops' was of critical importance for the resistance movement in the countryside, and victory here ensured the survival, relief and support of thousands of vulnerable families. Spyros Meletzis, known as the photographer of the national resistance, concluded:

> Thousands of men and women participated in the Battle for the Crops … [For the first time during the occupation] they planted the crops, cultivated and harvested them and were able to keep the produce for themselves. And they had so much that when the country was liberated, people and soldiers had wheat for many months. (Meletzis, cited in Karavasilis, 2006, p 24)

Women played a central role:

> Groups of women worked for whole weeks in the production and collection of the harvest. Sometimes they worked for more than 16 hours per day. In Epirus, the valleys and villages were literally 50 metres away from the enemy lines [and] during the collection of harvest, real battles were taking place. For example in Prespes villages, Nazis were bombing from the nearby hills, and this lasted for 3 days. [But] the farmers … kept working. Women farmers, before working on their own land, worked the land of the families whose members had joined the guerrilla army. The battle for the crops involved whole villages, men and women, old people and children, all participated enthusiastically. (Nasiotis, 1975, p 23)

The organised efforts of the popular classes, in both rural and urban areas, to secure, produce and distribute food literally protected hundreds of thousands from starvation. They were driven by a political commitment to protect the people's right to life and dignity. Such a commitment also shaped the popular administration of the Government of the Mountains.

Popular administration

The development of the popular administration, supported by a system of people's justice, meant that the EAM-controlled area entered a period of profound social transformation.

People's administration did not appear 'out of the blue', from distressed villagers in continental Greece, nor was it imposed by force by KKE.[1] Its growth was consistent with the ideals of EAM and further enriched by local traditions and people's expectations. The institution of popular administration was something new, indigenous and genuinely popular. Although most of the official documents relating to the popular administration have been lost or destroyed, analysing information from secondary sources has helped to identify three different layers of its operation. The first is related to the establishment of EAM's local committees, which attempted to enhance the liberation struggle. The second layer appeared as a result of localised efforts to deal with everyday issues in the villages of Free Greece; inspired by the model of EAM's local committees and using local, popular and traditional 'wisdom'. The third layer was the election of the Government of the Mountains in 1944 and the instant adoption of a general people's administration official code.

Before the war, communist strongholds were to be found in the cities rather than in rural areas. However, after the war broke out, the rural areas became EAM's main base. The reason lies in the fact that the mountainous geomorphology of these areas was ideal for the development of guerrilla warfare. Additionally, many proletarians from the cities were pushed, by unemployment and famine, to the villages. Some had previous experience in the trade union movement. EAM wanted to create resistance committees wherever possible; by the end of 1941 a number of committees started to appear in many villages. News of EAM's successes, combined with support from some local figures, saw the further development of the committees in order both to deal with the organisation of the resistance and to manage everyday life. In addition to the main committees there were usually subcommittees, which would address particular aspects of the struggle such as youth participation, supplies, recruitment and routine relief issues (Stavrianos, 1952; Beikos, 1979).

The committees were democratically run. The secretary of each local EAM committee (*ipefthinos*) was responsible for contacting the superior EAM structures and ensuring that decisions were carried out in their village. Secretaries from a group of villages comprised the district council and elected the district committee. In turn, these committees elected a district ipefthinos, and the ipefthinoi of several districts elected the prefecture committee. Repeating the same democratic procedure, regional committees were elected for large regions and cities (for example Thessaly, Peloponnesus, Athens and so on). Finally, representatives from the different regions met to discuss EAM's agenda and elect a 25-member central committee. Although only about a tenth of the total EAM membership were also members of KKE, most of the ipefthinoi were communists (Stavrianos, 1952, p 46).

Although the structure looks 'centralised', the reality of life under occupation meant there was significant local autonomy. The disruption caused by the war (transportation difficulties, battles, check-points and so on) made it very difficult for the different committees to meet regularly, and even to check whether committees were executing agreed directives. The committees developed a crucial function in the villages, covering all aspects of village life. Thus, popular administration developed organically out of addressing the needs and the struggles of everyday life. In contrast to the pre-war period, popular administration allowed the peasants, for the first time, to experience a system that allowed them to raise their voice, discuss and democratically decide about important issues affecting their lives. Such a system of popular administration was, of course, incompatible with the principles of the popular judicial and legal system. So EAM dissolved the pre-war judicial system and established a system of 'people's justice'.

The 'heart' of the new administrative and legal system was the general assembly of the village. This included all the people of the village aged over 18 years, without any exception. The assembly gathered each month to discuss openly, and in public, all issues affecting the village. It elected the local committee, but the general assembly was able to dissolve the committee and elect a new one at will, if its performance was not satisfactory. The newly elected committee chose a treasurer, a vice-president and a secretary. Reporting to the committee were four subcommittees with clear and distinct responsibilities: the school subcommittee, the church subcommittee, the local security subcommittee and the relief and welfare subcommittee. Each of these had three members, two elected and one appointed by the *epitropi*. The appointed member was usually a 'specialist' (the teacher on the school subcommittee, the priest on the church committee). Generally speaking, the main duties of the committee were related to all the issues affecting a village's life and varied from land disputes and food issues to support of the liberation struggle. Stavrianos (1952) explains:

> The duties of the council included the management of public property, levying of taxes, imposition of labour service in community projects and registration of births, marriages, and deaths. The security committee appointed rural guards to keep order and enforced the decisions of the people's court. The food and social welfare committee was responsible for the food supply of the community and for the general welfare of orphans, disabled soldiers and the locals. The activities ... were supervised by the control committee, particularly

as regards financial matters. None of the elected officials were paid, with the occasional exception of rural guards. (p 48)

Welfare and relief issues were discussed and were approached in an organic and democratic way.

Alongside this there was also a people's local court. Election to the court followed a pattern similar to that for the elections to the local committees. Mazower recalls the comment of an observer that 'village justice was ... very democratic' (1993, p 237).

These courts were not bound by the pre-war law but were based on oral law, local traditions, common opinion and 'collective wisdom'. They covered all issues apart from divorce (a sensitive issue within a patriarchal village atmosphere) and murders (which were tried by the guerrilla courts of EAM). When the system of people's justice covered the whole of 'Free Greece', appeal courts and a central supreme court were also created and there was an attempt to develop a new common written law with clear, constitutional principles.

The people's courts operated publicly every Sunday after church, in the school buildings. Vaggelis Sakkatos, a well-known novelist and journalist, was an active member of the resistance movement on Kefalonia Island. His account of people's justice was very clear when he recalled that:

> I would like to highlight a very important fact regarding people's justice and the implementation of the popular courts.... People from my village started – even from the first day of the new institution – to join it, wave after wave. They were going to resolve everyday farming differences. Well, nobody ever complained. I was very impressed because each verdict was accepted with no complaints and appeals. (Sakkatos, interviewed by Kouloglou, 2007)

By 1944 these developments had laid the basis for the election of 'the Government of the Mountains'. The greater part of the country had already been liberated, citizens had managed to rebuild the functions of the state and they were engaged in a range of democratic institutions. In a massive operation, the Political Committee of National Liberation (PEEA) launched national elections in which approximately 1,800,000 people voted (more than in the pre-war elections of 1936). People voted for delegates to the National Council and on 14 May 1944, in the village of Coryshades, the National Council gathered for the first and last time. Its mission was to elect a government and write a constitution that would encompass all the achievements of the liberation movement (Hadjis, 1981; KKE, 1981).

The elections and debate in Coryshades lasted for 13 days and resulted in the formation of a government and an extensive legislative programme (64 Acts, 79 Decisions and 2 declarations). In its official document PEEA declared that:

> All authority derives from and is carried out by the people. Local self-government and people's justice are the fundamental principles of the public life of Greece … the liberties of all people are sacred and inviolable. The nation in arms will defend its liberties against any danger from wherever it comes. All Greeks, men and women, have equal political and civil rights.… work is a fundamental social function and creates the right to the enjoyment of all the rewards of life. (Community of Coryshades, 1983, articles 2, 4, 5, 6)

The same spirit of optimism, equality and determination is discernible throughout the various documents, Acts and bills of the PEEA. It was the same spirit that informed the decision for the development of an advanced network of welfare and health services, covering the needs of the people during war time. For example, Act 54 created a Social Policy and Hygiene Secretariat, which was set the task of setting up:

> All necessary [central and regional] services that will cover all the welfare and health needs of the Greek population … These services should be staffed in such a way that – under the direction of experts' committees – they will be connected to the self-administration committees and the popular local health organisations. (PEEA Act 20, 5 September 1944)

Another Act set a minimum wage:

> The minimum limits of salaries should be able to secure the maintenance of the workers and their families. These salaries can be paid in the form of money, food and material. (Beikos, 1979, p 17)

The Social Policy and Hygiene Secretariat comprised three core services: (1) Social Policy Service organisations and institutions for mothers and children, (2) Services for the Relief of War Victims, and (3) Service for Hygiene and Medical Support. The secretary and supervisors in each service were to be elected by representatives from medical associations, trade unions, service users and local popular organisations. Every three months all the secretariat workers were required to meet and discuss the operation and functioning of the relevant social policy institution. The popular health and welfare measures announced in 'Free Greece' were embraced by the people and professionals. Leading academic figures from the medical profession joined EAM's efforts to develop a free and universal health and welfare system. The effectiveness of these services was acknowledged by people in the American mission:

> An American observer in Macedonia on 22 January 1945 reported that 'as in the case of other hospitals run by ELAS … Source was impressed

by the seriousness and devotion of the staff, and the degree of success they have obtained in the face of serious obstacles of all kinds' (OSS, report 112535, 23 January 1945). Such interest was shown at least as early as the spring of 1943, when ELAS organized a medical service, which established five or more regional hospitals, and screened military recruits for disease. The medical service worked with a Secretariat for Health and Welfare in the provisional government which EAM established in March 1944, and this gave free medical treatment to the population under its authority. (Close, 2004, p 8)

But the social work and welfare experiment wasn't restricted to meeting material hardship, dealing with famine and medical support. There was also a conscious attempt to address the wider educational, cultural and emotional needs of the people in the 'Free Greece' region.

Holistic development

Claiming that Greece went through a cultural and educational explosion during the occupation may seem odd. However, the resistance and the popular experimentation in the EAM-controlled areas led to vibrant cultural, artistic and educational debates and activities that were related to the movement's identification of education and culture as important means of relief and emotional support and of personal transformation and resistance.

There was significant cultural activity in the fields of literature and theatre, and considerable developments with regard to education and pedagogy. During the first period of the occupation most of the artists tried to follow a 'legal way' to behave and perform. But, under the lead of the guild of actors and the association of writers, many artists became involved in resistance work. Anna Kalouta, a famous actress, remembers that:

> The occupation authorities killed many actors. They killed Kasis because they found out he was 'sending' EAM's messages. Actually, throughout the period of occupation, we were all involved in EAM. One day every week we staged a play and we were secretly sending the money to EAM. It was the big theatrical group of 'Asson'. I mean, Maria Kalouta, Filipidis, Mayreas, Avlonitis, Kokkinis and the script was written by Sakelarios.[2] (Anna Kalouta interviewed by Stellios Kouloglou, 2007)

Kostas Varnalis (a famous poet) argued:

> Intellectuals should approach the People; they should put their heart over People's heart so it will beat in the same tone. They should make

the Nation's life and fertile hope more stable and uproot any illusions. (Cited in Argyriou, 2006, p 16)

The vast majority of artists (actors, poets and writers) joined EAM. They participated in the wave of strikes that shook the capital in 1941 and 1943, and some used their theatres as temporary shelters for strikers who were attacked by the police (Papadouka, 2001). By the middle of 1942, however, the occupation forces had increased their harassment and surveillance of oppositional intellectuals and artists. Censorship became very tight and a series of high-profile arrests forced many artists to move to the liberated parts of the country.

'Free Greece' provided a fertile ground for cultural experimentation. Inspired by the struggle and encouraged by EAM's vision, a number of artists contributed to the movement for liberation and social change. Cultural committees appeared in most villages, where professional artists mixed with amateurs, youth and local people to organise cultural events.

At the epicentre of this 'explosion' was the theatre of the mountains. Performers threw themselves into staging plays in most of the villages. The performances were interactive and gave people the opportunity to attend and to participate in cultural activities for the first time in their lives (Mazower, 1993, p 285). There were puppeteers and *karagkiozi* (a traditional theatre of shadows) players performing in the villages (Myrsiades, 1977, p 104). Over 1,000 cultural teams and more than 21,000 artists are documented as having been involved (Myrsiades and Myrsiades, 1999, p 137).

Haris Sakellariou was 21 years old when he joined the EAM cultural teams as a writer and he recalls that

> The conditions under which we were writing theatrical plays were unprecedented. Often when the liberation struggle required, we had to interrupt writing for days. We had to leave the pencil and take the gun. Some manuscripts were never completed as the writers sealed them with their blood. (Sakellariou, 1995, p 10)

In addition to these local drama teams, at least three central EAM–ELAS touring troupes were travelling and performing in the villages. Their plays were full of allegories and were aimed at entertaining the local people, boosting their confidence, supporting them psychologically and helping them to understand the political and historical context of the liberation struggle. Apart from renditions of classic theatrical plays, there were performances of new contemporary plays whose content was patriotic and highly political, often connecting the 1821 war of independence with the ongoing liberation struggle. 'In the future we will all be one, villagers and town-dwellers, rich and poor' was the message carried by a Kotzioulas play (Mazower, 1993, p 276). Kotzioulas was an iconic figure of the EAM cultural movement and wrote several very popular scripts, such as *The sufferings of Jews* and *The Traitor* (Sakellariou, 1995).

Similar to the artists' movement was the mobilisation of intellectuals in the field of education. Many eminent university professors left Athens and joined EAM, accepting its open invitation to promote social change. Many of the finest pre-war university educators participated in the struggle for liberation. Names like Roza Imvriotis, Sofia Vlachou, Petros Imvriotis, Demetrios Glinos and many others not only participated in the struggle but experienced some of the most productive periods of their academic careers (see Mazower, 1993; Varnalis, 1998).

EAM's educational drive was reflected in the motto 'A school in every village'. Each village elected a dedicated school committee responsible for the uninterrupted operation of local schools. Such an interest in education was also reflected by EAM's creation of a pedagogical academy for teachers, thereby ensuring that there would be no shortage of personnel in the schools (Ntona, 2004). This academy operated alongside the military school for officers. The teachers' trade unions had a history of radical campaigning over various school and educational issues (such as the struggle for the establishment of *demotiki*, a more accessible and popular form of the Greek language). Perhaps not surprisingly, according to research by Aggelos Elefantis, 32% of the overall number of *Kapetanios* (guerrilla commanders) were teachers (Elefantis, cited in Ntona, 2004).

In 1944 the Government of the Mountains decided to publish a new primary school text-book and Roza Imvriotis was invited to produce it. Imvrioty enthusiastically accepted, thinking that this mission was:

> Unique, special and unlike anything else she had written before since the children of occupied Greece were writing history themselves. (Kyriakidou, 1995, p 2)

The textbook was named *Ta aetopoula* (Little Eagles), after the 'little eagles organisations' of EAM. These organisations were made up of children aged between 7 and 13 who participated in the resistance by assisting in minor acts of sabotage, acting as messengers and actively contributing within the cultural teams. *Ta aetopoula* was the first textbook written in the demotike language, something which the Greek state didn't achieve until 1976 (Mazower, 1993, p 280). Unfortunately, all these inspired teachers were blacklisted after the war and either fled to other countries as refugees or remained marginalised within their own country:

> Greece was not to see such an impressive and dedicated effort to improve rural schooling for another 30 years. (Mazower, 1993, p 281)

Greece's 'road not taken'

In 1949, after the open military involvement of the US, the Democratic Front was defeated and thousands of fighters and their families escaped to neighbouring countries. Hundreds of thousands of EAM sympathisers who remained in the country experienced violence and oppression for more than 30 years. It was within this context that formal social work was developed 'from above', suppressing the legacy of grassroots welfare.

Formal social work in Greece emerged in 1946 as a response to the influence of EAM's informal, popular solidarity networks and grassroots welfare (Ioakimidis, 2009). It was imported as a profession by the American mission that supported the National Army in its effort to crush the Democratic Front. Not only did formal social work not adopt the successful orientation of 'popular social practice' from below, but its initial mission was to operate as a deterrent against it. It is not a coincidence that the decision to form social work as a recognised profession was taken during the civil war, a period characterised by violence, viciousness, devastation and systematic foreign intervention. It was US intervention that provided the expertise and financial assistance to establish social work as part of the broader Truman Doctrine.

By and large, social work academia and the professional elite in Greece never acknowledged the existence of the alternative welfare traditions of 'Free Greece'. This denial has meant that Greek social work has an official history that is, at best, partial. Historically, social work has been treated with suspicion by the popular classes. The professional elite tend to attribute this to ineffective public relations, rather than to the profession's unsavoury history in the immediate post-1949 period. But the experiences during the 'Free Greece' era show a different history, a different welfare, set to different principles of engagement. As Reisch and Andrew (2002, p 4) have suggested:

> In an increasingly a-historical culture, we are ignorant of those elements of the past that challenged the status quo and deny the roles that radical actors and ideas played in bettering the lives of people.

Even though the welfare movement of the 1940s can be described as the 'road not taken', its vision, radicalism, optimism and collective values can inspire contemporary social work and challenge the neoliberal and individualistic ethos of dominant Anglo-American models.

Notes

[1] Actually, even the most optimistic KKE member could not expect such a major change, given the pre-war weakness of the Party. This becomes more obvious when we observe the Party's weakness in grasping the degree of this transformation (see KKE Official Documents, 1981 and 1995).

[2] These are all names of first-order Greek actors of the middle of the 20th century.

NINE

Social welfare services to protect elderly victims of war in Cyprus

Gregory Neocleous

Introduction

Within a few months of the 1974 Turkish military invasion of Cyprus, new and extraordinary social needs emerged within Greek-Cypriot society. With thousands of people becoming refugees in their own country, there was an immediate need for the development or improvement of social support networks. Today there is much discussion of the way(s) in which crisis can lead to 'social shock' and disasters exploited by the rich and powerful to restructure society along neoliberal lines (Klein, 2007). But the case of Cyprus in 1974 presents another possibility: intervention by the state to speed up the process of developing new, or improving existing, social services and welfare programmes in order to meet the needs of the population.

The Cypriot case provides a clear example of how extreme circumstances and the grassroots mobilisation of 'affected people' can challenge traditional attitudes and force the authorities to promote progressive reforms. As will be discussed in this chapter, innovative and accessible social programmes emerged in the aftermath of the Turkish invasion and contributed to the creation of a more adequate welfare state.

At the time of the invasion in 1974, expenditure on public assistance was minimal: there was full employment and living standards were comparatively high; but immediately after the invasion public assistance expanded. The internal displacement of one-third of the population created many complex social problems and increased the dependency of vulnerable groups, such as the displaced elderly population, on state support. The situation led to an immediate need for the introduction of new services and programmes in order to support the 200,000 displaced Greek Cypriots (Sarris et al, 2008).

Cyprus at a glance

In order to understand Cypriot society it is necessary to understand the importance of its geo-political location and recent history. The island of Cyprus is located in the eastern Mediterranean Sea, 75 km (47 miles) south of Turkey and 243 km

(151 miles) north of Lebanon. The island has an area of 9,251 sq km (3,571 sq miles) and a coastline of 648 km (402 miles). Its population is made up of the Greek-Cypriot community (82%) and the Turkish-Cypriot community (18%). The capital city, Nicosia (or Lefkosia, as it is pronounced in Greek), is located in the central part of the island. The city is militarily divided, with the Cypriot government controlling the southern portion and the Turkish military controlling the northern portion. The south of the island has been a full member of the EU since May 2004.

Cyprus's location has always made it attractive to 'great powers'. Its recent history has been shaped by the aftermath of British colonialism (1878–60). When the British 'left' (there is still a large British military presence on the island), the Republic of Cyprus was formed. Almost immediately, serious differences arose between the Greek and Turkish communities over the implementation and interpretation of the constitution. The Greek Cypriots argued that the complex mechanisms introduced to protect Turkish-Cypriot interests were obstacles to the efficiency of the government. In November 1963, President Makarios advanced a series of constitutional amendments designed to eliminate some of those provisions. The Turkish-Cypriot community opposed any such changes, claiming that they were unconstitutional.

The confrontation of the two communities prompted widespread inter-communal fighting by militant groups from both sides (both EOKA B', for the Greek Cypriots, and TMT, for the Turkish Cypriots, engaged in terrorist acts against civilian, religious and government targets). Following the outbreak of inter-communal violence, many Turkish Cypriots (and some Greek Cypriots) living in mixed villages began to move into 'enclaves' where they felt secure. United Nations (UN) peacekeeping forces were deployed on the island in 1964 in an effort to prevent further conflict. During that year, the Turkish air force bombed residential areas in Tylliria (north-western Cyprus, between Paphos and Nicosia), killing and injuring hundreds of civilians.

Following another outbreak of inter-communal violence in 1967–68, a Turkish-Cypriot provisional administration was formed in the Turkish pockets in the north of the island. Consequently, the Turkish-Cypriot vice-president, ministers and members of the parliament, along with all Turkish-Cypriot government employees, resigned and withdrew to the northern part of the island. In the Greek-Cypriot community there was growing disagreement over the way in which President Makarios III was handling the situation. On 15 July the Greek Junta and its Greek-Cypriot counterparts organised a coup which saw tanks in the streets and attacks on the presidential palace, the Cyprus Broadcast Corporation, police stations and other strategic places in an effort to overthrow and assassinate President Makarios and replace the official government.

After five days of arrests, interrogations and assassinations against both Greek and Turkish Cypriots by the Greek-Cypriot militants, Turkey invaded the island. The Turkish invasion led to the occupation of 37% of the northern part of the island and the displacement of more than 200,000 people from both communities.

Six thousand people died and 1,619 were listed as 'missing', among them 355 elderly people.

Thirteen thousand out of a total of 27,547 elderly Greek Cypriots at that time became refugees and were scattered all over the southern part of the island. Two thousand elderly individuals were trapped in the northern part for several months, and it was only after UN intervention that they were able to flee to the south. Yiallouros (2007, p 26) describes the aftermath of the Turkish invasion as 'an extraordinary social drama that never happened before in the entire history of Cyprus'. Because of limitations on access to information in the Turkish-occupied area, this chapter will discuss the consequences of the invasion only for the Greek-Cypriot community.

As a result of the 1974 war, Cyprus has been divided de facto between the legal and recognised government of the Republic of Cyprus, which controls two-thirds (63%) of the island, and the remaining one-third (37%) of the island, which is administered by Turkish Cypriots and the Turkish army. A 'green line' or buffer zone or 'dead' zone, dividing the two parts along a line from Morphou in the north-west through Nicosia to Famagusta in the north-east, is patrolled by UN peacekeeping forces, which have maintained the buffer zone between the two sides since 1974.

Culture and social welfare

The Greek Cypriots and Turkish Cypriots share many common customs, but maintain distinct identities based on religion, language and close ties with their respective 'motherlands'. Although Greek, Turkish and English are considered the official languages in the Republic of Cyprus, Greek is predominantly spoken in the south and Turkish is spoken in the north. It is worth mentioning that travel restrictions have been eased since 2003, enabling people from either side to cross the 'green line' through specific check-points. Since 2003, people from both communities have started to share many social, professional and personal activities, proving the fact that they can live together and are all citizens of the same country.

The social welfare system of Cyprus was introduced by the British colonialists in 1946, with the establishment of the Social Welfare Services Department. According to the department, its initial objective was to provide assistance to low-income families, children, the elderly, delinquents and vulnerable groups. In particular, it was responsible for providing assistance to anybody who was in need of social support. It also established state institutions for children and hostels and other institutions for people in need (the poor, disabled and so on). After the independence of Cyprus, social welfare provision remained the responsibility of the Department of Social Welfare Services in the Ministry of Labour and Social Insurance.

By the 1970s, social welfare had evolved into a body of activities designed to enable individuals, families, groups and communities to cope with social problems. In 1973 every Cypriot citizen in need became eligible for financial assistance to maintain a minimum standard of living, satisfy basic needs and improve living conditions. The ultimate objective of the welfare services was to make the recipients of welfare socially and financially self-sufficient. By late 1980s, the state was providing five main categories of services: delinquency and social defence, child and family welfare, community work and youth services, social services to other departments and public financial assistance (Chrysostomou, 2009).

Mass internal displacement and the role of the state

Soon after the establishment of the independent Republic of Cyprus in 1960, the country began to experience bi-communal conflicts, especially during the years 1963–64 and 1967–68, which led to the Turkish invasion of 1974. During the war, approximately two thousand chronically ill elderly people were left by their families in the care of other elderly people in their villages in the north, mainly because their families had no means to transfer them to the south (many refugees had to walk long distances through the fields in order to flee from the occupied areas). They thought that it would be only a matter of days before they could return to their homes, and hence that there was no need to remove their elderly family members.

In 1983 the Minister of Health, in a speech at the Pancyprian Seminar on Ageing, stated that the consequences of the 1974 war for the elderly population had become apparent from the very first days of the war, as thousands of senior citizens had lost their means for survival and their social networks. In the face of the sudden changes, it took several months for the state to function again and resume its provision of services to the public, especially to elderly pensioners. The challenge for the government arose from the fact that the Turkish invasion had exacerbated the problems and needs of the elderly population. The change had been so sudden that neither a social policy plan for the elderly population nor any other plan for dealing with the social needs of the elderly existed. It was thus vital that social policies be developed as quickly as possible.

The displaced elderly were the population group most severely affected by the war. They became isolated and lost their traditional role in society, especially those of them who became refugees (National Committee for Ageing in Cyprus, 1983). The accumulated pressure of problems created feelings in them of despair and unhappiness. Soon after the war it became clear that families were unable to care adequately for their elderly parents (Theodorou, 1987) because of new social circumstances. Before the war, and because of the limited development of the welfare state, caring for the elderly had been the sole responsibility of the family, and of the women in particular.[1] In the socio-economic context of the post-invasion era, women were in the front line of family efforts to respond to the changed situation, and the number of women who sought employment in order to support the family budget increased sharply.

For years, Cypriots had considered the family to be both the cornerstone of their culture and the means of its maintenance, meeting physical, social and emotional needs. The strong ties and sense of solidarity among family members were the basis on which most national social policies had been developed. Theodorou (1987) writes that respect for one's parents, caring about them and for them, had for many years been one of the strongest values of Cypriot culture, transmitted from generation to generation. In many instances, children were criticised by society if they failed to care for their parents, and problems between parents and children were usually carefully concealed. A crisis among family members was considered to be a strictly internal matter, about which no one outside the family had a right to know. This situation was rarely questioned, especially in terms of family values, which were based on the assumption that families were morally and legally obliged to care for their elderly members and were the most basic unit for meeting elderly people's needs.

Before 1974, elderly people in Cyprus lived either with or close to their children or other relatives. Caring for elderly relatives was a moral responsibility for families. Old age was full of meaning, and the elderly maintained a productive role within the family and the family environment.

Family ties under pressure

Despite strong family bonds, the dispersal of thousands of refugee families all over the island (Social Welfare Services, 1979) made it very difficult for children, relatives and friends to maintain their responsibility to care for elderly family members. The social and economic problems that they faced were some of the basic causes preventing the children of displaced elderly persons from caring for their parents (Social Welfare Services, 1977). Families affected by the war were forced to live in tents and barrack quarters, creating problems of living space. Thousands of Greek Cypriots, including the elderly, lived in this manner for years after the Turkish invasion, until refugee camps were constructed. The Cypriot family system and the traditional system of care were unable to withstand this tremendous disruption and change, making it difficult for families to care for their elderly members.

The decomposition of the traditional family support systems made old age one of the most complicated social problems in the country. The initial response of the Department of Social Welfare Services was to encourage families and communities to continue their traditional roles as caregivers to the elderly, in an effort to keep them in their home and social environments (Ministry of Labour and Social Insurance, 1980), and it developed new support programmes that would enable families to avoid or postpone moving their elderly relatives into institutions.

A new era begins for the Cypriot social welfare system

Apart from losing their financial resources and property, which had provided them with a feeling of autonomy, power and status, elderly refugees now faced a new challenge. They were dependent on others for their social and personal care, primarily because of their physical and psychological distress. Panagi, a former general secretary of EKYSY (Union of Cypriot Pensioners) (EKYSY, 2003), has pointed out that many of the displaced elderly felt psychologically distressed as a result of losing the support of their local community and contact with relatives, friends and neighbours following the Turkish invasion. In addition, they experienced many difficulties in adjusting to new circumstances and environments. Most importantly, the absence of support services played a vital role in their psychological distress.

In the wake of the tremendous social changes created by the invasion and the substantial needs of the refugees, new forms of social services appeared. Their basic purpose was to provide support for the thousands of refugees who urgently needed shelter, food, clothes and medical and emotional care. In addition, various studies were conducted in order to identify the needs of the elderly people living in refugee camps. One such study, carried out by Michael (1979, p 13), indicated common characteristics among elderly refugees in the camps. The research focused on four problem areas: health, lack of family support, mobility and financial status. Based on the mounting needs, the Department of Social Welfare Services adopted a series of suggestions for the development and modification of social policies that would enable elderly refugees to overcome their difficulties and maintain their role in the community.

In addition to the distress of the population, the sudden (within a period of three months) and massive internal displacement of the population led to rapid changes in the structure, economy and functioning of the country. The displacement of thousands of Greek Cypriots and Turkish Cypriots, to the south and north respectively, created a new situation. A number of socio-economic problems arose, such as a 50% increase in unemployment and a 70% reduction in productivity

The high unemployment rate pushed the social security scheme to its limits (Lasettas, 1980). Thousands of people discontinued their contributions to the fund, while there was an increase in unemployment payments. The government responded to this by reducing retirement pensions by 14% and suspending the payment of unemployment benefits, marriage and funeral allowances. Other benefits, such as widow's allowance and maternity allowance, were also suspended (Ministry of Labour and Social Insurance, 1976).

Under these circumstances, discussions were held between the government and the trade unions. The trade unions, having long experience of grassroots organisation, submitted recommendations to the government and eventually a temporary consensus was reached. This consensus led eventually to the Social Security [Amendment] Law, 1975. Until the Social Security Fund was able to provide all the necessary benefits, the state introduced a new Public Assistance Law, which expanded the criteria for financial support, and made a large number of people eligible for support who either were not receiving any social security benefits, as a result of the benefit cuts, or were unemployed. The reduction in pensions had been a disaster for the elderly. The new Public Assistance Law minimised the risks that they faced and covered the extra needs created by the pension reduction.

Another issue to be solved as soon as possible was the provision of shelter for the 200,000 refugees. Until permanent houses could be constructed (a process that took several years), the vast majority of refugees had to live in tents and shanties in refugee camps. Old communities were split up and lost. In the camps people had a different culture and way of doing things. On top of this, refugees had to deal with the consequences of the war, such as the loss of family members, the psychological distress, their displacement from their land and the loss of their right to return.

Initially, government spending focused on meeting the basic survival needs of the refugees and others through cash grants and aid in kind. Since then, the social welfare system in Cyprus has gradually moved towards providing long-term care services, free secondary education, health services, a wage-related social insurance scheme, scholarships and loans for needy students to study abroad; and infrastructural buildings such as schools, hospitals and various welfare institutions such as nursing homes, community welfare centres, children's and youth homes, hostels and day-care centres for children and the elderly.

The introduction of domiciliary social services for elderly refugees

In 1953 the Department of Social Welfare Services introduced the Public Assistance Scheme, which provided financial assistance to elderly people who did not have the means to meet their basic needs for food, shelter and clothing. The philosophy of the scheme was to safeguard the rights of the elderly to a minimum standard of living by providing financial assistance and social services. The modification of the Public Assistance Regulation into a law in 1975, in order to fulfil the needs of thousands of refugees, especially the elderly, is considered to have met their needs, and provided 'substance to the constitutional right of all people who are entitled to enjoy a decent standard of living' (Papassava, 1993). The scheme resulted in an improved financial position for many elderly people.

Internal displacement created numerous problems for the elderly among the refugees: lack of appropriate housing and care, health issues, financial constraints, the adjustment to a new situation away from their homes and traditional environment, the wounds created by the displacement and the 'shattered dreams and hopes for them and their families' (Michael, 1979, p 13).

In addition to settling refugees, the government needed to construct nursing homes. It handed over abandoned houses, formerly owned by Turkish Cypriots who had now fled to the north, to elderly two-member families, and gave financial support to elderly people so that they could move with their children.

War and displacement resulted in the rapid development of institutional care, especially private nursing homes, in an effort to provide shelter for those elderly who had no social support network. The Department of Social Welfare Services constructed seven state nursing homes to provide shelter for 331 displaced elderly persons, while another 348 elderly refugees received shelter within the private sector. The number of elderly people residing in nursing homes tripled after the 1974 war.

Elderly people and families with elderly members were given priority for housing and received grants and loans from the government to build homes. However, this created some problems. For instance, in some refugee settlements the houses provided for the elderly people were not adapted to their needs and were sometimes a long way from community services and facilities.

The 1975 Annual Report of the Department of Social Welfare Services stated that the large number of displaced elderly refugees required immediate attention, and so, in 1976, the government began the construction of six state nursing homes, which were to be fully completed by 1978 (Social Welfare Services, 1977) and funded by the United Nations High Commission for Refugees (Social Welfare Services, 1975; Philelftheros, 1978). The Homes for the Elderly and Disabled People Bill 1979/81 (*Cyprus Gazette*, 1980) was passed into law in 1981 and provided for the registration and inspection of nursing homes, with the aim of achieving acceptable standards of care for residents.

Institutional care was a new form of service adopted by the government after the invasion. All the state nursing homes were operated by the Department of Social Welfare Services and provided accommodation, food and care on a 24-hour basis. One of the nursing homes set up by the government operated as a reception centre for close to two thousand elderly people who gradually fled from the Turkish occupied areas.

As an alternative to nursing homes, three other programmes were developed to provide for the basic needs of elderly people. The first, a home care services programme, provided services such as cooking, bathing and shopping for people living at home. The second was a programme to place elderly individuals with 'foster families'. The third was the funding of grassroots volunteer organisations in order to improve the services and programmes provided to elderly people (Michael, 1979).

The Department of Social Welfare Services also initiated an 'Intensive Programme for the Relief of the Aged'. Its purpose was to provide financial assistance to those elderly people who were not entitled to social security and were facing immediate risk of poverty (Social Welfare Services, 1976). In December 1977 the Department, in cooperation with the Cypriot Red Cross, initiated a 'Programme for the Financial Adoption of Displaced Elderly Persons' (Social Welfare Services, 1977), the main objective of which was to use contributions from the British Cypriot community to provide financial support for 100 elderly and destitute Cypriots.

In addition to state interventions, the establishment of the Pancyprian Association for the Welfare of the Elderly, with financial and technical support from the government, led to the coordination of all grassroots services for displaced elderly people. At the same time, Cyprus experienced a tremendous increase in the number of voluntary sector organisations that aimed to meet the needs of displaced elderly people. Senior Citizens' Centres were set up, mainly within the refugee camps. These open centres designed and put on various cultural and social events at a community level, 'investing' in the widespread sense of solidarity that emerged in the post–invasion era.

Despite state attempts to respond to the expectations and needs of elderly refugees, the Department of Social Welfare Services (1979) admitted that it was impossible to deal with the psychological distress of those elderly people residing in its nursing homes. The Department reported an increase in the death rate among those elderly people living in nursing homes, as compared to those living in their own homes.

Conclusion

All the available documentary evidence indicates that after the 1974 invasion the Department of Social Welfare Services implemented a series of relief measures in order to provide support for displaced elderly people. Its main objective was to fill the gap created by their displacement and the loss of their land and social networks.

The extreme circumstances that Cyprus faced as a result of the military coup and the Turkish military invasion led the government to implement a series of protective measures and other interventions. Although no protective measures could compensate for the tragedy of the war and its aftermath, the state's response and provision of welfare did help displaced elderly people to cope with the material, social and psychological hardships of post-invasion life. Under the extraordinary conditions created by the invasion, a more coherent, proactive and adequate welfare system emerged. Such a development would have been impossible without the solidarity and dynamism of the local, displaced communities.

Note

[1] A study carried out in 1970 in two rural areas of Cyprus (Michael, 1979) indicated that, despite the increase in the elderly population and some other minor problems associated with old age and health, strong family ties remained important in the support of the elderly.

TEN

Worker's eye view of neoliberalism and Hurricane Katrina

Marla S. McCulloch

Introduction

The profound physical destruction of Hurricane Katrina (and subsequent Hurricane Rita) was compounded by social and political problems already firmly entrenched before the storms hit. The disaster was a product not only of physical forces, but of neoliberal ideology as well.

My perspective is that of one of the more than 230,000 volunteers with the American Red Cross who responded during Hurricanes Katrina and Rita (Becker, 2008). I was dispatched as a Disaster Mental Health worker in the Central Louisiana region. I was one of 22 mental health workers in an area that had over 200 shelters at one point. It was all we could do to try to manage one crisis after another involving the chronically mentally ill, the chronically homeless, the addicts and the severely traumatised. I was 'a mobile crisis unit of one' driving from shelter to shelter, trying to help people obtain medications, mediate interpersonal conflicts, procure needed resources and function as a community. To further frustrate the situation, we were practising in isolation. The system of social and health services had temporarily stopped functioning. None of the hospitals or ambulance services would take psychiatric patients. Local mental health would not respond and Child and Adult Protective Services would not respond.

Additionally, immediately before and after Hurricane Rita hit, I ran a small Red Cross shelter and coordinated the initial intake of evacuees. We were at a small church camp and had a possible capacity of about 200 – with no medical staff, no other mental health staff and no manager. The shelter manager was delayed by the worsening conditions and exhausted from managing a shelter for the two weeks previous, during Hurricane Katrina.

The context

Physical

On 29 August 2005 Hurricane Katrina made landfall in south-eastern Louisiana. It was the largest natural disaster the United States has ever seen. The area affected was roughly equivalent to the size of the entire landmass of the United Kingdom (around 90,000 sq miles). At least 1,836 people died and more than 700 were listed as missing. Between 645,000 and 1.1 million people were displaced from their homes and communities – the largest displacement since the American Civil War of the 1860s. Less than a month later, Hurricane Rita hit in the same region (Knabb et al, 2006).

Hurricane Katrina was the fifth hurricane (and second category 5 hurricane) of an especially active 2005 Atlantic hurricane season. It was the sixth-strongest hurricane in recorded history and the third-strongest to come ashore in the United States. It was also the costliest, with a price tag of $75 billion in estimated damage (Knabb et al, 2006).

Hurricane Katrina's size alone resulted in devastation over 100 miles (160 km) from the storm's centre. The subsequent storm surge caused major or catastrophic damage along the coasts of Louisiana, Mississippi and Alabama. There were 33 tornadoes reported from the storm (Knabb et al, 2006).

Hurricane Rita, the fourth most intense Atlantic hurricane ever recorded and the fifth major hurricane of the season, made landfall on 23 September– less than a month after Hurricane Katrina – between Texas and Louisiana. This second hurricane re-flooded New Orleans, disrupted and damaged repairs to the toppled levees and caused approximately $11.3 billion more in damage (Brunsma et al, 2007).

Approximately 24% of the total annual production of the US oil industry was lost during the six-month shutdown after the storms (Fagot and Winbush, 2006). With 1.3 million acres of forestlands destroyed, the forestry industry in the state of Mississippi sustained losses estimated to be near $5 billion (Sheikh, 2005).

Social

The human impact caused by the storms can be paralleled to the impact caused by the American Civil War. There were massive displacement, economic differences based largely on race and other factors of 'deservingness', elements of opportunism and an attempt to reassert power and dominance along the lines of race and gender.

Obviously, the most immediate impact was the lives lost during and immediately after the storms. News stories started to paint a picture of those who were disproportionately affected – the poor, the elderly and the ill. There were stories of elderly, disabled nursing-home residents who drowned in their beds because no one came to evacuate them (Harris, 2005). A bus filled with elderly and disabled passengers exploded (along with medical oxygen tanks) during the chaotic evacuation efforts (Brubaker, 2005). At Danziger Bridge, unarmed poor people were shot and killed by police officers as they searched for food and tried to escape the floodwaters on foot. The police officers claimed to be protecting a wealthier neighbourhood from 'looters' and 'snipers'.

The area affected by the storms had an abundance of people living in poverty. In some neighbourhoods in New Orleans, poverty rates exceeded 40%. Overall, almost 50,000 poor New Orleans residents lived in neighbourhoods with a poverty rate of more than 40% (Katz, 2006).

Among the United States' 50 largest cities, New Orleans ranked second in neighbourhoods of concentrated poverty – such as the Lower Ninth Ward. For example, the average household earned less than $20,000 annually, only one in 12 adults held a college degree, four in five children were raised in single-parent families, and four in 10 working-age adults – many of them disabled – were not connected to the labour force (Katz, 2006). These neighbourhoods of concentrated poverty do not appear accidentally and it is no coincidence that they were devastated disproportionately. They have been created, in part, by generations of policies that isolate the poor into these urban poverty reservations and cut them off from the subsidised suburban sprawl and the housing, educational and economic opportunities that it monopolises. These neighbourhoods of concentrated poverty were built in the most flood-prone areas and protected by the weakest levee systems, which were not maintained and were systematically de-funded. Evacuating those neighbourhoods became impossible when the skeletal public transportation system was suspended well before Hurricane Katrina hit, with no plan of providing transportation to those reliant on it.

As a result of the storm, that poverty was compounded and concentrated even further. Hundreds of thousands were left unemployed, which will have a knock-on effect as lower taxes are paid to local governments.

Political

Hurricanes Katrina and Rita occurred in the second term of the George W. Bush presidency, post 9/11 and the declaration of the pre-emptive war in Iraq. The Supreme Court appointed President Bush after the election proved to be rife with irregularities. He had no popular support until after the 9/11 attacks, when a wave of fear and patriotism swept the country. Even then, this was short-lived favour.

President Bush was rightly criticised as being too aloof and removed in his response. He cut a mere day off his vacation, flew over the region several days later and waited two weeks to deliver an address. He, and the federal response, seemed to be perplexed and paralysed by the scale of the storms and their subsequent destruction. He spoke of the hurricane as being an 'unforeseeable event'. However, a storm of this scale and its potential damage had been predicted by numerous private sector and government scientists, journalists and the army corps of engineers. In an eerily similar exercise in July 2004, the Federal Emergency Management Agency (FEMA) had conducted a simulation of 'Hurricane Pam', with follow-up workshops that finished a mere five days before Katrina (FEMA, 2004). The simulation was managed by three for-profit firms hired by FEMA via a bidding process to conduct the training exercise. However, there did not seem to be any funding or political will to implement the recommendations of that simulation exercise.

Ideological

While an abundance of blame emerged after the disaster – from historically racist power structures to incompetent federal administration to the de-funding of critical services – they are all merely symptoms of a destructive ideological shift to neoliberalism.

Neoliberalism, as employed here, is a late-20th-century political movement that developed via unregulated capitalism and a conservative, pro-big-business political agenda. 'Neoliberalism is an effort to extend the reach of market logic, to apply it as an organising principle for all social and political relations' (Soss et al, 2009, p 13). Simply put, it is an effort to reorganise all of society on market terms, with market values, in order to serve market needs and market demands. In the US, this has manifested itself as a movement towards a rhetoric and practice of 'small government' and the use of private sector and charitable organisations to fulfil the role of government services.

The post-1970 economic landscape of the United States chronicles the rise of neoliberal ideology in the United States. Beginning with the presidency of Ronald Reagan in 1980, through to the Presidency of George W. Bush ending in 2008, almost three decades of neoliberal ideology have restructured social policy and the delivery of social services on market terms. That shift has had an important role in the growing income inequality that first started in the 1970s.

An example of this was in 1979, when Federal Reserve Chairman Paul Volker raised interest rates to unprecedented levels for the purported purpose of fighting inflation. In reality, this led to an era of falling living standards, increased unemployment and income inequality. The resulting increase in poverty and homelessness (and subsequent decrease in rates of economic growth) was supposed to be addressed by the 'trickle-down' effect of 'Reaganomics'. This neoliberal approach only served to accelerate these trends.

Certainly, the dissolution of the post-Depression regulatory structure was a prime example of this ideology reshaping policy stance (especially the 1999 Gramm-Leach-Bliley Act, which repealed the provision of the Glass-Steagall Act of 1933 that lowered risk by separating commercial and investment banks).

Beyond liberalisation of the financial market, the ideology of neoliberalism was applied to the provision of social services. The move towards privatisation of public industries and services proved to be disastrous during Hurricane Katrina. Inadequate public assistance to evacuate poor and ill residents was as much an effect of neoliberal ideology as was the failure to invest in an adequate levee system. These are symptoms of a systematic de-funding of the American welfare state. In essence, the botched government response had its origin in both incompetence and policy.

We see an example of this in the situation of the levee design, construction and maintenance in New Orleans. The levee failures were a result of system design flaws, combined with the lack of adequate maintenance. Their placement was highly suspect, with poorer neighbourhoods being under-protected. The National

Science Foundation found that those responsible for the conception, design, construction and maintenance of the region's flood-control system had apparently failed to pay sufficient attention to public safety (Warrick and Grunwald, 2005).

In a society organised around neoliberal ideology, the legitimate role of government in public safety is not the prevailing concern. Infrastructure jobs (such as designing and building levees) are sent out for contract in the private sector. The contract is awarded to the lowest bidder. Market forces, not public safety concerns, drive the entire process.

The people affected

Further, I can relate the growing concern that direct service response workers should challenge the lies that were being perpetrated by the government and media. These lies shaped the disaster as being the fault of the uneducated, lazy, ignorant and, ultimately, undeserving poor. Officials blamed those affected for not 'getting out of the way of the storm.'[1] Elements of racism and sexism further coded the erupting dominant discourse and justified the lack of governmental response, both prior to and following the disaster.

The initial needs of people were to escape the path of the storm. When that was not possible, they needed safe shelter from the storms and their aftermath. Once the storm was over, people were desperate for clean water and safe housing. The Red Cross volunteers and other charity organisations met these needs. In Red Cross shelters, large signs were displayed stating that these services were funded by donations as a 'gift from the American people'. The unspoken message was that it was a gift that one should be grateful to passively receive – not an entitlement. This functions within the neoliberal framework of religious and private organisations taking over the role of government.

However, being in the shelters during that time, I witnessed the experience of a growing consciousness and resistance among Red Cross and other disaster-response workers, who were outraged at the privatisation of service provision and the lack of government involvement in meeting the most basic and most desperate needs of the people. I saw a total of four FEMA (the agency is charged with 'disaster mitigation, preparedness, response, recovery, education and references') workers and two FEMA trucks the entire time I was in Central Louisiana. Two FEMA workers walked into one of our shelters of over 3,000 people – of course they concealed their identification badges for their own safety – approached the social workers and asked them to pick three families to receive housing. How do you make such a choice? How do you resist dominant discourse about the 'deserving' versus 'undeserving poor'? How do you resist a dynamic that reinscribes oppression? Ultimately, we had to choose someone. However, we did our best to enter into a dialogue about which families in the shelter had the least resources, the least potential for resources and the greatest needs.

Whom were we talking about? Who were the people affected by these storms? Our shelters were disproportionately populated with people of colour, the mentally ill, the elderly, the disabled and the poor. When employed, these are people who have been historically squeezed out of industrial jobs into service and retail jobs with few or no benefits. This meant that we were dealing with a population that often has health concerns at the forefront of its immediate needs.

However, even this group was highly diverse. There were working families with children, retired couples, gay and lesbian families trying to hide in order to survive congregate living and transfolks who spent an unbelievable amount of energy just trying to keep from being victimised when they needed to use the toilet or take a shower.

One transgender (male to female) evacuee caused quite a stir in one of the shelters. I was called in to help the volunteer staff sort out the situation. 'Joe' had initially appeared in the shelter with gender-typical attire and grooming. However, as time stretched on and laundry facilities were scarce, 'Joe' had run out of his gender-typical selections and had started cross-dressing – his preferred attire. The staff were concerned about bathrooms and showers and wanted to make some sort of policy. They were concerned that they needed to 'protect' other people in the shelter from Joe.

I introduced myself to 'Joe' and privately asked if he had another name. He smiled and reintroduced *herself* as 'Shontay'. When I asked how things were going and why everyone was concerned, she said that it was because she had been switching back and forth between the bathrooms. One week there were women in the shelter who had threatened her – so she felt safer using the men's room. The next week those women were gone, but she had been hassled by some of the men. She started using the women's room. She started to cry and spoke of her fears of being assaulted. 'I just want to be safe' was her only request in the shelter. That was a logical and reasonable request.

Social work networks

It was out of this neoliberal, sexist and racist murk that an alternative form of social work reasserted itself. (This alternative form has been present in other times of great need and disaster. It is a form of social work that is deeply concerned with human rights and informed by ground-level 'ways of knowing'.) This model of social work emerges when we reject the privileging of one form of knowledge over another, focus on relationship building and invert dominant power structures.

If you were watching the American news reports, you really have no idea what happened down there. I think that most people expect that I saw nothing but bloated bodies and storm damage. I didn't. What I experienced was a woefully inadequate social welfare system and public health system in total collapse.

Social workers were working within the context of the Southern experience to create and facilitate new networks. In the Deep South of the United States, the Evangelical and Pentecostal versions of Christianity have had profound influences on southern culture. It is referred to as the 'Bible Belt' as a result. Any effective social work intervention needs to be both inclusive of the church communities and mindful of those it may exclude as a result.

The church communities responded to the storms in full force. Many shelters were in church buildings, church schools or church camps and were staffed by church members. Volunteers from local churches cared for evacuees and Red Cross volunteers. They cooked meal after meal and washed our laundry for weeks. With electricity and gas being in short supply, they had little more than the evacuees themselves.

For all their generosity, social workers needed to be savvy of the fact that churches are still quite racially segregated. Additionally, churches have had vocal (and sometimes violent) opposition to sexual minorities, other religious groups and those who deviate from traditional gender roles. This was humorously articulated by a Disaster Mental Health worker upon driving up to a church with a rather large sign directing the reader to 'Take a Stand for Jesus.' Upon seeing the sign, he stated that those of us in the car were 'a Southern Baptist nightmare' because we were 'a dyke, a Jew and a man who likes to talk about feelings'.

Due to the dominant centrist position of the two-party system, there were no political parties with which to build any alliances. Additionally, organised labour has little to no influence in the Deep South.

Social work in action

Upon arrival in Louisiana, volunteers were sorted through an intake station, given orientation to the relief effort and the cultural context of their area and assigned to an area and function. Disaster Mental Health workers were assigned to a team of two or three and then issued a vehicle.

During this process, social workers were grouped with psychologists, marriage and family therapists and other professionals. I noticed that considerable effort was being made to identify and distribute the social workers among the teams. Unsure as to why this was, I asked if they were trying to create multi-disciplinary teams or some such effort. It turned out that all the shelters were requesting social workers exclusively. Social workers were considered to be the most useful to shelter staff and the evacuees because we knew how to negotiate systems and work with people effectively.

While the Red Cross model organised the shelter structure, social workers were able to quickly come in and facilitate the community that quickly emerged. People were in these shelters for several days or weeks at a time, with little or nothing to do. Social workers recognised that the evacuees needed something meaningful to occupy their time, children needed safe space in which to play and the shelter (and the evacuees and volunteers associated with them) had to interact with the larger community. Social workers were uniquely skilled in managing these multiple demands. Additionally, because this setting required clinically trained social workers, we were also able to respond to the stress and other mental health issues present in the evacuees and Red Cross volunteers.

To some extent or another, communities and a sense of solidarity evolved in almost all the shelters. Social workers identified and nurtured the development of systems of self-governance. Evacuees were encouraged to articulate and address their needs as a community. Evacuee-led security patrols, cooking collectives, inter-faith religious services and baby-sitting cooperatives were some of the examples of their creative expressions of self-determination. Some evacuees 'crossed over' and volunteered their time as official Red Cross volunteers within the shelters.

Social work community organisation – informed by a strong professional ethic of self-determination – may not have been the intention of the Disaster Mental Health model, but it proved to be highly effective in this setting. Paired with the doctors and nurses in Disaster Health Services, we were clearly intended to function within a medical model based on a macro/micro divide, where only micro-work and focus on the individual was valued. However, because social workers in this setting were trained and professionally oriented to intervene on both a micro and a macro level, we were far more effective in these community settings.

This was evident in one shelter where a Red Cross staff member pulled me aside to talk. He was both an evacuee and a staff member. He had been volunteering for over a month and his home had been destroyed by the storms. He stated that he'd watched the 'little girls' who were social workers come in and out of the shelters. He was older and had initially dismissed them, due to their age and gender. However, he quickly noticed that those 'little girls' were 'the only people who seem to really respect what people here have to say'. He recognised that those social workers weren't like the other Disaster Mental Health professionals in that 'they talk to us like we are real people ... they don't act like they are better than us'. It was in this context that he was able to talk to me about some very private and difficult information and seek advice. In essence, he trusted a 'little girl' because social workers had consistently modelled mutual respect for him and the larger community.

Social work lessons to be learned

The nature of any large-scale disaster is that it abounds in chaos and general disorganisation. While many may attempt to evaluate relief efforts and determine how to respond more effectively in the future, this line of enquiry has limited use. It is not possible to treat any disaster as a training exercise for the next disaster, as the same conditions will never exist in the same way again. Each disaster is unique. However, each disaster is an opportunity to glean information about local and larger community functioning.

Crisis does not bring out the best in people – it brings out the truth in people. There were examples of brutality and the ugly, reinscribing oppression. There were also thousands of caring, selfless people who set aside their own needs and their own families to help someone else.

Similarly, crisis exposes the truth in systems and structures. It shines an examiner's light on covert motivations and structural injustice.

It also exposes the truth in social justice and human rights movements and the profession of social work. How is it that 28% of the residents of New Orleans could be living in poverty and there was no outcry from social workers? (Brunsma, 2007). How could workers' rights be completely gutted in the South, with no attempts by social workers to join with labour movements? How can systematic racism still segregate much of the day-to-day life in the Deep South? How can social workers tolerate the brutality of sexism and homophobia being justified by history, culture or religion?

Social workers have been so co-opted by neoliberal ideology that there is more conversation in the professional organisations about 'title protection' (for mental health billing purposes) than there is about community organising. Clearly, Hurricane Katrina provided an opportunity to demonstrate to ourselves, other professionals and the larger community that social work models were far superior in addressing the complex issues presented by a large-scale natural disaster. It is my fervent hope that this lesson is not forgotten or dismissed.

Note

[1] Senator Rick Santorum, while 'criticizing the government's emergency response to hurricane victims' on 4 September 2005, was 'also criticizing the ones who chose to ride out the storm'. (Video, WTAE-TV CH 4 (ABC) Pittsburgh)

ELEVEN

Social work, social development and practice legitimacy in Central Asia

Terry Murphy

> On the seventh of March, I tore off my veil
> But before I got home
> I bought three new Paranjis
> To veil myself more darkly.
> (Satirical song heard among Uzbek women 1929[1])

This protest song originated as part of Uzbek women's cultural resistance to the imposed sovietisation and modernisation of Central Asia in the late 1920s and critiqued the forcible removal of the Islamic veil by Soviet authorities. This practice was presented by Soviet sources at the time as involving the liberation of women but in reality was often carried out at gun point and demonstrates dramatically the conflict generated when an outside model of development or empowerment is imposed on a society. Culturally ignorant development imposes change in a way which is experienced as alien and which negates the value and depth of the local cultures it is formally devoted to helping.

The conflict between the values of powerful outside imperial forces in Central Asia and their modernising project and often misrepresented or misunderstood local social and cultural norms is being acted out again, 80 years later, in the neighbouring country of Afghanistan, where a Western-led coalition propounding an ideology of modernity and human rights battles belief groups who hold paramount local tribal and religious or cultural affiliations.

At the very least, social work and social development practice which fails to engage with local political, communal and cultural realities is ineffective, and at worst, it can promote active conflict and place local social work practitioners at risk.

This chapter attempts to examine the basis for a theoretical understanding of the evolving role of social work in Central Asia's most populous country, Uzbekistan. It examines the tension between social work's claim to universal values and the more recent international moves toward models of practice which embody indigenisation of theory and methods and the broader incorporation of local culture.

An important cultural centre on the Silk Route, the territory of Uzbekistan has been home to artists and spiritual leaders such as Alisher Navoi (15th century), famous for the cyclical collection of poems *The Hamsa*; and leading medics like

Ibn Sina (11th century), who wrote *The Cannon of Medicine*, as well as historians such as Abu Rayhan al-Bruni (11th century), who wrote the history of India. The ancient Silk Road scholastic cities of Bukhara and Samarq, now in modern Uzbekistan, were central to the development of Islamic mathematics, philosophy and the sciences. Social work in Uzbekistan and Central Asia therefore builds upon an enormously rich cultural history (Dani and Masson, 1992). Demographically, the population of Uzbekistan is very young: 34.1% of its people are younger than 14 (2008 estimate). According to official sources, Uzbeks comprise a majority (80%) of the total population, with Russian, Tatar, Tajik, Karapkalpak and Korean citizens making up the remaining 20%.

In the modern context, all definitions of Central Asia consensually include the five former Soviet republics of Kazakhstan, Kyrgyzstan, Tajikistan, Turkmenistan and Uzbekistan, with a total population of 61.5 million as of 2009. Other areas are often included, such as the Republic of Mongolia, Afghanistan, northern and western Pakistan, north-eastern Iran, Jammu and Kashmir, and western parts of the People's Republic of China. Central Asia therefore remains an ethnically and culturally diverse area, heir to successive waves of immigration and conquest (Dani and Masson, 1992).

In the 20th century the Soviet areas of Central Asia saw significant industrialisation and construction of infrastructure, but also the suppression of local cultures and hundreds of thousands of deaths from failed collectivisation programmes. Soviet authorities deported millions of people, including entire nationalities, from western areas of the USSR to Central Asia and Siberia, producing massive cultural disruption (Poliakov and Olcott, 1992).

Later, from 1959 to 1970, about two million people from various parts of the Soviet Union migrated to Central Asia. These large-scale movements and the deliberate creation in the Stalinist period of divisive national boundaries which designedly did not match ethnic populations on the ground have left a lasting legacy of ethnic tensions and environmental problems (Mandelbaum, 1994).

Environmental issues dominate a complex regional politics. The contemporary use of scarce water resources for large-scale cotton monoculture has destroyed much of the Aral Sea region and produces political tension between neighbouring states and international concerns over the use of child labour for cotton picking in Uzbekistan, the world's second-largest producer of cotton. According to UNICEF in 2000, an estimated 22.6% of Uzbek children aged between 5 and 14 worked at least part time, primarily in cotton harvesting. In 2004, children in the Ferghana region reported that an average day's harvest of 10 kg of cotton would earn them 38 US cents. UNICEF itself has taken a lead role in looking to advocate the replacement of child labour in cotton production, which is a residual practice from the Soviet era (Ilkhamov, 2004; UNICEF, 2008).

The development of social work in the post-communist countries of Central Asia and the Caucasus has been subject to the dramatic and sometimes violent realities of regional political change in the last two decades, since they gained independence on the break-up of the former Soviet Union. Poverty remains a major issue in Uzbekistan, as Central Asia's most populous country. Estimated average wages in 2006 were $90–$120 per month, with an old-age pension at $30 per month. Labour migration remains a major issue for young children losing parents who need to live abroad in order to earn money. Russia's Federal Migration Service reports 2.5 million Uzbek migrant workers in Russia, and there are indications of up to 1 million Uzbek migrants working illegally in Kazakhstan. Uzbekistan's migrant workers may thus be around 3.5–4 million people, or 25% of the labour force of 14.8 million (IMF, 2008). This creates major issues for social work and, in cases involving the absence of financially capable grandparents, has resulted in the institutionalisation of many children whose parents have left the country to work. One of the major efforts of the developing professional social work services in Uzbekistan has been towards supporting these abandoned children's placement in extended family and foster placements, and moving away from Soviet-era large institutional solutions.

The U.S. Agency for International Development, whose mission was to assist the development of civil society in developing countries, announced in 2003 that civil society was only then 'beginning to develop in Uzbekistan', citing the more than 500 non-governmental organisations (NGOs) that had been established at that point. But following the political reaction caused by the 2005 Andijan incident, in which as many as 500 local people were killed when troops opened fire on protesters, more than 300 NGOs were forced to close operations, disrupting the development of educational, social care and public health projects.

This traumatic change in itself demonstrates one of the key skills required to deliver social work services in extremis, the need to be able to adapt radically to social policy landscapes which can be extremely vulnerable to outside events. Following any period of regional unrest or conflict, international projects and international NGOs may be seen by political decision makers as undermining local culture or as being actively hostile to national governments and may be rapidly closed down without debate.

In western donor countries and international organisations a development discourse focused on human rights and gender equality, for example, may be seen as embodying universal norms. However, from the perspective of decision makers in developing countries these discourses may be seen as directly attacking governmental competence, traditional values or national pride.

On a professional social work level, cultural and political naiveté in international practice can also place at risk local professionals working with outside development agencies when the attempt to develop projects fails to take into account local political and cultural reality. In 2009 an Uzbek psychologist, Maxim Popov, director of a sexual-health awareness NGO, was sentenced to seven years' imprisonment as punishment for his work to disseminate internationally produced materials to raise public awareness on prevention of sexually transmitted diseases. None of the international agencies which had promoted his work, including the US and UK government development organisations such as USAID, UNICEF, UNAIDS, and Global Development (UK) spoke out or publicly protested his imprisonment

(Elovich, 2010). In this case international bodies simply failed to understand how increasing state concerns over the role of independent, internationally funded NGOs and the complex nature of local Islamic values had not been fully understood or addressed by the international bodies at government level. Instead, a local professional was left to suffer severe punishment for the failure of international social work agencies to effectively engage with state and culture in ensuring that proper partnership and authorisation were built in before engaging on a highly sensitive social work and health project.

One of the key reasons for the limited effectiveness of NGOs within the Central Asian context has been that, structurally, Western NGOs tend to focus on a single issue or social problem; well-known examples may include Amnesty International for human rights, Greenpeace for environmental issues, and WWF for animal conservation. This single-issue structure is logical in an individualistic, consumerist Western context in which social advocacy is single-issue driven for clarity of marketing and 'brand' purposes.

However, this model fails to take into account the central importance of local and communal networks which form the central recognised mechanism for delivering social help within the Central Asian context. The importance and centrality of mahalla and, on a wider level, of the allegiance to clans and ethnic groupings forms a deeply embedded network of influence which single-interest social work development approaches can fail to take into account. An effective international impact in the Central Asian context requires that whole-community interventions are organised, and social work programmes need to examine issues of gender, family, support and risk within the organic extended-family and clan networks which dominate decision making and allegiance.

It is important, then, to examine the ways in which the empowerment-based values of social work can be in practice embodied in a series of practical programmes which negotiate the potential minefield of divergent international and national priorities and stakeholders. An approach to social work in extremis which fails to be able to negotiate the interests of powerful national stakeholders and identifies only with the sometimes more palatable values of international development organisations will guarantee long-term project failure.

To engage properly with the process of developing social work in extremis it is necessary to develop a model of practice which helps us to evaluate the ethical dimensions of practice in extreme contexts. This is of particular use when international social work consultants from established Western systems may be practising with social workers from a developing national system in a situation of conflict or of political norms and realities which differ from Western democratic ones.

Understanding the nature and history of Islam in Central Asia is important to any social work practice which attempts to understand local realities. During most of the 20th century, Sunni Islam (the dominant form of Islam in Central Asia) was heavily suppressed in the Central Asian republics which formed part of the Soviet Union. In particular, during the periods of Stalinist repression teaching institutes such as madrassas were destroyed or were turned over to secular use and large numbers of religious teachers and imams (Muslim religious leaders) were murdered by the Soviet secret police. A major part of the Soviet project was enforced secularisation, and Islam, in the same way as orthodox Christianity, was subject to severe repression. Subsequently, however, for essentially pragmatic political reasons during the Second World War and afterwards, the Soviet state chose to come to a practical accommodation with religious culture and to appeal to it as part of a patriotic national identity. While this allowed many cultural aspects of religion to continue, the massive accommodations required by religious figures and organisations in order to survive within the Soviet state caused religious figures and institutions to be seen, in general, as deeply compromised and unable to fulfil many of their traditional social functions.

Islamic cultures within the Soviet Union were diverse in Azerbaijan, and among the Volga Tartars an indigenous secularised intelligentsia had developed by the late 19th century. However, in the traditional khanates of Bukhara and Khiva and the Fergana valley and among the more latterly converted nomadic peoples of current-day Kyrgyzstan and Kazakhstan, local understandings of Islam continued to play a role in daily life for both rural and urban communities.

Following the establishment of the Soviet state in the early 20th century, Soviet policy as initially established by Stalin's Tatar advisor Sultan Galiev sought to distinguish between perceived fanatical elements to be destroyed and the larger community of Islamic believers (the *umma*) who could be treated as a potential instrument of social progress, with the eventual aim of complete laicisation. As the Stalinist terror progressed, however, particular attention was given to destroying the progressive Jadid movement, which had sought to produce a more reformed and modernised interpretation of Islam suitable for the 20th century, as this was seen as providing a direct competition to communist ideology.

This period, known as the onslaught or *Hujum*, in the 1920s and 1930s left most religious institutions destroyed, and formal religious observance disappeared from everyday life. While formal religious observance was suppressed, however, in private, family and communal arenas a local or folk practice remained strong.

What remained, then, throughout the 20th century were the deeply embedded folk practices of everyday life consisting of a traditional interweaving of Islamic culture with far older regional customs and practices. These syncretic practices are symbolised today by the world heritage Islamic Registan buildings of Samarqand, in which Islamic architecture is uniquely adorned with the representational animal figures of the earlier Zoroastrian faith.

These Islamic-based, syncretic folk practices remain embedded in everyday life in the region today. During the period of Soviet rule meetings and practices which shared a fundamental Islamic character were portrayed as purely shamanistic or folk practices, so as to escape surveillance and repression. This syncretic mixture of Islamic practice and older shamanistic or Zoroastrian belief systems has played a central role in the development of communal responses to social problems and to the communal provision of traditional welfare services.

As late as the 1980s a major Soviet sociological study of Islam within the Soviet Union showed that religious practice was comparatively wide scale among all strata of society and that previous sociological views that the practice of Islam within Central Asia and the Caucasus had become largely ritualistic in nature or *obriadovyi* were inaccurate, and that these beliefs played a significant role in the day-to-day life of the community and were handed down between generations.

Even many non-believers, it was found, perceived Islam to be a central thread of a national cultural patrimony and of the historical patchwork of ideas transmitted between generations which gave a core cultural identity and meaning to the indigenous peoples of Central Asia. Today, among the professionals and decision makers involved in social work in Uzbekistan in Central Asia, it is common to find a significant knowledge of aspects of Islamic thought among formally non-religious people.

At a ministerial conference I attended in 2009 a senior official discussing the provision of alternative forms of foster care and the current process of de-institutionalisation in Uzbekistan quoted the Koranic saying 'he who cares for the orphan will be close to me in paradise', which was clearly understood as part of a shared cultural and moral heritage by those present, whatever the ethnic and religious affiliation of the participants. Such cultural tags can help the development of a culturally relevant discourse about social work.

Precursors to social welfare in Central Asia have an ancient and highly structured history, itself predating the introduction of Islam. During the early Zoroastrian period in Central Asia familial charity as a modality of social support was traditional for all community members who were able to provide it. Formal religious institutions had the functions of social services – the rendering of support, help, and arrangement of charity. The local rulers, the Zoroastrian temples and wealthy citizens would arrange charitable festivals and almsgiving. Material support from collective funds was also given to families in need. These traditional mechanisms of social help within the community meant that every person received the formal social protection of the traditional communal structures that he or she belonged to. These structures comprised both the family and the wider community, delivering support to their members. On a wider level *khashar* – or disinterested and voluntary help by the community – was used for the communal building of social housing, bridges, dams and canals; this was one of the forms of large-scale traditional behaviour expected as part of codified and mutual social obligation.

The forms of social support to the poor began to be expanded after the Abbasid Caliphate defeated the Chinese Tang Dynasty for control of Central Asia in 751, which was the turning point for the beginning of mass conversion to Islam in the region.

Islamic Central Asia developed new kinds of cultural values. Islamisation in the region has also had the effect of blending Islam into native cultures, creating new forms of Islamic practices, known as folk Islam, the most prominent proponent of which was Khoja Akhmet Yassawi, whose Sufi Yeseviye sect appealed greatly to local nomads.

The functions of social support and help became entrusted to mosques and public-religious societies. The modalities of social support took both individual and collective forms. For individuals, one of the basic canons of Islam is almsgiving or *zakat* (sometimes referred to as *sadaqah*). The term 'zakat' refers to alms imposed by law, as opposed to dole or sadaqah, which is a voluntary donation by private persons in favour of the poor. Traditionally, in Central Asia zakat must be only used to meet the needs of the poorest in society. In addition to zakat there is also *sadakaye-fittir*, which refers to handouts arranged for the poor on the occasion of *edool-fittir*, meaning the celebration of ending of the fast. Sadakaye-fittir is culturally obligatory for all Muslims possessing any tax-free property, and remained in practice during the Soviet era and today. Within the social–cultural system of the country there also existed such indigenous social commitments as *savob* (good deed, benefaction) and *khimmat* (generosity), which served as an original 'instrument' of social support.

The most central social structure which effective social work regionally needs to understand, which was developed in Central Asia, is that of the *mahalla* (Arabic for site or locality). This essentially forms a local, community-based organisation which may cover a rural village, or a number of blocks of flats within a town or city. This form of community organisation has been subject to a degree of state standardisation in recent years. It developed originally as a means of providing local support and arbitrating in local disputes between and within families.

Originally, mahalla were organised and controlled by traditional elders and figures of respect within the community, literally *Oqsoquol* or white beards. State standardisation and control in Soviet and postSoviet times means that the *rais* or leader or manager of the mahalla is now appointed by the state and, unlike previously, does not have to live within the community itself. Each manager usually has two paid assistants to help in their work. Mahalla personnel, to date, however, do not receive social work training. On the street, views of the mahalla committees range from their being positive and helpful to their being an arm of state surveillance, with a significant view expressed informally to me by young people of their being 'interfering old busybodies'. It seems fair to assume that the reported wide range of competence, motivation and skill in different mahalla committees is accurate, and the quality of service seems to be linked to the idiosyncratic quality of the individual rais.

The work of the mahalla committee itself may involve a wide provision of unqualified social welfare help for isolated elderly individuals, for example, or offering to mediate in family disputes. It is, for example, compulsory for couples considering divorce to attempt mediation with the help of the mahalla before formal legal proceedings are initiated.

Given the economic resources and the cultural significance of the mahalla system, then, one of the most interesting questions for social work development in Uzbekistan is the way in which the new and developing systems of professional social work which are based upon professional competence, adherence to recognised codes of ethics and the use of international social work theory and practice engage with the traditional community-based system, based on concepts of character, cultural knowledge and the inherent fairness of elders and community. The strong cultural tendency to assimilation and syncretic fusion in the region, however, provides deeper cultural reasons to presuppose this can be achieved.

While mahalla are common in most areas of Uzbekistan, it is important to note that they are experienced in significantly different ways, depending on the ethnic and cultural origin of the residents of an area. Urban areas which are largely Uzbek in character may have residents who have been actively involved in various mahalla from childhood.

However, significant non-Uzbek ethnic groups in Uzbekistan and wider Central Asia, for example urban residents who are ethnically Russian, Korean or Tajik, may have been less involved in mahalla as a social organisation, as may have been the originally nomadic residents of Karakalpak origin in the Aral Sea region. Mahalla as a concept has always been of less interest to the nomadic peoples of the region and had more engagement with the settled Uzbek farming and agricultural way of life.

Mahalla is also an important political structure and concept – in addition to its existence as a welfare mechanism – which reports directly to central government. It is seen as a core social and cultural construct for the regulation of society and the promotion of cultural values. One of the important development tasks for professional social work development in Uzbekistan has been to clarify the difference in roles and the complementary nature of professional social work and the more social welfare-based practice of the mahalla system. During development meetings some policy makers were unclear about the need for the development of professional social work and expressed the belief that because of the mahalla system 'everyone in Uzbekistan is a social worker'.

However, the success of the country's first professional social work teams in the last five years has demonstrated in policy terms that professional social work and the community-based mahalla system can coexist and work together extremely well, providing complementary services. Undoubtedly, however, more work, both theoretical and in terms of concrete policy and procedure, needs to be undertaken in the next few years to embed a positive, multi-agency framework which makes explicit the roles and responsibilities of professional social work teams and mahalla and the ways in which they interface (Murphy, 2009).

Social work practice in Central Asia needs therefore to locate itself within these pervasive and shared cultural concepts and structures in order to develop an effective and indigenised practice. Central to the development of successful social work practice, therefore, has been the adoption of practice which respects and uses the forms of shared social obligation and social aid which have developed. The acceptance of communal responsibility for social problems is in itself a major source of strength for social work development.

However, there are recognisable difficulties as well as strengths in non-professional solutions developed by community organisations. It is difficult for community resources to meaningfully use research and social theory, and skills may be limited. Traditional responses to problems of spousal violence or child protection may be to blame the victim for bringing shame upon the family or wider community.

It is important to note that, in cultures where communal values have predominance over Western notions of individual rights and responsibilities, the issue of shame and family honour must be directly incorporated into social work training programmes. In particular, methodologies must include practical social work techniques to deal with the issue of pressure to conceal major social problems within the family and disavow victims. For this purpose, in developing social work training videos in Uzbekistan we particularly focused on developing positive responses to shame-based issues (Murphy, 2008).

Within the regional context, for example, mothers–in–law within extended traditional families are frequently cited as figures of abuse by young wives in domestic violence reports. Thus, social work and gender programmes based on Western models of domestic violence training, which take no account of abuse perpetrated on women by other more socially powerful women, are unlikely to be effective, as they fail to properly incorporate local clan realities. To be effectively indigenised, therefore, it is important to produce local educational and training materials which present recognisable local realities to local social workers in training. Video vignettes portraying recognisable local scenarios have proved to be significantly more effective than imported training material (Murphy, 2008, 2009).

Over the period 2005 to 2010, professional social workers in pilot family support teams were trained, with an explicit mandate to prevent institutionalisation wherever possible, and in discussions and consultation demonstrated clearly effective practice in allowing children to remain with their own families while social problems were worked through with the help of the social worker. This clearly demonstrated one of the possibilities opened up by the development of professional social work teams, to offer a greater range of possible solutions to children and families in crisis, based on assessment rather than community advice or, often, long–term institutionalisation of the child.

Olcott (1995) argues that understanding the clan networks is 'perhaps the single most crucial element' in understanding Central Asia, especially that clan politics 'convey privilege' and 'responsibility'. The key to successfully interfacing the social work paradigm and the mahalla or community systems is to work with this sense of communal responsibility and to use professional social workers to offer solutions and possibilities which the traditional systems would not themselves have arrived at. This model developed during the Teesside University consultancy from 2006 to 2010, essentially, attempts to indigenise a solution–focused approach to social work by allowing the social worker to offer new hypotheses to the traditional system as to both problem cause and solution. Mahalla committees are encouraged by attached professional social workers to develop new hypotheses to problems and to use solution–focused methodologies to create safety plans with the social worker and the family experiencing problems. This is achieved using models such as the Signs of Safety model (Turnell and Edwards, 1999) for child protection issues and community resource planning for poverty alleviation. The social worker's role is not to supplant or replace the mahalla committee but, in effect, to act as a solution-focused consultant to the mahalla as well as to the family experiencing social problems. In a systemic sense, social workers trained by the national social work team retraining programme developed from 2005 to 2010 are taught to look for and generate new possibilities for understanding and for solution which incorporate both the central needs of the child and family and the importance of sustaining communal acceptance and support.

In discussion, students and professionals are capable of balanced views of the mahalla system. As a system, it can work well in delivering locally based social welfare support for families that may be experiencing financial difficulties due to a breadwinner's illness or an elderly person's social isolation. However, the mahalla system has not shown itself capable of dealing with the more complex issues with which professional social work grapples. These include child abuse and child protection, complex issues of domestic violence, drug misuse and disability.

These more complex problems require well-trained professionals who are able to make difficult risk assessments in the interests of a vulnerable child or adult in cases where the community may, in fact, be unable to assess the risk or to accept, for example, that a popular community member may also be abusive to their spouse or children.

Moreover, previous disastrous attempts internationally at unqualified community-based child protection demonstrate the potential for active civil unrest if members of one community are seen as snatching or kidnapping the children of another community.

While working as a UNICEF consultant in Africa in 2000, I witnessed at first hand the enormous political problems that had resulted when a well-meaning minister decided herself, with her bodyguards, to personally remove a child whom she felt to be at risk from a different community. She was not felt by the community to be a neutral figure, in the way that a professional social worker can be, and communal problems resulted. Similarly, as a child protection manager in Northern Ireland toward the end of the 'troubles' or civil war, I found that it was clear that social workers needed to be seen as politically neutral figures who could negotiate not just with the formal government but also with banned organisations who represented polarised communities. This professionalism of social workers in the proper and positive sense of neutrality and clearly just behaviour enabled practice to be carried out in sensitive areas where any attempt by members of one community to interfere with the family lives of another would have led to violence.

Of particular interest in the development of social work within Uzbekistan has been the institutional location of social work education departments. Unlike in the UK or the US, where academic social work departments tend to be located in schools of social science or health, in Uzbekistan social work has been located within cultural institutes in a number of universities. This has presented a number of interesting development issues. Significant numbers of social work educators originally came from a cultural studies background, with backgrounds in performing or creative arts. This has given educators a reflective and in-depth knowledge of cultural issues within their own society and an appreciation of the need to develop theory and practice alongside each other. Broader issues remain, however, with significant levels of corruption within the wider education system. This was readily referred to by social work students in the universities, with particular individuals noted as being either corrupt or honest. Students presented an interesting perception that new experiential teaching methods in social work had been far more readily adopted by 'honest' academic staff, as those prone to corruption required a rigid and formal approach to students so as to maintain an atmosphere of intimidation and control.

In terms of theory, few new social work academics from cultural studies backgrounds have had training in any empirical social science, and they require methodological training to carry out small-scale empirical studies to develop a local, robust and evidence-based practices (Murphy, 2008; 2009). Over the last decade, however, extremely successful practice projects have been set up in parts of the country. Family support teams staffed by professionals from psychological and youth studies backgrounds have retrained as social workers and provide community-based case-work services which would be recognisable to any social worker from an established system. Parent-support programmes for children with a disability have enabled children to remain at home instead of facing institutionalisation. These successful projects demonstrate the possibility of social work taking root in Central Asia as a whole. However, they exist in parallel with large-scale institutions, and the wide-scale transfer of funding out of previous, outdated models and towards community-based social work is the goal of much international and local advocacy.

The Central Asian region provides a clear example of social work in extremis. In a region racked by inequality, poverty, corruption and a history of predatory rule, one of social work's core tasks is to locate its progressive but effective position with the complex and ancient cultures of the region. Effective practice necessitates an engagement with the traditional, communal and Islamic values of the area. It is important therefore to consider what obstacles hinder this engagement.

One of the core theoretical issues facing social work in extreme social environments is the nature of civil society within which social work normally finds a home. The working definition of the London School of Economics Centre for Civil Society is useful: 'Civil society refers to the arena of uncoerced collective action around shared interests, purposes and values.' Civil societies are often populated by organisations such as registered charities, development non-governmental organisations, community groups, women's organisations, faith-based organisations, professional associations, trade unions, self-help groups, social movements, business associations, coalitions and advocacy groups.

In the Central Asian context such a definition has little engagement with social reality. Such formal non-governmental organisations are so circumscribed and monitored as to provide few opportunities for developing the possibility of an independent social space for social work to operate. NGOs which may be effective vehicles to deliver social work in a Western context are located in too fragile a 'permissive social space' to attempt social work of real impact. In reality, extensive and informed permission by senior policy makers at the state level which addresses national concerns over social stability and social norms is necessary for the creation of effective, long-term social work organisations.

The clear distinction central to Western liberal thought of religion and the state cannot be considered in the same way in a Central Asian context. The classic notion of civil society essentially presupposes a Western-oriented set of beliefs and values focused on the individual and individual human rights. In the traditional model of development by means of the single-issue NGO as international partner, resources are spent on creating models that have little engagement with the main communal mechanisms that control everyday life for the vast majority of people.

It is extremely difficult, then, for traditional Western models of social work practice to allow for creative engagement with existing traditional structures – such as clan networks and the mahalla – that are tied to religion. These do not resonate for most social work theorists, who view pre-existing patriarchal cultural mechanisms as part of the problem, instead of as a social culture to be engaged with and as a potential space for social work to operate in.

Thus, many potential international development agencies promote NGOs that act as single-issue advocacy platforms on the Western model. Unfortunately, these NGOs simply do not do well in Central Asia, given that they fail to mesh with local communal realities.

It is essential in developing effective social work in Central Asia that we pay close attention to the pre-modern social affiliations of extended family and clan and that leaders and elites within clan structures are engaged to better represent those over whom they have degrees of influence or direct authority. Social work programmes will have to address the elites in a conversation to demonstrate to the relatively small numbers of effective power holders that social work offers a cost-effective and humane alternative to previous largely ineffective (but expensive) institutions. Secondly, the indigenous communal structures of mahalla and clan need to be engaged with in order to create a complementary rather than a competitive space for professional social work. Finally, significant adaptation of social work models and methods needs to take place in order to create a local curriculum for social work education which engages with and represents the communal and traditional as well as the individual and the modern.

What is clear is that the development of social work in Central Asia will have to be intimately connected with an engagement with the local forms of Islam in all its complex, folk and syncretic manifestations. The development of an empowerment-based practice in Central Asia must be done in a way that is congruent with its culture. The transformation of a traditional society must begin by engaging with the traditions of that society. Islam will be central, as it is unlikely that anything akin to civil society will develop and prosper in Central Asia without the incorporation of elements of the cultural and moral framework provided by Islam. The search for progressive solutions which effectively engage with traditional culture, and the emergence of social work structures which offer the region the possibility of more effective and creative solutions for those in need is the next stage of the development of social work in Central Asia.

Note
[1] In Northrop (2004).

Social work in extremis – some general conclusions

Vasilios Ioakimidis

We started our Introduction by including discussion of the recent disaster in Haiti and its aftermath. But the book's completion also coincided with another crisis: the dramatic sharpening of the financial crisis in Greece and the response it generated from both the governing and working classes (and, of course, the Greek example finds echoes in recent events in Ireland, Spain, Iceland, France and, more recently, the UK). The crisis exposed the long-term failure of the policies being pursued by the ruling classes, which resorted to 'calling in' the International Monetary Fund (IMF) to promote rehabilitation and reinstate order. The government turned to the IMF by resorting to the 'rhetoric of fear'. The Greek finance minister invited and legitimised the actions of the IMF in the country, declaring that there is a 'basic choice between collapse or salvation' (BBC, 2010). But, in the face of the proposed onslaught on public services, the Greek trade unions and popular grassroots networks organised for political change. In the case of Greece, the state responses and grassroots demands occurred simultaneously. The tension created by these responses highlights the class nature of 'disaster management'. This is a dynamic that often occurs in periods of crisis.

The Greek political and financial elites responded to the crisis by unconditionally adopting the IMF's proposals to deepen the neoliberal regime in Greece. This included the implementation of the most draconian austerity package in recent Greek history: threats to dismiss public sector employees, direct cuts in salaries, restructuring of the national insurance system, increased taxation, reduction of the minimum wage and spending cuts on front-line services. These measures did not include or affect the banking, trade and marine-business capital which had accumulated unprecedented profits in the immediate period before the crisis.

The government resorted to the psychological intimidation of the public (pointing to a 'forthcoming disaster'), the generation of feelings of collective guilt ('we are all responsible for the situation'), curtailment of basic democratic principles (the agreement with the IMF was not ratified by the parliament but was signed by the appointed, and not elected, finance minister), weakening of civil liberties (police brutality, random arrests, operation of vigilantes) and promotion of individualism in an attempt to divide and rule (see Eleftherotypia online edition, 2010)

The austerity package forced the Greek popular classes, already experiencing high poverty rates, to fight for survival. Hundreds of thousands of people organised strikes and demonstrations that were the largest in decades (*Guardian*, 2010). In this way, the popular classes declared that the management of the crisis should be fundamentally different to that dictated by the IMF and the Greek ruling class. The emphasis of the reaction from below was not limited to the defence of their working conditions and salaries but was politically broader, challenging the existing political and economic structures within Greece. Such a militant response was also reflected in the decision of hundreds of grassroots trade unionists to ignore and by-pass the bureaucratic and state-allied national confederation of trade unions. And within these grassroots networks new visions and new solutions are being discussed which hark back to the radical and popular social welfare projects of the Greek civil war era.

The developments in Greece were still ongoing as we completed this book. However, the extraordinary political and social upheaval provides another example of our thesis that periods of crisis potentially act as a catalyst for the creation and flourishing of grassroots social and welfare practices. What is particularly interesting about Greece is the reaffirmation of the fact that grassroots and ruling class responses can emerge in parallel, but rarely in consensus. When such a condition occurs it eventually takes the form of either open or subtle class conflict. Such a dynamic has not been adequately discussed in this book, but we believe that our analysis can offer a starting point for a further debate within social work.

As we have argued in this book, the apocalyptic post-crisis consequences that the 'rhetoric of fear' predicts can be challenged. In fact, there are several cases where extreme circumstances provided opportunities for people to by-pass the authorities and directly respond to the mounting needs of their affected communities in a collective and creative manner. During these processes, informal welfare networks develop from below, reflecting the resilience, hope and determination of the people.

Most chapters described cases that occurred in very different historical, political and social contexts. Such diversity demands that we develop our basic argument, avoiding over generalisation and simplification. Therefore, our intention is not to provide definite answers and quick-fix solutions but rather to start a debate and shift attention to the various forms of popular social work that can develop in extremis.

However, there are a number of themes and issues that arise from the case studies and which offer a 'glimpse' of alternative social work practices.

The 'live and let die' myth

Margaret Thatcher's phrase 'there is not such a thing as society' encapsulates the epitome of neoliberal politics. The supremacy of the market and individualism are promoted as natural and rational conditions of human culture. Every attempt to diverge from these principles is presented generally as absurd and, at best, as utopian. Within such a context it is predicted that, in urgent circumstances, when the authorities are unable to ensure order, the dog-eat-dog instincts of human nature will prevail and inevitable catastrophe will follow. Violence, panic, systematic looting, anarchy and chaos will replace the order that only a well-functioning state can ensure.

According to such perspectives, in times of crisis sometimes it is necessary to curb democratic functions and mobilise the army in order to restore order. A review of the basic arguments behind most military juntas of the last 50 years confirms the above. Further, when the 'disaster' occurs it offers an opportunity for markets to make a profit, as part of a one-way road to rehabilitation. As the IMF explains:

> The transfer of risks to international capital markets has substantial benefits because it greatly expands the pool of insurance capital available to developing countries. Nonetheless, a number of uncertainties are associated with the insurance of natural disaster risk. Even though there are well-established markets for insuring certain catastrophe risks, it cannot be taken for granted that all natural disaster risks can be insured in the market at an affordable cost. (Hofman, 2007)

However, many of the case studies in this book indicate otherwise. The extreme circumstances we have described did not lead inevitably to a pandemonium that reflected 'selfish human nature'. On the contrary, in all cases the dog-eat-dog axiom was found wanting. People did not run away and, more importantly, did not turn against each other. In fact, it was the authorities that appeared to be exposed and unable to control the situation. For example, as I described in my chapter, the extreme circumstances that followed the defeat of Greece in the Second World War led to the massive withdrawal of the political establishment and its complete unwieldiness and inability to respond to the urgent needs of the people. Within a very different context, Marla McCulloch highlights that communities affected by Hurricane Katrina in the US witnessed a similar unwillingness and inability on the part of the authorities to respond proactively to the situation.

The extreme circumstances brought local communities together. Creative and grassroots networks appeared instantly and replaced the role of the authorities. These networks developed organically within the communities and enjoyed the trust of local people. The networks were the catalysts inspiring local populations to explore alternative ways of organising and, more importantly, alternative visions for social change.

Democratic processes from below

Another similarity that characterises many of the cases we have presented in this book is that, when communities respond, they start to challenge and redefine existing hierarchies.

As Jones and Lavalette and Lavalette and Levin highlight in their chapters, the grassroots procedures in Palestine and Lebanon involve the creation of multiple committees, created from below, that directly involve local people and activists in the decision-making process. Teloni, in a similar fashion, claims that such committees not only respond to the needs of the affected people (in her case, refugees) but involve an educational dimension that helps the communities to redefine their political understanding and envisages long-term changes. Ioakimidis describes how, in the case of the Greek Liberation Front, grassroots politics and direct involvement of the popular classes in decision making led to the creation of an embryonic system of self-administration and popular justice recognised by millions of people.

Throughout most chapters of this book, such a determination for social change in the long term is evident. What starts as a small-scale and localised response to an extreme situation may soon develop into a political movement for emancipation. The collective and democratic experience of the people, who in most cases feel in control of their own fate for the first time, provides an opportunity for them to expose the inadequacies, irrationalities and oppression of the 'pre-disaster' status and seek long-term change.

Holistic welfare practice

Another common characteristic in the case studies is the holistic nature of these alternative welfare practices. In fact, as some of the authors have highlighted (Xavier, Teloni, Ioakimidis, Hinestroza and Ioakimidis and Maglajlic), it is very difficult to distinguish the welfare element from the other dimensions of the community engagement. The practice of the grassroots committees organised to address the needs of the population is holistic. The main priority in all cases appears to be the struggle for survival. However, the notion and content of the term 'needs' is much broader than the official definition of the authorities and might also include informal education, cultural development and collective participation. Thus, it is difficult to differentiate the welfare practices from the political, cultural and educational elements. What keeps these elements together is a common sense of solidarity.

Given the difficulties or unwillingness to access the existing official/bureaucratic welfare resources, grassroots welfare initiatives are forced to develop alternative methods and techniques. These new methods reflect the creativity and resourcefulness of the communities. Neocleous indicates that, in the case of Cyprus, the mounting needs of the affected communities and their grassroots responses directed the state in the creation of an inclusive and holistic welfare state. Ioakimidis and Teloni demonstrate how collective cultural events are used to address emotional and psychological tensions within the community, a theme that is also taken up by Jones and Lavalette.

Rebecca Solnit has argued elsewhere that 'the constellations of solidarity, altruism, and improvisation are within most of us and reappear at these times. People know what to do in a disaster' (2009, p 10). To this observation we can add that people's reactions in periods of crisis offer an alternative perspective on social work and welfare practice. A new paradigm focuses on the needs and aspirations of communities and, more importantly, is based on the active and equal participation of the people from below in the creation of a new vision of society. However, such developments usually remain short glimpses of alternative realities. In most cases the official social work profession, the state and big NGOs reclaim their territory and reinstate the institutional hierarchies and systemic 'normality'.

Rethinking social work?

In his introduction Michael Lavalette suggested that the case studies in this book force us to reconsider what we think social work can and should be. He suggested that the activities of workers on the ground during extreme circumstances offer a broader social work engagement than that offered by narrow models of the profession that are increasingly dominant in the UK and the US.

We suggest that the case studies speak to an alternative social work tradition, that they offer examples of social work that is politically oriented, that is organic and non-hierarchical. Our aim is not to denigrate existing models of social work but to suggest that there is an important tradition of community, popular and engaged social work that is enriched by its connections with broader social movement activity – but which is often ignored or written out of social work's history. We hope that these 'glimpses' of alternative social work realities can inspire a broader discussion about the role, nature and direction of the profession.

References

Achar, G. and Warschawski, M. (2007) *The 33 Day War*, London: SAQI.

Adams, G. (2010) 'Hollywood star shows how aid can help Haiti', *Independent on Sunday*, 11 July, www.independent.co.uk/news/world/americas/hollywood-star-how-aid-can-help-Haiti-2023810.html

Alayon, N. (2005) *Trabajo Social Latinoamericano a 40 años de la Reconceptualización*, Buenos Aires: Editorial Espacio.

al-Hout, B.N. (2004) *Sabra and Shatila: September 1982*, London: Pluto.

Alinsky, S. (1971) *Rules for Radicals*, New York: Vintage Books.

American Center for International Labor Solidarity (2006) *Justice for all: The struggle for worker rights in Colombia*, www.solidaritycenter.org/files/ColombiaFinal.pdf [accessed 6 October 2010].

Amnesty International (2007) *Lebanon: Exiled and suffering: Palestinian refugees in Lebanon*, www.amnesty.org/en/library/asset/MDE18/010/2007/en/35eba2ba-d367-11dd-a329-2f46302a8cc6/mde180102007en.html

Amnesty International (2008) Colombia:'"Leave us in peace!"Targeting civilians in the internal armed conflict – FACTS AND FIGURES', www.amnesty.org/en/for-media/press-releases/colombia-%E2%80%98leave-us-peace%E2%80%99-targeting-civilians-internal-armed-conflict-facts [accessed 5 October 2010].

Amnesty International (2009) 'Thousands more people forced to flee from Colombia's armed conflict', www.amnesty.org/en/news-and-updates/report/thousands-more-people-forced-flee-from-colombia-armed-conflict-20090716 [accessed 6 October 2010].

Anand, M. (2009) 'Gender in social work education and practice in India', *Social Work Education*, 28(1): 96–105.

Antoniou, M. (2009) Social insurance scheme in Cyprus [interview by G. Neocleous], Larnaca, 4 June.

Argyriou, E. (2006) 'On the way: art in resistance', *Rizospastis* daily newspaper 28 October, p 16.

Balata (nd) *Balata Refugee Camp West Bank*. Background leaflet available from the Yafa Cultural Centre, www.yafacult.org

Bandarage, A. (2009) *The separatist conflict in Sri Lanka*, Bloomington, IN: Authors Choice Press.

Barker, C. (ed) (1987) *Revolutionary rehearsals*, London: Bookmarks.

Baroud, R. (ed) (2003) *Searching Jenin: Eyewitness accounts of the Israeli invasion*, Seattle: Cune Press.

BBC (2010) 'Eurozone approves massive Greece bail-out', 2 May, http://news.bbc.co.uk/1/hi/world/europe/8656649.stm [accessed 17 February 2011].

Becker, J.C. (2008) *The testimony of the Senior Vice President, Disaster Services, American Red Cross before the Committee on Transportation and Infrastructure Subcommittee on Economic Development, Public Buildings and Emergency Management*, US House of Representatives, 23 September.

Beikos, G. (1979) *People's administration in Free Greece*, Athens: Themelio. [In Greek]

Berger, J. (2007) *Hold everything dear: Dispatches on survival and resistance*, London: Verso.

Blaikie, P. et al (1994) *At risk: Natural hazards, people's vulnerability, and disasters*, Canada: Routledge.

Blanchard, B. (2008) 'Billion dollar U.S. disasters', 8 October, Federal Emergency Management Agency.

Bröning, M. (2008) 'The myth of the Shia crescent', *Project Syndicate*, www.project-syndicate.org/commentary/broening1/English [accessed 19 February 2010].

Brubaker, B. (2005) 'Numerous violations alleged in bus fire', *The Washington Post*, 18 October.

Brunsma, D.L., Overfelt, D. and Picou, J.S. (eds) (2007) The *sociology of Katrina: Perspectives on a modern catastrophe*, Plymouth, UK: Rowman and Littlefield.

Burke, J. (2006) 'Are the Shias on the brink of taking over the Middle East?', *The Observer*, 23 July, www.guardian.co.uk/world/2006/jul/23/israel.syria [accessed 19 February 2010].

Cabrera, J.P. (2009) 'An examination of the persistence of the residual child welfare system in the United States: Addressing charges of radical theoretical myopia with implications for social work practice', *Journal of Progressive Human Services*, 20(1): 26–44.

Callinicos, A. (2009) *Imperialism and the global economy*, Cambridge: Polity.

Carey, L. (2007) 'Teaching macro practice: an experiential learning project', *Journal of Teaching in Social Work*, 27(1): 61–71.

Carroll, R. (2010) 'Quake-torn Haiti hit by floods', *Guardian*, 1 March, www.guardian.co.uk/world/2010/mar/01/quake-haiti-floods/print.

Carroll, R., Addley, E. and Meikle, J. (2010) 'Haiti homeless reach 2 million', *The Guardian*, 21 January, www.guardian.co.uk/world/2010/jan/21/haiti-homeless-reach-2-million

Ceric, I. and Jensen, S.B. (1996) *Community oriented mental health care in BiH: Strategy and model projects*, Sarajevo: WHO.

Chit, B. (2008) *Lessons from the July War*, Beirut: Mansoor. [In Arabic, English version provided by author as personal correspondence.]

Chomsky, N. (1999) *The fateful triangle*, 2nd edn, London: Pluto.

Chrysostomou, T. (2009) 'Social Welfare Department' [interview by G. Neocleous], Nicosia, 7 September.

Chu, W.C.K. et al (2009) 'Social work as a moral and political practice', *International Social Work*, 52(3): 287–98.

Clarence, W. (2007) *Ethnic war fare in Sri Lanka and the UN crisis*, London: Pluto Books.

Close, D.H. (2004) 'War, medical advance and the improvement of health in Greece, 1944–53', *South European Society & Politics*, 9(3): 1–27.

Cockburn, P. (2008) *Muqtada Al-Sadr and the fall of Iraq*, London: Faber and Faber.

Collins, S. (2009) 'Some critical perspectives on social work and collectives', *British Journal of Social Work*, 39: 334–52.

Community of Coryshades (1983) *Official records of PEEA National Council*, Coryshades: Community of Coryshades. [In Greek]

Cook, C., Hanieh, A. and Kay, A. (2004) *Stolen youth: The politics of Israel's detention of Palestinian children*, London: Pluto.

Cree, V. and Myers, S. (2008) *Social work: Making a difference*, Bristol: The Policy Press.

Cyprus Gazette (1980) No 1941, 16 July.

Daily Star (Beirut) (2006) 'Timeline on war', 19 August, www.dailystar.com.lb/July_War06.asp [accessed 17 February 2011].

Dani, A.H. and Masson, V.M. (eds) (1992) *UNESCO history of civilizations of Central Asia*, Paris: UNESCO.

Darby, J. (2001) *The effects of violence on peace processes*, Washington, DC: United States Institute of Peace.

Deacon, B. (1995) 'Nadnacionalne agencije i socijalna politika postsocijalistickih zemalja' (Supranational Agencies and Social Policy in Post-Socialist Countries), *Croatian Journal of Social Policy*, 2(4), 281–94.

dci-pal (Defence for Children International – Palestine Section) (2008) 'Statistics', www.dci-pal.org/english/home.cfm [accessed 9 July 2008].

Doctors Without Borders (2005) 'Displaced Colombians struggle to survive in urban slums', www.doctorswithoutborders.org/news/article.cfm?id=1547 [accessed 10 October 2010].

Dominelli, L. (2002) *Feminist social work theory and practice,* London: Palgrave.

Eaton, G. (2010) 'Saving Haiti from disaster capitalism', *New Statesman*, 17 January, www.newstatesman.com/blogs/the-staggers/2010/01/economic-shock-haiti-disaster [accessed 17 February 2011].

EKYSY (Enosi Kyprion Syntaxiouhon) (2003) *30 years of offering: Where we came from, where we stand, where we go...*, Nicosia: EKYSY.

Eleftheri Ellada (Athens) (1943) 'Editorial – Front Page', 12 March, 14: 1.

Eleftherotypia online edition (2010), 'Condemning report about the pre-emptive arrests', www.enet.gr/?i=news.el.article&id=143687 [accessed 17 February 2011].

Elovich, R. (2010) 'Prison and no backup from the U.S. Government for work on AIDS', www.huffingtonpost.com/richard-elovich/from-the-american-people_b_651479.html

ETAEE (Eidiko Tameio Antimetopisis Ektakton Anagkon) (Special Fund for Emergency Responses of the Ministry of Economics and Finances) (2010) 'Action', www.etaea.gr/drasi.html [accessed 5 May 2010].

Europa (2010) 'Summaries of EU Legislation', http://europa.eu/legislation_summaries/justice_freedom_security/free_movement_of_persons_asylum_immigration/l33081_en.htm [accessed 17 March 2010].

European Council on Refugees and Exiles (2008) *Sharing responsibility for refugee protection in Europe. Dublin Reconsidered*, www.ecre.org/files/Sharing%20Responsibility_Dublin%20Reconsidered.pdf [accessed 15 March 2010].

Fagot, C. and Winbush, D. (2006) 'Hurricane Katrina/Hurricane Rita evacuation and production shut-in statistics report', U.S. Government Minerals Management Service.

Fair, C. (2004) *Urban battlefields of South Asia*, Santa Monica, Arlington, Pittsburg: Rand Corporation.

FEMA (Federal Emergency Management Agency) (2004) 'Hurricane Pam exercise concludes', news release, 23 July.

Ferguson, I. (2008) *Reclaiming social work: Challenging neo-liberalism and promoting social justice*, London: Sage.

Ferguson, I. and Lavalette, M. (2006) 'Globalization and global justice', *International Social Work*, 49: 309–18.

Ferguson, I. and Lavalette, M. (2007) 'Democratic language and neo-liberal practice: the problem with "civil society"', *International Social Work*, 50(4): 447-59.

Ferguson, I. and Woodward, R. (2009) *Radical social work in practice: Making a difference*, Bristol: The Policy Press.

Ferguson, I. and Lavalette, M. (2009) *Social work after baby P: Issues, debates and alternative perspectives*, Liverpool: Hope University Press.

Fisk, R. (1990) *Pity the nation: Lebanon at war*, Oxford: Oxford University Press.

Fook, J. (2002) *Social work: A critical approach to practice*, London, Sage.

Fortress Europe (2010), http://fortresseurope.blogspot.com/2006/01/m.html.

Freire, P. (2009) *Teachers as cultural workers; Letters to those who dare teach*, Thessalonica: Epikendro. [In Greek]

Fromkin, D. (1989) *A peace to end all peace: The fall of the Ottoman Empire and the creation of the modern Middle East*, New York: Owl.

Frontex (2010) 'The official website of Frontex', www.frontex.europa.eu/ [accessed 5/3/2010].

Gagnon, V.P. (2002) 'International NGOs in Bosnia-Herzegovina: attempting to build civil society', in S.E. Mendelson and J.K. Glenn (eds) *The power and limits of NGOs: A critical look at building democracy in Eastern Europe and Eurasia*, New York: Columbia University Press, pp 207–64.

Gardner, S. (2005) *Cities, counties, kids, and families*, Maryland: University Press of the Americas.

Garrett, P.M. (2002) 'Social work and the just society: diversity, difference and the sequestration of poverty', *Journal of Social Work*, 2: 187–210.

German, L. and Murray, A. (2005) *Stop the war: The story of Britain's biggest mass movement*, London: Bookmarks).

Glinos, D. (1941) *What EAM is and what does it want*, Athens: EAM, available in Harilaos Florakis Historical Archives.

Gonzalez, M. (2010a) 'Building a new Haiti', *Guardian*, 4 February, www.guardian. co.uk/commentisfree/2010/Feb/04/haiti-rebuilding-funds-un/print.

Gonzalez, M. (2010b) 'Haiti – the making of a tragedy', *Socialist Review*, February, pp 10-12.

Greek Helsinki Monitor (2008), 'Dublin II Convention, European asylum policy and problems in Greece', press announcement, http://cm.greekhelsinki.gr/index.php?sec=192&cid=3312 [accessed 5 March 2010].

Greek Ombudsman (2008) *Department of Human Rights: Special Report summary*, November, http://www.synigoros.gr/_01/8928_1____EIDIKES_ADEIES_KRATOUM._2008-3.2.11.pdf.

Guardian (2010) 'Greek protesters storm the Acropolis', Guardian online edition, 4 May, www.guardian.co.uk/business/2010/may/04/greek-protesters-storm-acropolis

Gutierrez, G. (1971) *A theology of liberation: History, politics and salvation*, New York: Orbis.

Hadjis, T. (1981) *The victorious revolution that was lost*, Athens: Dorikos.

Harik, J.P. (2004) *Hezbollah: The changing face of terrorism*, London: I.B. Tauris.

Harris, G. (2005) 'In nursing home, a fight lost to rising waters', *New York Times*, 7 September.

Harris, J. and White, V. (eds) (2009) *Modernising social work: Critical considerations*, Bristol: The Policy Press.

Herbert-Boyd, M. (2007) *Enriched by catastrophe: Social work and social conflict after the Halifax explosion*, Nova Scotia: Fernwood Publishing.

Hewitt, K. (1997) *Regions of risk: A geographical introduction to disasters*, Harlow: Longman.

Hionidou, V. (2004) 'Black market, hyperinflation and hunger: Greece 1941–1944', *Food and Foodways*, 12(2): 81–106.

Hofman, D. (2007) 'Time to master disaster', *Finance and Development*, 44(1).

Hourani, A. (1991) *A history of the Arab peoples*, London: Faber and Faber.

Human Rights Watch (2007) *Why they died: Civilian casualties in Lebanon during the 2006 war*, www.hrw.org/en/reports/2007/09/05/why-they-died-0 [accessed 4 April 2010].

Human Rights Watch (2010) *Paramilitaries' heirs: The new face of violence in Colombia*, New York: HRW publications.

Hylton, F. (2006) *Evil hour in Colombia*, London: Verso.

IDMC (Internal Displacement Monitoring Centre) (2010) 'Colombia: new displacement continues, response still ineffective', www.internal-displacement.org/countries/Colombia [accessed 5 October 2010].

Ife, J. (2008) *Human rights and social work: Towards rights-based practice*, Sydney: Cambridge University Press.

IFSW (2000) Definition of social work, http://www.ifsw.org/f38000138.html [accessed 3 December 2009].

Ilkhamov, V. (2004) 'The limits of centralization', in P.J. Luong (ed) *The transformation of Central Asia: States and societies from Soviet rule to independence*, Ithaca: Cornell University Press, pp 161-72.

IMF (2008) *Republic of Uzbekistan: Poverty strategy reduction paper*, IMF Country Report 08/34, January 2008, No. 58, Brussels.

International Disaster Database (2010) Country profile. Center for Research on the Epidemiology of Disasters, http://emdat.be/result-country-profile [accessed5 April 2010].

International Federation of Journalists (2008) 'IFJ condemns beating of journalists, calls on Greece to act', www.ifj.org/en/articles/efj-calls-for-investigation-into-attack-on-greek-journalist [accessed 4 May 2010].

Ioakimidis, V. (2009) 'A critical examination of the political construction and function of Greek social work', PhD thesis, University of Liverpool, Liverpool.

ITUC (2010) 'Haiti – trade union assistance arrives', 22 January, www.ituc-csi.org/haiti-trade-union-assistance.html [accessed 5 April 2010].

James, C.L.R. (1938/1980) *The black Jacobins*, Tiptree: Anchor Press.

Johnson, R. (2005) *A region in turmoil, South Asian conflicts since 1947*, London: Reaktion Books.

Jones, C (1983) *State social work and the working class,* Basingstoke, Macmillan.

Jones, C. (2007) 'What is to be done', in M. Lavalette and I. Ferguson (eds) *International social work and the radical tradition*, Birmingham: Venture Press.

Jones, C. (2011) 'The best and worst of times: reflections on the impact of radicalism on British social work education in the 1970s', in M. Lavalette (ed) *Radical social work today*, Bristol: The Policy Press.

Jones, P. (2009) 'Teaching for change in social work: A discipline-based argument for the use of transformative approaches to teaching and learning', *Journal of Transformative Education*, 7: 8–25.

Jordan, B (2000) *Social work and the Third Way*, London, Sage.

Karamichas, J. (2007) 'The impact of the summer 2007 forest fires in Greece: Recent environmental mobilizations, cyber-activism and electoral performance', *South European Society and Politics*, 12(4): 521–33.

Karavasilis, P. (1996) 'The battle for crops', *Rizospastis* daily newspaper, 29 July, p 24.

Katz, B. (2006) 'Concentrated poverty in New Orleans and other American cities', *The Chronicle of Higher Education*, 4 August, p 15.

Kimber, C. (2010) 'Hell in Haiti as aid turns to occupation', *Socialist Worker*, 13 January, p 6.

King, N. (2005) *Education under occupation … learning to improvise*, London: Discovery Analytical Resourcing.

King, R.J. (2006) *Big, easy money: Disaster profiteering on the American gulf coast*, Oakland, CA: CorpWatch.

KKE (1981) *Documents from the National Resistance*, Athens: Syghroni Epohi.

KKE (1995) *KKE's history; official documents*, Athens: Syghroni Epohi.

Klein, N. (2007a) *The shock doctrine: The rise of disaster capitalism*, London: Allen Lane.

Klein, N. (2007b) 'Information is shock resistance: Arm Yourself – the shock doctrine', http://www.naomiklein.org/shock-doctrine [accessed 1 February 2010].

Klein, N. (2010) 'Forgiveness for Haiti? We should be begging theirs', *Guardian*, 11 February, www.guardian.co.uk/commentisfree/2010/Feb/11/we-should-beg-haitis-forgiveness/print.

Knabb, R., Rhome, J. and Brown, D. (2006) 'Tropical cyclone report: Hurricane Katrina: 23–30 August 2005', National Hurricane Center, 10 August.

Kostarelou, E. (2007) 'Paraliaka fileta gis toy priropliktou nomou Hleias ksepoylaei I kivernisi, tesseris meres prin tis ekloges' ['The government sells off seaside parcels of (public) land of the fire-affected prefecture of Ilias just four days before the election'], *Eleytherotipia*, 13 September.

Koulouglou, S. (2007) *Hitler's Greece: Greek history*, Greek State Television (ET), Lynx Productions SA for Reporters Without Borders.

Kumin, J. (2007) 'Control vs. protection: refugees, migrants and the EU', *Refugees Magazine*, 148(4), UNHCR.

Lasettas, C. (1980) 'Social security', *Haravgi*, 1 February, p 2.

Lavalette, M. (2006) *Palestine journey*, London: Respect.

Lavalette, M. (ed) (2011) *Radical social work today: Social work at the crossroads*, Bristol: The Policy Press.

Lavalette, M. and Ferguson, I. (eds) (2007a) *International social work and the radical tradition*, Birmingham: Venture Press.

Lavalette, M. and Ferguson, I. (2007b) 'Democratic language and neo-liberal practice: the problem with "civil society"', *International Social Work* 50(4) pp 447-59.

Linardatos, S. (1975) *The 4th of August dictatorship*, Athens: Dialogos.

Livieratos, D. (2006) *The great times of working class*, Athens: Paraskimio.

MacKinnon, S.T. (2009) 'Social work intellectuals in the twenty first century: critical social theory, critical social work and public engagement', *Social Work Education*, 28: 512–27.

Makdisi, U. (2008) 'Understanding sectarianism', in N. Hovsepian (ed) *The war on Lebanon: A reader*, Northampton, MA: Olive Branch Press.

Mandelbaum, M. (ed) (1994) *Central Asia and the world: Kazakhstan, Uzbekistan, Tajikistan, Kyrgyzstan, and Turkmenistan*, Council on Foreign Relations Press.

Marshall, P. (1989) *Intifada: Zionism, imperialism and Palestinian resistance*, London: Bookmarks.

Martin-Ortega, O. (2008), 'Deadly ventures? Multinational corporations and paramilitaries in Colombia', *Revista electrónica de estudios internacionales*, www.reei.org/reei%2016/doc/MARTINORTEGA_Olga.pdf [accessed 17 February 2011].

Mavrikos, G. (2004) *The labour and trade unionist movement 1918–1948; two lines in constant conflict*, Athens: Sygxroni epohi.

Mazower, M. (1993) *Inside Hitler's Greece*, New Haven and London: Yale University Press.

Meertens, D. (2002) 'Colombia: Internally displaced persons and the conditions for socio-economic reintegration', www.unhcr.org/refworld/pdfid/3de62e427.pdf [accessed 10 October 2010].

Mendes, P. (2009) 'Teaching community development to social work students: a critical reflection', *Community Development Journal*, 44(2): 248–62.

Michael, D. (1979) *Shack: the last station. A report on the living conditions for elderly in Cyprus refugee camps no 2*, Nicosia: Social Welfare Services.

Migreurop (2010) *Europe's murderous borders*, www.migreurop.org/rubrique289. html?lang=en [accessed 10 March 2010].

Miliband, R. (1989) *Divided societies*, Oxford and New York: Oxford University Press.

Ministry of Labour and Social Insurance (1976) *Annual Report of the Ministry of Labour and Social Insurance*, Nicosia: Cyprus Government Printing Office.

Ministry of Labour and Social Insurance (1980) *Annual Report of the Ministry of Labour and Social Insurance*, Nicosia: Cyprus Government Printing Office.

Mmatli, T. (2008) 'Political activism as a social work strategy in Africa', *International Social Work*, 51: 297–310.

Mohan, B. (2005) 'New internationalism: social work's dilemmas, dreams and delusion', *International Social Work*, 48: 241–50.

Morley, C. (2008) 'Teaching critical practice: resisting structural domination through critical reflection', *Social Work Education*, 27(4): 407–21.

Muminović, A. and Mustafovski, F. (2000) 'Žrtva kao pomagać' (A victim as a helper), unpublished thesis for the Education of Supervisors in Psychosocial Work 1998–2000, University of Sarajevo, 2000 (paper available from the chapter author [Maglajlic]).

Murillo, L.G. (2001) 'El Chocó: the African heart of Colombia', speech given at the American Museum of Natural History in New York, 23 February, http:// colhrnet.igc.org/newsletter/y2001/spring01art/africanheart101.htm

Murphy, T.P. (2008) 'Development of social work in Uzbekistan in an international context', *Materials of the international forum 'Inclusive education and modern trends in developing of forms of social support of children'*, Tashkent: Republican Center for Social Adaptation of Children, pp 23–8.

Murphy, T.P. (2009) 'Social work in Uzbekistan: perspectives for the development of cost effective services', *Materials of the international forum 'Inclusive education and modern trends in developing of forms of social support of children'*, Tashkent: Republican Center for Social Adaptation of Children, pp 117–22.

Myrsiades, L. (1977) 'Greek Resistance theatre in World War II', *The Drama Review*, 21(1): 99–106.

Myrsiades, L. and Myrsiades, K. (1999) *Cultural representation in historical resistance: Complexity and construction in Greek guerrilla theater*, Lewisburg: Bucknell University Press.

Nasiotis, G. (1975) *Greek women during the National Struggle*, Athens: Nasiotis.

National Committee for Ageing in Cyprus (1983) 'Pancyprian seminar on ageing'.

New Statesman (2010) 'Haiti death toll rises to 230,000', 10 February, www. newstatesman.com/2010/02/haiti-thought-injured-season.

Newsroom DOL (2007) 'The General Wind prohibits the fire fighting efforts', 27 August, www.in.gr/news/article.asp?lngEntityID=826902 [accessed 5 May 2010].

NOAS, Aitima and Norwegian Helsinki Committee (2009a) 'Unwanted people: The illegal deportations of the asylum seekers by Greece', 22 October, www. aitima.gr/demo/?q=en/en/home [accessed 12 May 2010].

NOAS, Aitima and Norwegian Helsinki Committee (2009b) 'Out the back door: illegal deportations of refugees by Greece', press release, Oslo–Athens, 22 October [accessed 12 May 2010].

Nodaros, M (2008a) 'Kataggelia sok gia to dimo Zaxaros. Parembasi toy Erithrou Stayrou kai tis Aystrialianis presvias. Xtizoun aythereto dimarxeio me 1.8 ekat. Euro ton piroplikton', ['Shocking denunciation for the city government of Zacharo. They are building an unlicensed City Hall with 1.8 million Euro donated for the fire'affected people. Red Cross and the Australian Embassy is intervening', *Eleytherotipia*, 25 August.

Nodaros, M (2008b) 'Ileia ping pong me to authaireto dimarxeio', ['Ileia ping pong with the unlicensed City Hall'], *Eleytherotipia*, 26 August.

Northrop, D (2004) *Veiled empire: Gender and power in Stalinist Central Asia*, New York: Cornell University Press.

Norton, A.R. (2007) *Hezbollah*, Princeton: Princeton University Press.

Ntona, K. (2004) 'Teachers and collective action, 1941–1944: structure, discourse, practice', 3rd International Conference; History of Education, University of Patras.

NTUA (National Technical University School of Architecture) (2008) *Planning for the fire affected communities*, www.arch.ntua.gr/pyroplikta [accessed 5 December 2008]. [In Greek]

Olcott, M. (1995) 'Islam and fundamentalism in Central Asia', in Y. Roi (ed) *Muslim Eurasia: Conflicting legacies*, London: Frank Cass, p 25.

Oliver B. and Fernando Y. (2006) 'La población negra en la Colombia de hoy: dinámicas sociodemográficas, culturales y políticas', *Estudios afro-asiáticos*, 25(1): 9-21.

Ozerkan, F. (2010) 'Turkey, Greece join EU project to share illegal migration burden', in *Hürriyet Daily News* (Ankara), 12 March.

Papadouka, O.V. (2001) *The Athenian theatre: Occupation, resistance, prosecution*, Athens: K.P. Sbilias Publications.

Papageorgakakis, N. (2006) 'The public servants' movement during the occupation', in *ADEDY Annual Conference 2006*, Athens: ADEDY.

Papassava, E. (1993) *Turkish invasion and the appearance of social problems*, Nicosia: University of Nicosia.

Pappe, I. (2006) *The ethnic cleansing of Palestine*, Oxford: One World.

Paternostro, S. (2007) *My Colombian war: A journey through the country I left behind*, New York: Henry Holt.

Payne, M (2006) *What is professional social work?*, Bristol, The Policy Press.

PCBS (Palestinian Central Bureau of Statistics) (2008) 'Poverty and living conditions in the Palestinian Territory', www.pcbs.gov.ps/Portals/_pcbs/PressRelease/poverty_ee.pdf [accessed 2 July 2008].

Pecnik, N. and Stubbs, P. (1994) *Working with refugees and displaced persons in Croatia: From dependency to development?* http://gaspp.stakes.fi/NR/rdonlyres/68A172BC-FD88-437A-828E-785061347F37/4866/Croatiafromdependencytodevelopment.pdf [accessed 10 July 2010].

Pendaraki, M. (2010) 'Reinforcing class privileges through post disaster restoration policies: the example of Ilias, Greece: lessons for social development, social work and community organizing', Presentation submitted for inclusion in the proceedings of the 2010 Joint World Conference on Social Work and Social Development: the Agenda, Hong Kong, June.

Pendaraki, M. and Skandamis, M. (2009) 'A critical review of the European policies of asylum: the re-positioning of asylum seekers from refugees/victims in need of protection to criminal/illegal immigrants', *Social Work, SKLE*, 94: 71–92.

Peppiatt, D. (2010) 'Communities will make Haiti strong', *Guardian*, 21 February, www.guardian.co.uk/commentisfree/2010/Feb/21/haiti-displaced-social-networks/print

Petropoulos, G. (2004) 'February 1943, The cancellation of the political forced recruitment', *Rizospastis* Daily Newspaper, 22 February, p 14.

Philelftheros (1978) 'ETYK reacts to the new social security scheme', 17 February, p 1.

Pilger, J. (2010) 'The kidnapping of Haiti', *New Statesman*, 28 January, www.newstatesman.com/international-politics/2010/02/haiti-pilger-obama-venezuela

Poliakov, S. and Olcott, M. (eds) (1992) *Everyday Islam, religion and tradition in rural Central Asia*, Armonk: M.E. Sharpe.

Popay, J. and Dhooge, Y. (1989) 'Unemployment, cod's head soup and radical social work' in M. Langan and P. Lee (eds), *Radical social work today*, London: Unwin Hyman.

Posada-Carb, E. (1998) 'Fiction as history: The bananeras and Gabriel Garcia Marquez's one hundred years of solitude', *Journal of Latin American Studies*, 30(2): 395–414.

Pratt, D. (2006) *Intifada: The long day of rage*, Glasgow: Sunday Herald Books.

Pyles, L. (2007) 'Community organizing for post-disaster social development: locating social work', *International Social Work*, May, 50: 321-33.

Rappaport, M. (2006) 'IDF commander: We fired more than a million cluster bombs in Lebanon', *Haaretz*, 12 September, www.haaretz.com/news/idf-commander-we-fired-more-than-a-million-cluster-bombs-in-lebanon-1.197099 [accessed 24 April 2010].

Razack, N. (1999) 'Anti-discriminatory practice: pedagogical struggles and challenges', *British Journal of Social Work*, 29: 231–50.

Reisch, M. and Andrew J. (2002) *The road not taken: A history of radical social work in the United States*, New York: Brunner-Routledge.

Richardson, J. (2005) *Paradise poisoned – learning about conflict, terrorism and development from Sri Lanka's civil wars*, Kandy: International Center for Ethnic Studies.

Robinson, S. (2010) 'Haiti: overthrowing slavery and resisting the IMF', *Socialist Worker*, 23 January, p 7.

Rose, J. (1986) *Israel: The hijack state*, London: Bookmarks)

Saad-Ghorayeb, A. (2002) *Hizbu'llah: Politics and religion*, London: Pluto.

Sakellariou, H. (1995) *The theatre of resistance*, Athens: Synhroni Epohi.

Sarris, M., Soulis, S., Marinie, P. and Antaras, G. (2008) *Open care services in the Cyprus model of social welfare*, Nicosia: Social Welfare Services.

Sheikh, P. (2005) 'The impact of Hurricane Katrina on biological resources', Congressional Research Service, 18 October.

Smith, I (1989) 'Community work in recession: A practitoner's perspective' in M. Langan and P. Lee (eds), *Radical social work today*, London: Unwin Hyman.

Social Welfare Services (1975) *Annual report of the Department of Social Welfare Services*, Nicosia: Cyprus Government Printing Office.

Social Welfare Services (1976) *Annual report of the Department of Social Welfare Services*, Nicosia: Cyprus Government Printing Office.

Social Welfare Services (1977) *Annual report of the Department of Social Welfare Services*, Nicosia: Cyprus Government Printing Office.

Social Welfare Services (1979) *Annual report of the Department of Social Welfare Services*, Nicosia: Cyprus Government Printing Office.

Solas, J. (2008) 'Social work and social justice: what are we fighting for?', *Australian Social Work*, 61(2): 124–36.

Solnit, R. (2009) *A paradise built in hell*, New York: Viking.

Solnit, R. (2010) 'Covering Haiti: when the media is the disaster', *Guernica: a magazine of art and politics*, www.guernicamag.com/blog/1514/when_the_media_is_the/

Somasundaram, R., Sritharan, D., Hoole, D. and Rajani, T. (1992) *The broken Palmyra, the Tamil crisis in Sri Lanka, an inside account*, Jaffna: UTHR.

Soss, J., Fording, R. and Schram, S. (2009) 'Governing the poor: the rise of the neoliberal paternalist state', paper presented at the 2009 Annual Meeting of the American Political Science Association, Toronto, Canada.

Stavrianos, L.S. (1952) 'The Greek National Liberation Front (EAM): a study in resistance organization and administration', *The Journal of Modern History*, 24(1): 42–55.

Stiglitz, J. (2007) 'Bleakonomics', *New York Times*, 30 September, p 7.

Strier, R. (2008) 'Class-competent social work: a preliminary definition', *International Journal of Social Welfare*, 18: 237–42.

SYTE (2006) 'History of SYTE', www.syte.gr/history.asp [accessed 14 March 2007].

Tarrow, S. (1994) *Power in movement: Social movements and contentious politics*, Cambridge, Cambridge University Press.

Teloni, D. and Pendaraki, M. (2010) 'Proposals for the redevelopment of the curriculum of the social work department of TEI Patras', TEI Patras: Social Work Department Committee of Curriculum Development.

Theodorou, A. (1987) 'Caring for ageing people in Cyprus after 1974', unpublished paper.

Traboulsi, F. (2007) *A history of modern Lebanon*, London: Pluto Press.

TUC (2010a) 'Haiti Aid Earthquake Appeal', www.tuc.org.uk/international/tuc-17424-fo-cfm

TUC (2010b) 'ITUC interview with Haiti's trade union leader Loulou Cherry', www.tuc.org.uk/internetional/tuc-17532-fo.cfm

Turnell, A. and Edwards, S. (1999) *Signs of safety: A solution and safety oriented approach to child protection casework*, New York: W. W. Norton and Company.

UN-Habitat (2003) *Global report on human settlements 2003, The challenge of slums*, London: Earthscan.

UNHCR (2008) *Refugees of the world 2006*, Athens: Ellinika Grammata.

UNHCR (2009) Statistical data on the official website of the Greek department, www.unhcr.gr/exec/BOSTATS%20table2009EL.pdf.

UNHCR (2010) 'UNHCR express its deep sorrow for the deaths of refugees in the sea near Samos', Press announcement, www.unhcr.gr/Press_Rel/02_2010_12Feb.htm [accessed 25 February 2010].

UNICEF (2008) 'Child labour in cotton production', www.unicef.org/uzbekistan/protection.html.

UNRWA (2006) *West Bank refugee camp profiles*, www.un.org/unrwa/refugees/westbank.html [accessed 9 July 2008].

Uyangoda, J. (2007) *Ethnic conflict in Sri Lanka: Changing dynamics*, Washington: East West Center.

Varnalis, K. (1998) *Literature memoires*, Greek–French edition, Athens: Kedros.

Veracini, L. (2006) *Israel and settler society*, London: Pluto.

Vournas, T. (2000) *Modern history of Greece*, Athens: Tolidis.

Warrick, T. and Grunwald, M. (2005) 'Investigators link levee failures to design flaws', *Washington Post*, 24 October, p 8.

Watkins, M. and Shulman, H. (2008) *Toward psychologies of liberation*, New York: Palgrave Macmillan.

WHO (World Health Organisation, Regional Office for Europe, Bosnia and Herzegovina Office) (1997a) *Public health and health care: A general overview*, Federation of BiH, Sarajevo: WHO Office BiH.

WHO (World Health Organisation, Regional Office for Europe, Bosnia and Herzegovina Office) (1997b) *Health reform and reconstruction programme BiH*, PHC programme, Sarajevo, February.

Witner, L. (1982) *American intervention in Greece, 1943–1949*, New York: Columbia University Press.

Wood, G. (2009) 'Colombia's False Positives', Council on Hemispheric Affairs, 10 June.

World Bank (1999) *Poverty reduction and the World Bank: Progress in fiscal 1998*, World Bank Publications.

World Bank (2000a) *Poverty reduction and the World Bank: Progress in fiscal 1999*, World Bank Publications.

World Bank (2000b) *Emergency war victims rehabilitation project: Draft implementation completion report.* [Copy available with R.A. Maglajlic, chapter author]

Yaakov, R. (1995) *Muslim Eurasia: Conflicting legacies*, New York: Routledge.

Yiallouros, P. (2007) *The evolution of the Social Insurance Scheme: 7 January 1957–8*, Nicosia: Social Insurance Services.

Younge, G. (2010) 'The West owes Haiti a bailout. And it would be a hand-back, not a handout', *Guardian*, 31 January, www.guardian.co.uk/commentisfree/2010/jan/31/west-haiti-bailout-reimbursed-brutality/prin

Zirogiannis, N. (2009) 'Wildfire prevention and mitigation: the case of southern Greece', Master's thesis, Paper 254, http://scholarworks.umass.edu/theses/254/ [accessed 2 April 2010].

Index

Page references for notes are followed by n

9/11 34
33-Day War 31–2, 34–50

A

Achar, G. 33
Adams, G. 12–13
Afghanistan 34–5, 153, 154
Agia Anna 54
aid
  Haiti 9, 12–13
  Ilias 52–6
  Palestinian West Bank 21–4
Albania 111
Alinsky, Saul 62
Am'ari Refugee Camp 15–29
Amithalingam, Appapillai 95
Amnesty International 33, 84
Andrew, J. 132
anti-capitalist movement 37
Arnstein, Sherry 62
Asia 153–65
Asian tsunami 5, 13–14
asylum seekers 65
  see also refugees
Athens 122–3
Autodefensas Unidas de Colombia (AUC)
  83
Azerbaijan 157

B

Balata Refugee Camp 15–29
Baroud, R. 29n
Basaglia, Franco 109
Beikos, G. 128
Beirut 31–2, 33
Berger, John 24
Blaikie, P. 61
Bogota 84–91
Bosnia and Herzegovina (BiH) 105,
  108–11, 113n
Britain
  and Cyprus 134, 135
  Falklands War 12

and Greece 119
and Lebanon 32–3
social work 2, 3, 4
War on Terror 34–5, 36
Bröning, M. 35
Bulgaria 111
Burke, Jason 35–6
Bush, George W. 145

C

Carey, L. 60
Central Asia 153–65
Chelvanayagam, S.J.V. 94
children
  abuse and protection 162
  Croatia 107–9
  Greece 116
  Palestinian West Bank 15–29
  Samidoun 48–9
  Uzbekistan 154, 155
Chile 11
China 154
Chit, B. 31, 40, 50
civil society 11, 38, 163, 164
  see also NGOs
clan networks 156, 161, 164
class 54–5
Close, D.H. 128–9
Colombia 81–91
community organising
  Hurricane Katrina 150
  Ilias 56–62
conscientisation 89–90
Cree, V. 2
Croatia 105, 107–9
culture
  Greece 129–31
  Palestinian West Bank 25–6
Cyprus 133–5
  culture and social welfare 135–6
  elderly refugees 133, 134–5, 136–41

D

democracy 169–70
  despalzados 88–9
  EAM 125–9
  Kinisi 70
  Samidoun 39–40
  Sri Lanka 98
despalzados 81–2, 84–6
  conscientisation and emancipation 89–91
  future 91
  meeting urgent needs/mediation 86–7
  trust building/participation and
    democracy 88–9
Dhooge, Y. 78
disaster capitalism 10–11
  Ilias fire 55–6, 58–9
Doctors Without Borders 85
Dublin II Convention 67–8

E

E-EAM (Labour EAM) 120–1
EAM (National Liberation Front) 116, 118,
  119–20, 131–2
  fight for survival 120–5
  holistic development 129–31
  popular administration 125–9
earthquakes 6–10
education 131
ELAS (Popular Liberation Army) 116,
  118–19, 124
elderly people 133, 134–5, 136–41
Elefantos, Aggelos 131
Eleftheri Ellada 122
emancipation 90–1
Eurodac Regulations 67
European Council on Refugees and Exiles
  67–8
European Union (EU)
  accession processes 111, 112
  anti-immigration policy 65–8

F

famine 117–18, 120–1, 123–5
FARC 83, 84
FEMA (Federal Emergency Management
  Agency) 145, 147
Ferguson, Iain 3, 61, 62, 71, 78
fires 51–62, 63n
food
  Greek occupation 117–18, 120–1, 123–5
  Kinisi 75
forest fires 51–62, 63n

France 32–3
Freire, Paulo 75, 81
Frontex 65–6, 67

G

Germany 117, 119, 122, 124
Glinos, Demetrios 118, 121, 131
Global Justice movement 37
Greece
  1940s welfare movement 115–32
  and Cyprus 134
  disaster capitalism 11
  financial crisis 61, 167–8
  Ilias fire 51–62
  Kinisi 65, 70–9
  refugees 66, 68–9
Guatemala 7
Gutierrez, Gustavo 91

H

Haiti 6–10, 11, 12–13
Hamas 35, 36
Hamlet Trust 110
health care 75
HealthNet International (HNI) 110–11
Herbert-Boyd, Michelle 5–6, 14
Hewitt, Kenneth 7
Hezbollah 34, 36, 39, 46, 47
Hionidou, V. 117
Hofman, D. 169
holistic welfare practice 170–1
  EAM 129–31
  Kinisi 78
Human Rights Watch 31, 83
Hurricane Katrina 5, 143
  ideological context 146–7
  people affected 147–8
  physical context 143–4
  political context 145
  social context 144–5
  social work networks 148–9
Hurricane Rita 143, 144

I

Ife, J. 61–2
Ilias 51–2
  class nature of politics 54–5
  government response 52–3
  profiteering 55–6
  social work intervention 56–60
Imvriotis, Petros 131
Imvriotis, Roza 131

inclusion 99
India 95
internal displacement
  Colombia 81–2, 84–91
  Cyprus 133, 134–5, 136–41
  Samidoun 36–50
  Sri Lanka 96, 101–2
International Federation of Social Workers
  (IFSW) 2–3, 105
International Monetary Fund (IMF)
  111–12, 169
  Greece 61, 167, 168
international organisations 105, 112–13
  Bosnia and Herzegovina 109–11
  Croatia 107–9
  World Bank and EU 111–12
Iran 35, 154
Iraq 5, 11, 34–5
Islam
  Central Asia 156–9, 164–5
  Sri Lanka 94, 97
  see also Shia
Israel
  and Hamas 36
  and Hezbollah 36
  and Lebanon 31, 33–4, 36, 43, 44
  and Palestinian West Bank 15, 16–19,
    24–6, 28

J

J/P Haiti Relief Organisation 12–13
Jenin Refugee Camp 15–29, 38
Jones, C. 72, 79n
July War 31–2, 34–50

K

Kaifa, Lake 55–6
Kalouta, Anna 129
Karamichas, J. 63n
Katrina *see* Hurricane Katrina
Kazakhstan 154, 157
khashar 158
Kinisi 65, 69
  community work on multiple levels 71–2
  creation 70–1
  gains 76
  grassroots networks 73–4
  implications for social work 76–9
  political action 74
  welfare structures 74–6
KKE (Communist Party) 118, 120, 122,
  125, 126, 132n

Klein, Naomi 4–5, 8, 10–12, 13–14, 55, 133
Kotzioulas, Giorgos 130
Kyrgyzstan 154, 157
Kyriakos, Mpistas 52, 53, 54, 56

L

language
  Cyprus 135
  Kinisi 75
  Sri Lanka 94, 96–7, 100
Lavalette, Michael 3, 61, 62
Lebanon 32–4
  July War 31
  Samidoun 31–2, 36–50
lesbian, gay and transgender (LGBT) people
  39, 47, 148
London School of Economics Centre for
  Civil Society 163
looting 9
Lousiana 143–51

M

MacKinnon, S.T. 62
mahalla 156, 159–60, 161–2, 164
Marshall, P. 19
Mazower, M. 117–18, 123–4, 127, 131
media
  community organising 59
  refugees 71–2, 73
Meletzis, Spyros 124
memory 24–6
mental health services 109–10
Michael, D. 138, 139, 141n
migrants 65
  see also refugees
Migreurop 68
Miliband, Ralph 119
Mills, C. Wright 29
Mongolia 154
Muminovic, A. 106
Muslims *see* Islam
Mustafovski, F. 106
Myers, S. 2

N

Nablus 16, 17, 24, 26, 38
Nakba 25, 33
Nasiotis, G. 124
neoliberalism 10–12
  Greece 167
  Hurricane Katrina 146–7
networks 169

Greek financial crisis 167–8
Kinisi 73–4
New Orleans 5, 144–5, 146–7, 151
NGOs
  Central Asia 163–4
  Haiti 12, 13
  Lebanon 38–9
  Palestinian West Bank 22–3, 24
  Uzbekistan 155–6
Nodaros, Makis 55

O

Olcott, M. 161
older people 133, 134–5, 136–41
Ozerkan, F. 67

P

Pakistan 154
Palestine 33, 34, 36, 38
Palestinian West Bank 15–29, 38
  funding 21–4
  memory 24–6
  organic projects 19–21
  trust 26–8
  undefeated dismay 28–9
Papageorgakakis, N. 123
Papassava, E. 139
participation 171
  despalzados 88–9
  Sri Lanka 98
Paternostro, Silvana 81–2
Patras refugee camp 68, 69–79
peace building 96–7, 99–101, 102–4
Pecnik, Nina 108
PEEA (Political Committee of National
  Liberation) 127–8
Pendaraki, M. 62, 78
Penn, Sean 12–13
Peppiatt, David 6, 12
Pilger, John 9
Polidoras, Mr 51
Popay, J. 78
Popov, Maxim 155–6
popular social work 1–2, 3–4, 6, 115, 171
  Asian tsunami 13–14
  despalzados 84–91
  Greece 115–17, 119–32
  Kinisi 70–9
Palestinian West Bank 15–29
  Samidoun 31–50
poverty
  Haiti 7–8

New Orleans 144–5, 151
Palestinian West Bank 16, 21
  Uzbekistan 154–5
Preston 4
professionalisation 3
profiteering 55–6, 58
Pyles, Loretta 57–8, 61

R

radical social work 57, 61, 79n
Ramallah 16, 24, 38
Red Cross 143, 147, 149
refugees 106
  Croatia 108–9
  Cyprus 133, 134–5, 136–41
  EU policy 65–8
  Greece 68–79
  Palestinian West Bank 15–19
  Samidoun 36–50
  Sri Lanka 96, 101–2
  see also internal displacement
Reisch, M. 132
restorative justice 99

S

sadakaye-fittir 159
sadaqah 159
Saddam Nagar 102–4
Sakellariou, Haris 130
Sakkatos, Vaggelis 127
Samidoun 31–2, 50
  creation 36–41
  meeting human need 41–50
Santorum, Rick 151n
Savudrija refugee camp 108–9
Seattle 37
Serbia 111
shame 161
Shia 33, 35–6
shock doctrine 4–5, 10–14
Shulman, H. 91
Sinhalese 93–7, 99–104
Skandamis, M. 78
Smith, I. 76–7
social capital 98
social justice 58, 60
social shocks 4–5, 10–14, 133
social work 2, 3, 4, 115
  Central Asia 160–5
  definitions 23
  Greece 57, 115, 116, 119, 132

Hurricane Katrina 148–51
see also popular social work
social work education
   Ilias 56–60
   Uzbekistan 162–3
Solnit, Rebecca 1, 5, 9, 12, 170
Soss, J. 146
Soviet Union 153, 154, 156–8
Sri Lanka 93–5
   issues confronting peace-building
      initiatives 96–7
   philosophical foundations 97–9
   social work interventions 99–104
Stavrianos, L.S. 126–7
Stiglitz, Joseph 11
Strier, R. 62
Sunni 156

T

Ta aetopoula (Imvriotis) 131
Tajikistan 154
Tamils 93–7, 99–104
Thailand 13–14
Thatcher, Margaret 168
Theodorou, A. 137
Torres, Camilo 91
transgender people 148
Trincomalee 101–2
trust
   despalzados 88
   Palestinian West Bank 26–8
   Sri Lanka 98
tsunami 5, 13–14
Turkey
   and Cyprus 133, 134, 135
   refugees 66–7, 68
Turkmenistan 154

U

UK *see* Britain
UN Millennium Development Goals 105,
   111
undefeated dismay 24, 28–9
UNICEF 111
   Croatia 107–9
Uzbekistan 154
Uribe, Alvaro 82, 84
US
   9/11 5, 12
   and Greece 131, 132
   and Haiti 7, 8–9, 10, 11

and Hezbollah 34
Hurricane Katrina 143–51
and Lebanon 33, 34
War on Terror 34–5, 36, 66
USAID 22
Uzbekistan 153–65

V

Varnalis, Kostas 129–30
Vavuniya 99–101
Vlachou, Sofia 131
Volker, Paul 146
Vournas, T. 122

W

war 105–6
   Bosnia and Herzegovina 109–11
   Colombia 83–91
   Croatia 107–9
   Cyprus 134–5, 136
   Greece 116–31
   Lebanon 31–2, 34–50
   Sri Lanka 95–104
Warschawski, M. 33
Watkins, M. 91
welfare 6
   Cyprus 135–41
   Palestinian West Bank 15–29
   Samidoun 31–50
West Bank *see* Palestinian West Bank
women
   Central Asia 153, 161
   Cyprus 136
   Greece 124
   Sri Lanka 98, 102, 103
Woodward, R. 71, 78
World Bank 111–12
World Health Organisation (WHO) 109

Y

Yaffa Youth Centre 15–29
Yiallouros, P. 135
Younge, Gary 6–7, 8, 11
Yugoslav Republic of Macedonia 111

Z

zakat 159